T0260513

Praise for *AWS Cookbook*

There's something sorely missing from official AWS documentation: a sense of reality. Most of us aren't attempting to win points for collecting as many AWS services as we can; we're trying to complete a task somewhere that isn't a whiteboard. *AWS Cookbook* speaks to real users with a collection of recipes and pragmatic examples we can all benefit from.

—*Corey Quinn,*
Chief Cloud Economist, The Duckbill Group

Inside you'll find a great deal of information on typical AWS use cases plus a reference implementation that's easy to follow. If you like to learn AWS concepts in a practice-driven, example-based, hands-on manner, I highly recommend this book.

—*Gaurav Raje,*
author of Security and Microservice Architecture on AWS

I've never read a book packed so densely with ninja level tips and tricks for AWS; it's the book I wish I had five years ago. If you use AWS day to day, you need this in your toolkit, not only for the things it contains but also for the inspiration it provides. In my view, it's the best AWS book there is.

—*Adrian Cantrill,*
AWS Trainer, learn.cantrill.io

Putting AWS into practice with hands-on experience is the difference between cloud literacy and cloud fluency. *AWS Cookbook* serves up practical scenarios for working in the cloud to help individuals level up their career.

—*Drew Firment,*
AWS Community Hero and Head Enterprise Strategist, Pluralsight

AWS Cookbook
Recipes for Success on AWS

John Culkin and Mike Zazon

Beijing · Boston · Farnham · Sebastopol · Tokyo

AWS Cookbook

by John Culkin and Mike Zazon

Copyright © 2022 Culkins Coffee Shop LLC and Mike Zazon. All rights reserved.

Published by O'Reilly Media, Inc., 1005 Gravenstein Highway North, Sebastopol, CA 95472.

O'Reilly books may be purchased for educational, business, or sales promotional use. Online editions are also available for most titles (*http://oreilly.com*). For more information, contact our corporate/institutional sales department: 800-998-9938 or *corporate@oreilly.com*.

Acquisitions Editor: Jennifer Pollock	**Indexer:** Ellen Troutman-Zaig
Development Editor: Virginia Wilson	**Interior Designer:** David Futato
Production Editor: Christopher Faucher	**Cover Designer:** Karen Montgomery
Copyeditor: nSight, Inc.	**Illustrator:** Kate Dullea
Proofreader: Sharon Wilkey	

December 2021:   First Edition

Revision History for the First Edition
2021-12-02:   First Release

See *http://oreilly.com/catalog/errata.csp?isbn=9781492092605* for release details.

The O'Reilly logo is a registered trademark of O'Reilly Media, Inc. *AWS Cookbook*, the cover image, and related trade dress are trademarks of O'Reilly Media, Inc.

The views expressed in this work are those of the authors and do not represent the publisher's views. While the publisher and the authors have used good faith efforts to ensure that the information and instructions contained in this work are accurate, the publisher and the authors disclaim all responsibility for errors or omissions, including without limitation responsibility for damages resulting from the use of or reliance on this work. Use of the information and instructions contained in this work is at your own risk. If any code samples or other technology this work contains or describes is subject to open source licenses or the intellectual property rights of others, it is your responsibility to ensure that your use thereof complies with such licenses and/or rights.

978-1-492-09260-5

[LSI]

Dedicated to my father, who taught me that a spreadsheet could be used for much more than totaling up columns.

—John

Dedicated to my aunt, Judy Dunn. Thank you for the Tandy 1000 PC that sparked my fascination with computer programming and technology.

—Mike

Table of Contents

Foreword. xi

Preface. xiii

1. Security. 1
   1.0 Introduction   1
   1.1 Creating and Assuming an IAM Role for Developer Access   2
   1.2 Generating a Least Privilege IAM Policy Based on Access Patterns   6
   1.3 Enforcing IAM User Password Policies in Your AWS Account   9
   1.4 Testing IAM Policies with the IAM Policy Simulator   13
   1.5 Delegating IAM Administrative Capabilities Using Permissions
       Boundaries   17
   1.6 Connecting to EC2 Instances Using AWS SSM Session Manager   25
   1.7 Encrypting EBS Volumes Using KMS Keys   30
   1.8 Storing, Encrypting, and Accessing Passwords Using Secrets Manager   33
   1.9 Blocking Public Access for an S3 Bucket   36
   1.10 Serving Web Content Securely from S3 with CloudFront   39

2. Networking. 43
   2.0 Introduction   43
   2.1 Defining Your Private Virtual Network in the Cloud by Creating an
       Amazon VPC   44
   2.2 Creating a Network Tier with Subnets and a Route Table in a VPC   47
   2.3 Connecting Your VPC to the Internet Using an Internet Gateway   51
   2.4 Using a NAT Gateway for Outbound Internet Access from Private Subnets   55
   2.5 Granting Dynamic Access by Referencing Security Groups   59

2.6 Using VPC Reachability Analyzer to Verify and Troubleshoot Network
   Paths   63
2.7 Redirecting HTTP Traffic to HTTPS with an Application Load Balancer   67
2.8 Simplifying Management of CIDRs in Security Groups with Prefix Lists   74
2.9 Controlling Network Access to S3 from Your VPC Using VPC Endpoints   78
2.10 Enabling Transitive Cross-VPC Connections Using Transit Gateway   82
2.11 Peering Two VPCs Together for Inter-VPC Network Communication   88

3. Storage.. 93
3.0 Introduction   93
3.1 Using S3 Lifecycle Policies to Reduce Storage Costs   94
3.2 Using S3 Intelligent-Tiering Archive Policies to Automatically Archive S3
   Objects   97
3.3 Replicating S3 Buckets to Meet Recovery Point Objectives   100
3.4 Observing S3 Storage and Access Metrics Using Storage Lens   105
3.5 Configuring Application-Specific Access to S3 Buckets with S3 Access
   Points   110
3.6 Using Amazon S3 Bucket Keys with KMS to Encrypt Objects   114
3.7 Creating and Restoring EC2 Backups to Another Region Using AWS
   Backup   118
3.8 Restoring a File from an EBS Snapshot   125
3.9 Replicating Data Between EFS and S3 with DataSync   128

4. Databases... 133
4.0 Introduction   133
4.1 Creating an Amazon Aurora Serverless PostgreSQL Database   134
4.2 Using IAM Authentication with an RDS Database   140
4.3 Leveraging RDS Proxy for Database Connections from Lambda   146
4.4 Encrypting the Storage of an Existing Amazon RDS for MySQL Database   153
4.5 Automating Password Rotation for RDS Databases   157
4.6 Autoscaling DynamoDB Table Provisioned Capacity   163
4.7 Migrating Databases to Amazon RDS Using AWS DMS   167
4.8 Enabling REST Access to Aurora Serverless Using RDS Data API   171

5. Serverless.. 177
5.0 Introduction   177
5.1 Configuring an ALB to Invoke a Lambda Function   179
5.2 Packaging Libraries with Lambda Layers   181
5.3 Invoking Lambda Functions on a Schedule   185
5.4 Configuring a Lambda Function to Access an EFS File System   188
5.5 Running Trusted Code in Lambda Using AWS Signer   191

    5.6 Packaging Lambda Code in a Container Image   194
    5.7 Automating CSV Import into DynamoDB from S3 with Lambda   198
    5.8 Reducing Lambda Startup Times with Provisioned Concurrency   201
    5.9 Accessing VPC Resources with Lambda   204

6. Containers...**207**
    6.0 Introduction   207
    6.1 Building, Tagging, and Pushing a Container Image to Amazon ECR   209
    6.2 Scanning Images for Security Vulnerabilities on Push to Amazon ECR   214
    6.3 Deploying a Container Using Amazon Lightsail   217
    6.4 Deploying Containers Using AWS Copilot   220
    6.5 Updating Containers with Blue/Green Deployments   223
    6.6 Autoscaling Container Workloads on Amazon ECS   228
    6.7 Launching a Fargate Container Task in Response to an Event   231
    6.8 Capturing Logs from Containers Running on Amazon ECS   235

7. Big Data..**241**
    7.0 Introduction   241
    7.1 Using a Kinesis Stream for Ingestion of Streaming Data   242
    7.2 Streaming Data to Amazon S3 Using Amazon Kinesis Data Firehose   245
    7.3 Automatically Discovering Metadata with AWS Glue Crawlers   249
    7.4 Querying Files on S3 Using Amazon Athena   256
    7.5 Transforming Data with AWS Glue DataBrew   261

8. AI/ML..**267**
    8.0 Introduction   267
    8.1 Transcribing a Podcast   268
    8.2 Converting Text to Speech   270
    8.3 Computer Vision Analysis of Form Data   272
    8.4 Redacting PII from Text Using Comprehend   275
    8.5 Detecting Text in a Video   279
    8.6 Physician Dictation Analysis Using Amazon Transcribe Medical and
        Comprehend Medical   281
    8.7 Determining Location of Text in an Image   285

9. Account Management..**289**
    9.0 Introduction   289
    9.1 Using EC2 Global View for Account Resource Analysis   290
    9.2 Modifying Tags for Many Resources at One Time with Tag Editor   292
    9.3 Enabling CloudTrail Logging for Your AWS Account   297
    9.4 Setting Up Email Alerts for Root Login   300

9.5 Setting Up Multi-Factor Authentication for a Root User   302
9.6 Setting Up AWS Organizations and AWS Single Sign-On   307

Appendix. Fast Fixes. **315**

Index. **319**

Foreword

As part of the Amazon Web Services (AWS) team since the beginning, I have been able to watch it grow in scale, richness, and complexity from a unique vantage point. Even after writing thousands of blog posts and millions of words, I learn something new and useful about AWS just about every day.

With well over two hundred services in production and more launching regularly, AWS could easily leave you feeling overwhelmed. In addition to tens of thousands of pages of official AWS documentation, bloggers, AWS Heroes, AWS Partners, and others have created innumerable pieces of content—including blog posts, videos, webinars, overviews, and code samples.

While there's no substitute for having a full and complete understanding of a particular AWS service, the reality is that you often simply need to solve a "point" problem. Even after you understand a service, remembering how to use it to solve that problem can be a challenge—at least it is for me.

And that is where this cookbook comes in. Because of its broad selection of topics and carefully chosen recipes, I am confident that you will be able to quickly find one that addresses your immediate need and to put it into practice in short order. You can solve your problem, refresh your knowledge of that aspect of AWS, and move forward to create value for your customers!

My favorite aspect of this book is that it does not hand-wave past any of the details. Each recipe assumes that you start fresh and then helps you to cook up a perfectly seasoned solution. Nothing is left to chance, and you can use the recipes as is in most cases. The recipes also cover the all-important cleanup phase and ensure that you leave your AWS environment as you found it.

Where appropriate, the recipes use the AWS Cloud Development Kit (CDK) and include all of the necessary "moving parts." The CDK provides a double benefit; in addition to helping you to move forward more quickly, these CDK elements can help you learn more about how to put infrastructure as code (IaC) into practice.

Most cookbooks are designed to be browsed and savored, and this one is no exception. Flip through it, read an entire chapter, or use just a recipe or two, as you wish. I also recommend that you go through all of Chapter 1, just to make sure that your environment is set up and ready to go. Then, when you are presented with a problem to solve, find the appropriate recipe, put it into practice, and reap the benefits.

—Jeff Barr

—VP and Chief Evangelist at AWS
Seattle, WA
November 2021

Preface

The vast majority of workloads will go to the cloud.
We're just at the beginning—there's so much more to happen.
—Andy Jassy (https://oreil.ly/7Ube0)

Cloud usage has been gaining traction with enterprises and small businesses over the last decade and continues to accelerate. Gartner said the worldwide infrastructure as a service (IaaS) public cloud services market grew 40.7% in 2020 (*https://oreil.ly/ bJ5Sb*). The rapid growth of the cloud has led to a huge demand (*https://oreil.ly/kstre*) for cloud skills by many organizations. Many IT professionals understand the basic concepts of the cloud but want to become more comfortable working in the cloud. This gap between the supply and demand of cloud skills presents a significant opportunity for individuals to level up their career.

Through our combined 20+ years of cloud experience, we have had the benefit of working on Amazon Web Services (AWS) projects in many different roles. We have provided guidance to hundreds of developers on how and when to use AWS services. This has allowed us to understand the common challenges and easy wins of the cloud. We would like to share these lessons with you and give you a leg up for your own advancement. We wrote this book to share some of our knowledge and enable you to quickly acquire useful skills for working in the cloud. We hope that you will find yourself using this book as reference material for many years to come.

Who This Book Is For

This book is for developers, engineers, and architects of all levels, from beginner to expert. Beginners will learn cloud concepts and become comfortable working with cloud services. Experts will be able to examine code used to stand up recipe foundations, explore new services, and gain additional perspectives. If the plethora of cloud services and combinations seem overwhelming to you, then this book is for you. The recipes in this book aim to provide "Hello, World" proofs of concept and components of enterprise-grade applications. This will be accomplished using common use cases with guided walk-throughs of scenarios that you can directly apply to your current or future work. These curated and experience-building recipes are meant to demystify services and will immediately deliver value, regardless of your AWS experience level.

What You Will Learn

In addition to opening up new career opportunities, being able to harness the power of AWS will give you the ability to create powerful systems and applications that solve many interesting and demanding problems in our world today. Would you like to handle 60,000 cyber threats per second using AWS machine learning like Siemens (*https://oreil.ly/Qpyvy*) does? Or reduce your organization's on-premises footprint and expand its use of microservices like Capital One (*https://oreil.ly/vI0ZY*) has? If so, the practical examples in this book will help expedite your learning by providing tangible examples showing how you can put the building blocks of AWS together to form practical solutions that address common scenarios. The on-demand consumption model, vast capacity, advanced capabilities, and global footprint of the cloud create new possibilities that need to be explored.

The Recipes

We break the book into chapters that focus on general areas of technology (e.g., security, networking, artificial intelligence, etc.). The recipes contained within the chapters are bite-sized, self-contained, and easily consumable. Recipes vary in length and complexity. Each recipe has a problem statement, solution (with diagram), and discussion. Problem statements are tightly defined to avoid confusion. Solutions contain required preparation and steps to walk you through the work needed to accomplish the goal. When appropriate, explicit validation checks will be provided. We've also added extra challenges to the recipes to help you advance your learning if you wish to do so. Finally, we end each recipe with a short discussion to help you understand the solution and why it matters, suggestions to extend the solution, and ways to utilize it for real impact.

 To keep your AWS bill low and keep your account tidy, each recipe has cleanup steps provided in the repositories associated with the book.

Each chapter has its own repository at *https://github.com/awscookbook*. The repository contains preparation steps for easy copying and pasting, required files, and infrastructure as code. We have also created GitHub templates for reporting bugs and suggesting new recipes. We encourage you to leverage GitHub to submit issues, create requests for new recipes, and submit your own pull requests. We will actively maintain the chapter repositories with updates for recipe steps and code in the README files of each recipe. Be sure to check these for any new or alternative approaches. We look forward to interacting with you on GitHub with new fun challenges and hints to assist you.

Some recipes are "built from scratch," and others include preparation steps to allow you to interact with common scenarios seen in the real world. We have provided code to enable you to easily deploy the prerequisites. For example, Recipe 6.5, "Updating Containers with Blue/Green Deployments", assumes that you are a container developer creating an application deployment that requires an existing network stack. When prerequisites exist, they can be "pre-baked" with preparation steps using code provided in the repositories. When substantial preparation for a recipe is needed, you will use the AWS Cloud Development Kit (CDK), which is a fantastic tool for intelligently defining and declaring infrastructure. The majority of the recipes are CLI based; when appropriate, we use console walk-throughs including screenshots or descriptive text.

> There are many ways to achieve similar outcomes on AWS; this book will not be an exhaustive list. Many factors will dictate the best overall solution for your use case. We have selected recipe topics to help you learn about AWS and make the best choices for your specific needs.

You'll find recipes for things like the following:

- Redacting personally identifiable information (PII) from text by using Amazon Comprehend
- Automating password rotation for Amazon Relational Database Service (RDS) databases
- Using VPC Reachability Analyzer to verify and troubleshoot network paths

Along with the recipes, we also provide short lines of code in the Appendix that will quickly accomplish valuable and routine tasks. We feel that these are great tidbits to add to your cloud toolbox.

> AWS has a free tier (*https://aws.amazon.com/free*), but implementing recipes in this book could incur costs. We provide cleanup instructions, but you are responsible for any costs in your account. We recommend checking out the Well-Architected Labs (*https://www.wellarchitectedlabs.com*) developed by AWS on expenditure awareness and leveraging AWS Budgets actions (*https://oreil.ly/4OVCc*) to control costs.

What You Will Need

Here are the requirements to get started and some tips on where to find assistance:

- AWS account
  - Setup instructions (*https://oreil.ly/opuXX*)
  - An IAM user with console and programmatic access
  - Administrator privileges for your IAM user
- Personal computer/laptop
- Software
  - Web browser (e.g., Microsoft Edge, Google Chrome, or Mozilla Firefox)
  - Terminal with bash or Z shell (Zsh)
  - Git
    - Install instructions (*https://github.com/git-guides/install-git*)
  - Homebrew (optional but recommended to install other requirements)
    - Install instructions (*https://docs.brew.sh/Installation*)
  - Code editor (e.g., VSCodium or AWS Cloud9)
    - Recommended install: `brew install --cask vscodium`
  - AWS CLI version 2 (2.1.26 or later)
    - Install guide (*https://oreil.ly/uYhyX*)
    - Recommended install: `brew install awscli@2`
  - Python 3.7.9 (and pip) or later
    - Example install: `brew install python@3.7`
  - AWS Cloud Development Kit version 2.0 or later
    - Getting started guide (*https://oreil.ly/OmDu1*)
    - Recommended install: `brew install npm` and `npm i -g aws-cdk@next`
- Recommended: Create a folder in your home directory called *AWSCookbook*. This will allow you to clone each chapter's repository in one place:

```
AWSCookbook:$ tree -L 1
.
├── AccountManagement
├── ArtificialIntelligence
├── BigData
...
```

At the time of publishing, the AWS CDK has two versions: version 1 and version 2 (developer preview). The code we have provided is written for version 2. You can find out more information about how to migrate to and install CDK version 2 in this AWS CDK v2 article (*https://oreil.ly/jNyXH*).

Getting Started

This section provides examples of techniques and approaches we perform throughout the book to make the recipe steps easier to follow. You can skip over these topics if you feel comfortable with them. You can always come back and reference this section.

Setups

In addition to the installation of the prerequisites listed previously, you will need the following access.

AWS account setup

You will need a user with administrative permissions. Some of the recipes require the ability to create AWS Identity and Access Management (IAM) resources. You can follow the AWS guide for creating your first IAM admin user and user group (*https://oreil.ly/moVjA*).

General workstation setup steps for CLI recipes

We have created a group of code repositories available at *https://github.com/awscookbook*. Create a folder called *AWSCookbook* in your home directory (or any place of your choosing) and cd there:

```
mkdir ~/AWSCookbook && cd ~/AWSCookbook
```

This will give you a place to check out chapter repositories (e.g., *Security*):

```
git clone https://github.com/AWSCookbook/Security
```

Set and export your default Region in your terminal:

```
export AWS_REGION=us-east-1
```

 AWS offers many Regions across the world for cloud deployments. We'll be using the us-east-1 Region for simplicity. As long as the services are available, there is no reason these recipes won't work in other Regions. AWS has a list of Regions and services (*https://oreil.ly/I3eVB*).

Set your AWS `ACCOUNT_ID` by parsing output from the `aws sts get-caller-identity` operation:

```
AWS_ACCOUNT_ID=$(aws sts get-caller-identity \
    --query Account --output text)
```

> The `aws sts get-caller-identity` operation "returns details about the IAM user or role (*https://oreil.ly/XJMDp*) whose credentials are used to call the operation."

Validate AWS Command Line Interface (AWS CLI) setup and access:

```
aws ec2 describe-instances
```

If you don't have any EC2 instances deployed, you should see output similar to the following:

```
{
  "Reservations": []
}
```

> AWS CLI version 2 will by default send command output with multiple lines to `less` in your terminal. You can type **q** to exit. If you want to override this behavior, you can modify your *~/.aws/config* file to remove this default functionality (*https://oreil.ly/SU9gk*).

> AWS CloudShell (*https://aws.amazon.com/cloudshell*) is a browser-based terminal that you can use to quickly create a terminal environment in your authenticated AWS Console session to run AWS CLI commands from. By default, it uses the identity of your browser session to interact with the AWS APIs. Many of the recipes can be run using CloudShell. You can use CloudShell to run recipe steps, clean up commands, and other AWS CLI commands as your authenticated user, if you do not want to create a session that you use in your own local terminal environment on your workstation.

Techniques and Approaches Used in This Book

The next few sections will explain and give examples of some ways of using the CLI to help you with recipes.

Querying outputs, environment variables, and command substitution

Sometimes when subsequent commands depend on outputs from the command you are currently running. The AWS CLI provides the ability for client-side filtering of output (*https://oreil.ly/oV3cx*). At times, we will set environment variables (*https://oreil.ly/39qp6*) that contain these outputs by leveraging command substitution (*https://oreil.ly/FG9yl*).

We'll combine these three techniques to make things easier for you as you proceed through steps in the book. Here is an example:

Use the AWS Security Token Service (AWS STS) to retrieve your IAM user (or role) Amazon Resource Name (ARN) with the AWS CLI:

```
aws sts get-caller-identity
```

You should see output similar to the following:

```
{
  "UserId": "EXAMPLE",
  "Account": "111111111111",
  "Arn": "arn:aws:iam::111111111111:user/UserName"
}
```

An example of querying for the ARN value and outputting it to the terminal follows:

```
aws sts get-caller-identity --query Arn --output text
```

You should see output similar to the following:

```
arn:aws:iam::111111111111:user/UserName
```

Query for the ARN value and set it as an environment variable using command substitution:

```
PRINCIPAL_ARN=$(aws sts get-caller-identity --query Arn --output text)
```

To check the value of an environment variable, for example, you can echo it to the terminal:

```
echo $PRINCIPAL_ARN
```

You should see output similar to the following:

```
arn:aws:iam::111111111111:user/UserName
```

 Using the --dry-run flag is always a good idea when performing an operation that makes changes—for example, aws ec2 create-vpc --dry-run --cidr-block 10.10.0.0/16.

Replacing values in provided template files

Where possible, to simplify the learning experience for you, we have provided template files in the chapter code repositories that you can use as a starting point as input to some of the commands you will run in recipe steps. For example, when you create an AWS CodeDeploy configuration in Recipe 6.5, "Updating Containers with Blue/

Green Deployments", we provide *codedeploy-template.json* with `AWS_ACCOUNT_ID`, `PROD_LISTENER_ARN`, and `TEST_LISTENER_ARN` placeholders in the JSON file. We expect you to replace these placeholder values and save the file as *codedeploy.json*.

To further simplify your experience, if you follow the steps exactly and save these to environment variables, you can use the `sed` command to replace the values. Where possible, we provide you a command to do this, such as this example from Chapter 6:

Use the `sed` command to replace the values with the environment variables you exported with the *helper.py* script:

```
sed -e "s/AWS_ACCOUNT_ID/${AWS_ACCOUNT_ID}/g" \
    -e "s|PROD_LISTENER_ARN|${PROD_LISTENER_ARN}|g" \
    -e "s|TEST_LISTENER_ARN|${TEST_LISTENER_ARN}|g" \
    codedeploy-template.json > codedeploy.json
```

Passwords

During some of the steps in the recipes, you will create passwords and temporarily save them as environment variables to use in subsequent steps. Make sure you unset the environment variables by following the cleanup steps when you complete the recipe. We use this approach for simplicity of understanding. A more secure method (such as the method in Recipe 1.8) should be used in production environments by leveraging AWS Secrets Manager.

Generation. You can use AWS Secrets Manager via the AWS CLI to generate passwords (*https://oreil.ly/7TxP4*) with specific requirements. An example from Chapter 4 looks like this:

```
ADMIN_PASSWORD=$(aws secretsmanager get-random-password \
    --exclude-punctuation \
    --password-length 41 --require-each-included-type \
    --output text \
    --query RandomPassword)
```

Usage and storage. In production environments, you should use AWS Secrets Manager (*https://oreil.ly/PUyzf*) or AWS Systems Manager Parameter Store (*https://oreil.ly/HDMgB*) (using secure strings) with IAM policies to control who and what can access the secrets. For simplicity, some of the policies of passwords and secrets used in the recipes might not be as locked down from a policy perspective as you would want in a production environment. Be sure to always write your own IAM policies to control this behavior in practice.

Random suffixes

We generate a lot of random suffixes when we deal with global services like Amazon S3. These are needed because S3 bucket names need to be globally unique across the entire AWS customer base. Secrets Manager can be used via the CLI to generate a string that satisfies the naming convention and adds this random element to ensure all book readers can create resources and follow along using the same commands:

```
RANDOM_STRING=$(aws secretsmanager get-random-password \
    --exclude-punctuation --exclude-uppercase \
    --password-length 6 --require-each-included-type \
    --output text \
    --query RandomPassword)
```

You can also use any other utilities to generate random strings. Some local tools may be preferred.

AWS Cloud Development Kit and helper.py

A good place to start is the "Getting started with the AWS CDK" guide (*https://oreil.ly/OmDu1*). After you have CDK 2.0 installed, if this is the first time you are using the AWS CDK, you'll need to bootstrap with the Region you are working on with the AWS CDK toolkit:

```
cdk bootstrap aws://$AWS_ACCOUNT_ID/$AWS_REGION
```

We use the AWS CDK when needed throughout the book to give you the ability to deploy a consistent scenario that aligns with the problem statement you see in the recipe. You can also choose to execute the recipe steps in your own existing environments, as long as you have the input variables required for the recipe steps. If things don't work in your environment, you can stand up the provided environment and compare.

The CDK code we included in the repositories deploys resources using the AWS CloudFormation service, and we wrote output variables that you use in recipe steps. We created a Python script called *helper.py* which you can run in your terminal to take the CloudFormation output and set local variables to make the recipe steps easier to follow—in most cases, even copy and paste.

An example set of commands for deploying CDK code for a recipe after checking out the chapter repository for Chapter 4, looks like the following:

```
cd 401-Creating-an-Aurora-Serverless-DB/cdk-AWS-Cookbook-401/
test -d .venv || python3 -m venv .venv
source .venv/bin/activate
pip install --upgrade pip setuptools wheel
pip install -r requirements.txt
cdk deploy
```

You can easily copy and paste the preceding code from the root of the chapter repository (assuming you have Python, pip, and CDK installed as prerequisites) to deploy the scenario that the solution will address in the solution steps of the recipe.

The *helper.py* tool we created can then be run in your terminal after the cdk deploy is complete:

```
python helper.py
```

You should see output that you can copy and paste into your terminal to set environment variables from the CDK CloudFormation stack outputs:

```
$ python helper.py
Copy and paste the commands below into your terminal
ROLE_NAME='cdk-aws-cookbook-108-InstanceSS1PK7LB631QYEF'
INSTANCE_ID='random string here'
```

 Finally, a reminder that although we work for AWS, the opinions expressed in this book are our own.

Put on your apron, and let's get cooking with AWS!

Conventions Used in This Book

The following typographical conventions are used in this book:

Italic
: Indicates new terms, URLs, email addresses, filenames, and file extensions.

`Constant width`
: Used for program listings, as well as within paragraphs to refer to program elements such as variable or function names, databases, data types, environment variables, statements, and keywords.

`Constant width bold`
: Shows commands or other text that should be typed literally by the user.

`Constant width italic`
: Shows text that should be replaced with user-supplied values or by values determined by context.

 This element signifies a tip or suggestion.

 This element signifies a general note.

This element indicates a warning or caution.

Using Code Examples

Supplemental material (code examples, exercises, etc.) is available for download at *https://github.com/awscookbook*.

If you have a technical question or a problem using the code examples, please send email to *bookquestions@oreilly.com*.

This book is here to help you get your job done. In general, if example code is offered with this book, you may use it in your programs and documentation. You do not need to contact us for permission unless you're reproducing a significant portion of the code. For example, writing a program that uses several chunks of code from this book does not require permission. Selling or distributing examples from O'Reilly books does require permission. Answering a question by citing this book and quoting example code does not require permission. Incorporating a significant amount of example code from this book into your product's documentation does require permission.

We appreciate, but generally do not require, attribution. An attribution usually includes the title, author, publisher, and ISBN. For example: "*AWS Cookbook* by John Culkin and Mike Zazon (O'Reilly). Copyright 2022 Culkins Coffee Shop LLC and Mike Zazon, 978-1-492-09260-5."

If you feel your use of code examples falls outside fair use or the permission given above, feel free to contact us at *permissions@oreilly.com*.

O'Reilly Online Learning

 For more than 40 years, *O'Reilly Media* has provided technology and business training, knowledge, and insight to help companies succeed.

Our unique network of experts and innovators share their knowledge and expertise through books, articles, and our online learning platform. O'Reilly's online learning platform gives you on-demand access to live training courses, in-depth learning paths, interactive coding environments, and a vast collection of text and video from O'Reilly and 200+ other publishers. For more information, visit *http://oreilly.com*.

How to Contact Us

Please address comments and questions concerning this book to the publisher:

O'Reilly Media, Inc.
1005 Gravenstein Highway North
Sebastopol, CA 95472
800-998-9938 (in the United States or Canada)
707-829-0515 (international or local)
707-829-0104 (fax)

We have a web page for this book, where we list errata, examples, and any additional information. You can access this page at *https://oreil.ly/AWS-cookbook*.

Email *bookquestions@oreilly.com* to comment or ask technical questions about this book.

For news and information about our books and courses, visit *http://oreilly.com*.

Find us on Facebook: *http://facebook.com/oreilly*

Follow us on Twitter: *http://twitter.com/oreillymedia*

Watch us on YouTube: *http://youtube.com/oreillymedia*

Acknowledgments

Thank you to Jeff Armstrong, author of *Migrating to AWS, A Manager's Guide* for introducing us to O'Reilly.

We want to recognize the tech reviewers who helped get this book to where it is today. Their keen eyes, opinions, and technical prowess are greatly appreciated. Jess Males, Gaurav Raje, Jeff Barr, Paul Bayer, Neil Stewart, David Kheyman, Justin Domingus, Justin Garrison, Julian Pittas, Mark Wilkins, and Virginia Chu—thank you.

Thanks to the knowledgeable community at r/aws for always providing great insights and opinions.

Thank you to our production editor, Christopher Faucher, for getting the book in tip-top shape for release. Thanks also to our editor, Virginia Wilson, for taking the time to work with first-time authors during a pandemic. Your patience, suggestions, and guidance allowed us to complete this book and remain (somewhat) sane :-)

CHAPTER 1

Security

1.0 Introduction

The average cost of a data breach in 2021 reached a new high of USD 4.24 million as reported by the IBM/Ponemon Institute Report (*https://oreil.ly/YayAP*). When you choose to run your applications in the cloud, you trust AWS to provide a secure infrastructure that runs cloud services so that you can focus on your own innovation and value-added activities.

But security in the cloud is a shared responsibility (*https://oreil.ly/4Sv24*) between you and AWS. You are responsible for the configuration of things like AWS Identity and Access Management (IAM) policies, Amazon EC2 security groups, and host based firewalls. In other words, the security *of* the hardware and software platform that make up the AWS cloud is an AWS responsibility. The security of software and configurations that you implement *in* your AWS account(s) are your responsibility.

As you deploy cloud resources in AWS and apply configuration, it is critical to understand the security settings required to maintain a secure environment. This chapter's recipes include best practices and use cases focused on security. As security is a part of everything, you will use these recipes in conjunction with other recipes and chapters in this book. For example, you will see usage of AWS Systems Manager Session Manager used throughout the book when connecting to your EC2 instances. These foundational security recipes will give you the tools you need to build secure solutions on AWS.

In addition to the content in this chapter, so many great resources are available for you to dive deeper into security topics on AWS. "The Fundamentals of AWS Cloud Security" (*https://oreil.ly/7rDIX*), presented at the 2019 AWS security conference re:Inforce, gives a great overview. A more advanced talk, "Encryption: It Was the Best of Controls, It Was the Worst of Controls" (*https://oreil.ly/qnO16*), from AWS re:Invent, explores encryption scenarios explained in detail.

AWS publishes a best practices guide (*https://oreil.ly/BZQRt*) for securing your account, and all AWS account holders should be familiar with the best practices as they continue to evolve.

We cover important security topics in this chapter. It is not possible to cover every topic as the list of services and configurations (with respect to security on AWS) continues to grow and evolve. AWS keeps its Best Practices for Security, Identity, and Compliance web page (*https://oreil.ly/Us5oz*) up-to-date.

Workstation Configuration

You will need a few things installed to be ready for the recipes in this chapter.

General setup

Follow the "General workstation setup steps for CLI recipes" on page xvii to validate your configuration and set up the required environment variables. Then, clone the chapter code repository:

```
git clone https://github.com/AWSCookbook/Security
```

1.1 Creating and Assuming an IAM Role for Developer Access

Problem

To ensure that you are not always using administrative permissions, you need to create an IAM role for development use in your AWS account.

Solution

Create a role using an IAM policy that will allow the role to be assumed later. Attach the AWS managed `PowerUserAccess` IAM policy to the role (see Figure 1-1).

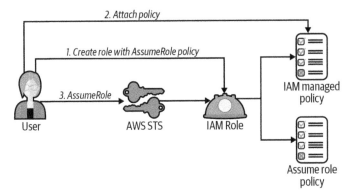

Figure 1-1. Create role, attach policy, and assume role

Steps

1. Create a file named *assume-role-policy-template.json* with the following content. This will allow an IAM principal to assume the role you will create next (file provided in the repository):

```
{
  "Version": "2012-10-17",
  "Statement": [
    {
      "Effect": "Allow",
      "Principal": {
        "AWS": "PRINCIPAL_ARN"
      },
      "Action": "sts:AssumeRole"
    }
  ]
}
```

 If you are using an IAM user, and you delete and re-create the IAM user, this policy will not continue to work because of the way that the IAM service helps mitigate the risk of privilege escalation. For more information, see the Note in the IAM documentation (*https://oreil.ly/wR02t*) about this.

2. Retrieve the ARN (*https://oreil.ly/BDayp*) for your user and set it as a variable:

```
PRINCIPAL_ARN=$(aws sts get-caller-identity --query Arn --output text)
```

3. Use the sed command to replace *PRINCIPAL_ARN* in the *assume-role-policy-template.json* file and generate the *assume-role-policy.json* file:

```
sed -e "s|PRINCIPAL_ARN|${PRINCIPAL_ARN}|g" \
    assume-role-policy-template.json > assume-role-policy.json
```

4. Create a role and specify the assume role policy file:

```
ROLE_ARN=$(aws iam create-role --role-name AWSCookbook101Role \
    --assume-role-policy-document file://assume-role-policy.json \
    --output text --query Role.Arn)
```

5. Attach the AWS managed `PowerUserAccess` policy to the role:

```
aws iam attach-role-policy --role-name AWSCookbook101Role \
    --policy-arn arn:aws:iam::aws:policy/PowerUserAccess
```

AWS provides access policies for common job functions (*https://oreil.ly/iyKFx*) for your convenience. These policies may be a good starting point for you to delegate user access to your account for specific job functions; however, it is best to define a least-privilege policy for your own specific requirements for every access need.

Validation checks.   Assume the role:

```
aws sts assume-role --role-arn $ROLE_ARN \
    --role-session-name AWSCookbook101
```

You should see output similar to the following:

```
{
  "Credentials": {
    "AccessKeyId": "<snip>",
    "SecretAccessKey": "<snip>",
    "SessionToken": "<snip>",
    "Expiration": "2021-09-12T23:34:56+00:00"
  },
  "AssumedRoleUser": {
    "AssumedRoleId": "EXAMPLE:AWSCookbook101",
    "Arn": "arn:aws:sts::11111111111:assumed-role/AWSCookbook101Role/AWSCookbook101"
  }
}
```

The AssumeRole API (*https://oreil.ly/dX1je*) returns a set of temporary credentials for a role session from the AWS Security Token Service (*https://oreil.ly/AdUrq*) (STS) to the caller as long as the permissions in the `AssumeRole` policy for the role allow. All IAM roles have an `AssumeRole` policy associated with them. You can use the output of this to configure the credentials for the AWS CLI (*https://oreil.ly/F7ril*); set the AccessKey, SecretAccessKey, and SessionToken as environment variables (*https://oreil.ly/UWNWd*); and also assume the role in the AWS Console using the Switch Role (*https://oreil.ly/dSfuG*) feature. When your applications need to make AWS API calls, the AWS SDK for your programming language of choice handles this for them.

Cleanup

Follow the steps in this recipe's folder in the chapter code repository (*https://github.com/AWSCookbook/Security*).

Discussion

Using administrative access for routine development tasks is not a security best practice. Giving unneeded permissions can result in unauthorized actions being performed. Using the `PowerUserAccess` AWS managed policy for development purposes is a better alternative to start rather than using `AdministratorAccess`. Later, you should define your own customer managed policy (*https://oreil.ly/hfQ3p*) granting only the specific actions for your needs. For example, if you need to log in often to check the status of your EC2 instances, you can create a read-only policy for this purpose and attach it to a role. Similarly, you can create a role for billing access and use it to access the AWS Billing console only. The more you practice using the principle of least privilege (*https://oreil.ly/jMW6h*), the more security will become a natural part of what you do.

You used an IAM user in this recipe to perform the steps. If you are using an AWS account that leverages federation (*https://oreil.ly/hmUw3*) for access (e.g., a sandbox or development AWS account at your employer), you should use temporary credentials from the AWS STS rather than an IAM user. This type of access uses time-based tokens that expire after an amount of time, rather than "long-lived" credentials like access keys or passwords. When you performed the `AssumeRole` in the validation steps, you called the STS service for temporary credentials. To help with frequent `AssumeRole` operations, the AWS CLI supports named profiles (*https://oreil.ly/fZSQ9*) that can automatically assume and refresh your temporary credentials for your role when you specify the `role_arn` parameter in the named profile.

> You can require multi-factor authentication (MFA) as a condition within the `AssumeRole` policies you create. This would allow the role to be assumed only by an identity that has been authenticated with MFA. For more information about requiring MFA for `AssumeRole`, see the support document (*https://oreil.ly/djRQI*).

See Recipe 9.4 to create an alert when a root login occurs.

> You can grant cross-account access to your AWS resources. The resource you define in the policy in this recipe would reference the AWS account and principal within that account that you would like to delegate access to. You should always use an `ExternalID` when enabling cross-account access. For more information, see the official tutorial for cross-account access (*https://oreil.ly/wwlF4*).

Challenge

Create additional IAM roles for each of the AWS managed policies for job functions (e.g., billing, database administrator, networking, etc.)

1.2 Generating a Least Privilege IAM Policy Based on Access Patterns

Problem

You would like to implement least privilege access for your user and scope down the permissions to allow access to only the services, resources, and actions you need to use in your AWS account.

Solution

Use the IAM Access Analyzer in the IAM console to generate an IAM policy based on the CloudTrail activity in your AWS account, as shown in Figure 1-2.

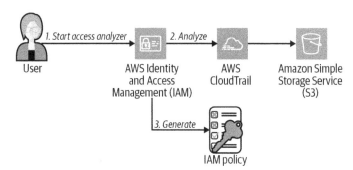

Figure 1-2. IAM Access Analyzer workflow

Prerequisite

- CloudTrail logging enabled for your account to a configured S3 bucket (see Recipe 9.3)

Steps

1. Navigate to the IAM console (*https://console.aws.amazon.com/iam*) and select your IAM role or IAM user that you would like to generate a policy for.

2. On the Permissions tab (the default active tab when viewing your principal), scroll to the bottom, expand the "Generate policy based on CloudTrail events" section, and click the "Generate policy" button.

For a quick view of the AWS services accessed from your principal, click the Access Advisor tab and view the service list and access time. While the IAM Access Advisor is not as powerful as the Access Analyzer, it can be helpful when auditing or troubleshooting IAM principals in your AWS account.

3. Select the time period of CloudTrail events you would like to evaluate, select your CloudTrail trail, choose your Region (or select "All regions"), and choose "Create and use a new service role." IAM Access Analyzer will create a role for the service to use for read access to your trail that you selected. Finally, click "Generate policy." See Figure 1-3 for an example.

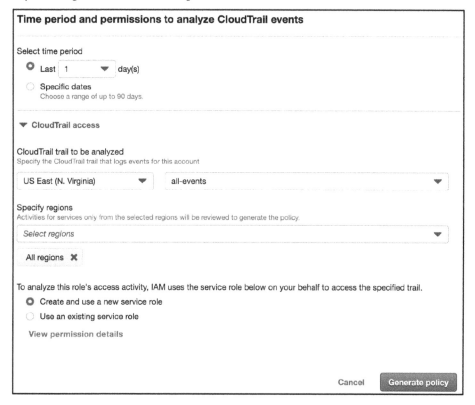

Figure 1-3. Generating a policy in the IAM Access Analyzer configuration

 The role creation can take up to 30 seconds. Once the role is created, the policy generation will take an amount of time depending on how much activity is in your CloudTrail trail.

4. Once the analyzer has completed, scroll to the bottom of the permissions tab and click "View generated policy," as shown in Figure 1-4.

Figure 1-4. Viewing the generated policy

5. Click Next, and you will see a generated policy in JSON format that is based on the activity that your IAM principal has made. You can edit this policy in the interface if you wish to add additional permissions. Click Next again, choose a name, and you can deploy this generated policy as an IAM policy.

You should see a generated IAM policy in the IAM console similar to this:

```
{
  "Version": "2012-10-17",
  "Statement": [
    {
      "Effect": "Allow",
      "Action": [
        "access-analyzer:ListPolicyGenerations",
        "cloudtrail:DescribeTrails",
        "cloudtrail:LookupEvents",
        "iam:GetAccountPasswordPolicy",
        "iam:GetAccountSummary",
        "iam:GetServiceLastAccessedDetails",
        "iam:ListAccountAliases",
        "iam:ListGroups",
        "iam:ListMFADevices",
        "iam:ListUsers",
        "s3:ListAllMyBuckets",
        "sts:GetCallerIdentity"
      ],
      "Resource": "*"
    }, ...
}
```

Validation checks. Create a new IAM user or role and attach the newly created IAM policy to it. Perform an action granted by the policy to verify that the policy allows your IAM principal to perform the actions that you need it to.

Discussion

You should always seek to implement least privilege IAM policies when you are scoping them for your users and applications. Oftentimes, you might not know exactly what permissions you may need when you start. With IAM Access Analyzer, you can start by granting your users and applications a larger scope in a development environment, enable CloudTrail logging (Recipe 9.3), and then run IAM Access Analyzer after you have a window of time that provides a good representation of the usual activity (choose this time period in the Access Analyzer configuration as you did in step 3). The generated policy will contain all of the necessary permissions to allow your application or users to work as they did during that time period that you chose to analyze, helping you implement the principle of least privilege (*https://oreil.ly/ jMW6h*).

You should also be aware of the list of services (*https://oreil.ly/ KPEFh*) that Access Analyzer supports.

Challenge

Use the IAM Policy Simulator (see Recipe 1.4) on the generated policy to verify that the policy contains the access you need.

1.3 Enforcing IAM User Password Policies in Your AWS Account

Special thanks to Gaurav Raje for his contribution to this recipe.

Problem

Your security policy requires that you must enforce a password policy for all the users within your AWS account. The password policy sets a 90-day expiration, and passwords must be made up of a minimum of 32 characters including lowercase and uppercase letters, numbers, and symbols.

Solution

Set a password policy for IAM users in your AWS account. Create an IAM group, an IAM user, and add the user to the group to verify that the policy is being enforced (see Figure 1-5).

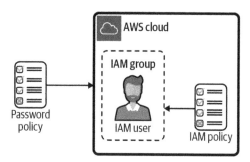

Figure 1-5. Using password policies with IAM users

If your organization has a central user directory, we recommend using identity federation to access your AWS accounts using AWS Single Sign-On (SSO) (*https://aws.amazon.com/single-sign-on*) rather than create individual IAM users and groups. Federation allows you to use an identity provider (IdP) where you already maintain users and groups. AWS publishes a guide (*https://aws.amazon.com/identity/federation*) that explains federated access configurations available. You can follow Recipe 9.6 to enable AWS SSO for your account even if you do not have an IdP available (AWS SSO provides a directory you can use by default).

Steps

1. Set an IAM password policy using the AWS CLI to require lowercase and upper-case letters, symbols, and numbers. The policy should indicate a minimum length of 32 characters, a maximum password age of 90 days, and password reuse prevented:

```
aws iam update-account-password-policy \
    --minimum-password-length 32 \
    --require-symbols \
    --require-numbers \
    --require-uppercase-characters \
    --require-lowercase-characters \
    --allow-users-to-change-password \
    --max-password-age 90 \
    --password-reuse-prevention true
```

2. Create an IAM group:

```
aws iam create-group --group-name AWSCookbook103Group
```

You should see output similar to the following:

```
{
  "Group": {
    "Path": "/",
    "GroupName": "AWSCookbook103Group",
    "GroupId": "<snip>",
```

```
        "Arn": "arn:aws:iam::111111111111:group/AWSCookbook103Group",
        "CreateDate": "2021-11-06T19:26:01+00:00"
    }
}
```

3. Attach the `ReadOnlyAccess` policy to the group:

```
aws iam attach-group-policy --group-name AWSCookbook103Group \
    --policy-arn arn:aws:iam::aws:policy/AWSBillingReadOnlyAccess
```

 It is best to attach policies to groups and not directly to users. As the number of users grows, it is easier to use IAM groups to delegate permissions for manageability. This also helps to meet compliance for standards like CIS Level 1 (*https://oreil.ly/ i211Q*).

4. Create an IAM user:

```
aws iam create-user --user-name awscookbook103user
```

You should see output similar to the following:

```
{
  "User": {
    "Path": "/",
    "UserName": "awscookbook103user",
    "UserId": "<snip>",
    "Arn": "arn:aws:iam::111111111111:user/awscookbook103user",
    "CreateDate": "2021-11-06T21:01:47+00:00"
  }
}
```

5. Use Secrets Manager to generate a password that conforms to your password policy:

```
RANDOM_STRING=$(aws secretsmanager get-random-password \
--password-length 32 --require-each-included-type \
--output text \
--query RandomPassword)
```

6. Create a login profile for the user that specifies a password:

```
aws iam create-login-profile --user-name awscookbook103user \
    --password $RANDOM_STRING
```

You should see output similar to the following:

```
{
  "LoginProfile": {
    "UserName": "awscookbook103user",
    "CreateDate": "2021-11-06T21:11:43+00:00",
    "PasswordResetRequired": false
  }
}
```

7. Add the user to the group you created for billing view-only access:

```
aws iam add-user-to-group --group-name AWSCookbook103Group \
    --user-name awscookbook103user
```

Validation checks.   Verify that the password policy you set is now active:

```
aws iam get-account-password-policy
```

You should see output similar to:

```
{
  "PasswordPolicy": {
    "MinimumPasswordLength": 32,
    "RequireSymbols": true,
    "RequireNumbers": true,
    "RequireUppercaseCharacters": true,
    "RequireLowercaseCharacters": true,
    "AllowUsersToChangePassword": true,
    "ExpirePasswords": true,
    "MaxPasswordAge": 90,
    "PasswordReusePrevention": 1
  }
}
```

Try to create a new user by using the AWS CLI with a password that violates the password policy. AWS will not allow you to create such a user:

```
aws iam create-user --user-name awscookbook103user2
```

Use Secrets Manager to generate a password that does not adhere to your password policy:

```
RANDOM_STRING2=$(aws secretsmanager get-random-password \
--password-length 16 --require-each-included-type \
--output text \
--query RandomPassword)
```

Create a login profile for the user that specifies the password:

```
aws iam create-login-profile --user-name awscookbook103user2 \
--password $RANDOM_STRING2
```

This command should fail and you should see output similar to:

```
An error occurred (PasswordPolicyViolation) when calling the CreateLoginProfile
operation: Password should have a minimum length of 32
```

Cleanup

Follow the steps in this recipe's folder in the chapter code repository (*https://github.com/AWSCookbook/Security*).

Discussion

For users logging in with passwords, AWS allows administrators to enforce password policies to their accounts that conform to the security requirements of your organization. This way, administrators can ensure that individual users don't compromise the security of the organization by choosing weak passwords or by not regularly changing their passwords.

Multi-factor authentication is encouraged for IAM users. You can use a software-based virtual MFA device or a hardware device for a second factor on IAM users. AWS keeps an updated list of supported devices (*https://aws.amazon.com/iam/features/mfa*).

Multi-factor authentication is a great way to add another layer of security on top of existing password-based security. It combines "what you know" and "what you have"; so, in cases where your password might be exposed to a malicious third-party actor, they would still need the additional factor to authenticate.

Challenge

Download the credential report (*https://oreil.ly/GFTke*) to analyze the IAM users and the password ages in your account.

1.4 Testing IAM Policies with the IAM Policy Simulator

Problem

You have an IAM policy that you would like to put into use but would like to test its effectiveness first.

Solution

Attach an IAM policy to an IAM role and simulate actions with the IAM Policy Simulator, as shown in Figure 1-6.

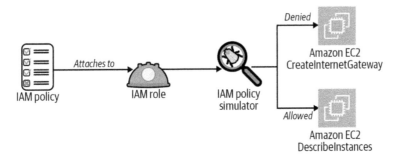

Figure 1-6. Simulating IAM policies attached to an IAM role

Steps

1. Create a file called *assume-role-policy.json* with the following content (file provided in the repository):

```
{
  "Version": "2012-10-17",
  "Statement": [
    {
      "Effect": "Allow",
      "Principal": {
        "Service": "ec2.amazonaws.com"
      },
      "Action": "sts:AssumeRole"
    }
  ]
}
```

2. Create an IAM role using the *assume-role-policy.json* file:

```
aws iam create-role --assume-role-policy-document \
    file://assume-role-policy.json --role-name AWSCookbook104IamRole
```

You should see output similar to the following:

```
{
  "Role": {
  "Path": "/",
  "RoleName": "AWSCookbook104IamRole",
  "RoleId": "<<UniqueID>>",
  "Arn": "arn:aws:iam::111111111111:role/AWSCookbook104IamRole",
  "CreateDate": "2021-09-22T23:37:44+00:00",
  "AssumeRolePolicyDocument": {
    "Version": "2012-10-17",
    "Statement": [
      ...
```

3. Attach the IAM managed policy for `AmazonEC2ReadOnlyAccess` to the IAM role:

```
aws iam attach-role-policy --role-name AWSCookbook104IamRole \
    --policy-arn arn:aws:iam::aws:policy/AmazonEC2ReadOnlyAccess
```

> You can find a list of all the actions, resources, and condition keys for EC2 in this AWS article (*https://oreil.ly/EjuR3*). The IAM global condition context keys (*https://oreil.ly/IUVkw*) are also useful in authoring fine-grained policies.

Validation checks.   Simulate the effect of the IAM policy you are using, testing several different types of actions on the EC2 service.

Test the `ec2:CreateInternetGateway` action:

```
aws iam simulate-principal-policy \
    --policy-source-arn arn:aws:iam::$AWS_ACCOUNT_ARN:role/AWSCookbook104IamRole \
    --action-names ec2:CreateInternetGateway
```

You should see output similar to the following (note the `EvalDecision`):

```
{
  "EvaluationResults": [
```

```
{
    "EvalActionName": "ec2:CreateInternetGateway",
    "EvalResourceName": "*",
    "EvalDecision": "implicitDeny",
    "MatchedStatements": [],
    "MissingContextValues": []
  }
 ]
}
```

Since you attached only the AWS managed AmazonEC2ReadOnlyAc
cess IAM policy to the role in this recipe, you will see an implicit
deny for the CreateInternetGateway action. This is expected
behavior. AmazonEC2ReadOnlyAccess does not grant any "create"
capabilities for the EC2 service.

Test the ec2:DescribeInstances action:

```
aws iam simulate-principal-policy \
    --policy-source-arn arn:aws:iam::$AWS_ACCOUNT_ARN:role/AWSCookbook104IamRole \
    --action-names ec2:DescribeInstances
```

You should see output similar to the following:

```
{
  "EvaluationResults": [
    {
    "EvalActionName": "ec2:DescribeInstances",
    "EvalResourceName": "*",
    "EvalDecision": "allowed",
    "MatchedStatements": [
        {
        "SourcePolicyId": "AmazonEC2ReadOnlyAccess",
        "SourcePolicyType": "IAM Policy",
        "StartPosition": {
          "Line": 3,
          "Column": 17
        },
        "EndPosition": {
          "Line": 8,
          "Column": 6
        }
        }
      ],
    "MissingContextValues": []
  }
 ]
}
```

The AmazonEC2ReadOnlyAccess policy allows read operations on
the EC2 service, so the DescribeInstances operation succeeds
when you simulate this action.

Cleanup

Follow the steps in this recipe's folder in the chapter code repository (*https://github.com/AWSCookbook/Security*).

Discussion

IAM policies (*https://oreil.ly/uy1uB*) let you define permissions for managing access in AWS. Policies can be attached to principals that allow you to grant (or deny) permissions to resources, users, groups and services. It is always best to scope your policies to the minimal set of permissions required as a security best practice. The IAM Policy Simulator (*https://oreil.ly/9qscF*) can be extremely helpful when designing and managing your own IAM policies for least-privileged access.

The IAM Policy Simulator also exposes a web interface you can use to test and troubleshoot IAM policies and understand their net effect with the policy you define. You can test all the policies or a subset of policies that you have attached to users, groups, and roles.

 The IAM Policy Simulator can help you simulate the effect of the following:

- Identity-based policies
- IAM permissions boundaries
- AWS Organizations service control policies (SCPs)
- Resource-based policies

After you review the Policy Simulator results, you can add additional statements to your policies that either solve your issue (from a troubleshooting standpoint) or attach newly created policies to users, groups, and roles with the confidence that the net effect of the policy was what you intended.

 To help you easily build IAM policies from scratch, AWS provides the AWS Policy Generator (*https://oreil.ly/Ny8HI*).

Challenge

Simulate the effect of a permissions boundary on an IAM principal (see Recipe 1.5).

1.5 Delegating IAM Administrative Capabilities Using Permissions Boundaries

Problem

You need to grant team members the ability to deploy Lambda functions and create IAM roles for them. You need to limit the effective permissions of the IAM roles created so that they allow only actions needed by the function.

Solution

Create a permissions boundary (*https://oreil.ly/dtZ7X*) policy, create an IAM role for Lambda developers, create an IAM policy that specifies the boundary policy, and attach the policy to the role you created. Figure 1-7 illustrates the effective permissions of the identity-based policy with the permissions boundary.

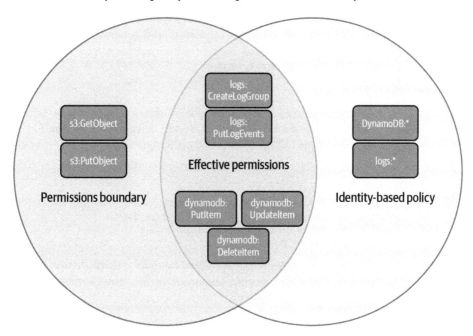

Figure 1-7. Effective permissions of identity-based policy with permissions boundary

Prerequisite

- An IAM user or federated identity for your AWS account with administrative privileges (follow the AWS guide for creating your first IAM admin user and user group (*https://oreil.ly/2MPmL*)).

Steps

1. Create a file named *assume-role-policy-template.json* with the following content (file provided in the repository):

```
{
  "Version": "2012-10-17",
  "Statement": [
    {
      "Effect": "Allow",
      "Principal": {
        "AWS": "PRINCIPAL_ARN"
      },
      "Action": "sts:AssumeRole"
    }
  ]
}
```

2. Retrieve the ARN for your user and set it as a variable:

```
PRINCIPAL_ARN=$(aws sts get-caller-identity --query Arn --output text)
```

3. Use the `sed` command to replace *PRINCIPAL_ARN* in the *assume-role-policy-template.json* file that we provided in the repository and generate the *assume-role-policy.json* file:

```
sed -e "s|PRINCIPAL_ARN|${PRINCIPAL_ARN}|g" \
assume-role-policy-template.json > assume-role-policy.json
```

> For the purposes of this recipe, you set the allowed IAM principal to your own user (User 1). To test delegated access, you would set the IAM principal to something else.

4. Create a role and specify the assume role policy file:

```
ROLE_ARN=$(aws iam create-role --role-name AWSCookbook105Role \
    --assume-role-policy-document file://assume-role-policy.json \
    --output text --query Role.Arn)
```

5. Create a permissions boundary JSON file named *boundary-template.json* with the following content. This allows specific DynamoDB, S3, and CloudWatch Logs actions (file provided in the repository):

```
{
  "Version": "2012-10-17",
  "Statement": [
    {
      "Sid": "CreateLogGroup",
      "Effect": "Allow",
      "Action": "logs:CreateLogGroup",
      "Resource": "arn:aws:logs:*:AWS_ACCOUNT_ID:*"
    },
    {
      "Sid": "CreateLogStreamandEvents",
      "Effect": "Allow",
```

```
      "Action": [
        "logs:CreateLogStream",
        "logs:PutLogEvents"
      ],
      "Resource": "arn:aws:logs:*:AWS_ACCOUNT_ID:*"
    },
    {
      "Sid": "DynamoDBPermissions",
      "Effect": "Allow",
      "Action": [
        "dynamodb:PutItem",
        "dynamodb:UpdateItem",
        "dynamodb:DeleteItem"
      ],
      "Resource": "arn:aws:dynamodb:*:AWS_ACCOUNT_ID:table/AWSCookbook*"
    },
    {
      "Sid": "S3Permissions",
      "Effect": "Allow",
      "Action": [
        "s3:GetObject",
        "s3:PutObject"
      ],
      "Resource": "arn:aws:s3:::AWSCookbook*/*"
    }
  ]
}
```

6. Use the `sed` command to replace *AWS_ACCOUNT_ID* in the *boundary-policy-template.json* file and generate the *boundary-policy.json* file:

```
sed -e "s|AWS_ACCOUNT_ID|${AWS_ACCOUNT_ID}|g" \
    boundary-policy-template.json > boundary-policy.json
```

7. Create the permissions boundary policy by using the AWS CLI:

```
aws iam create-policy --policy-name AWSCookbook105PB \
    --policy-document file://boundary-policy.json
```

You should see output similar to the following:

```
{
  "Policy": {
    "PolicyName": "AWSCookbook105PB",
    "PolicyId": "EXAMPLE",
    "Arn": "arn:aws:iam::111111111111:policy/AWSCookbook105PB",
    "Path": "/",
    "DefaultVersionId": "v1",
    "AttachmentCount": 0,
    "PermissionsBoundaryUsageCount": 0,
    "IsAttachable": true,
    "CreateDate": "2021-09-24T00:36:53+00:00",
    "UpdateDate": "2021-09-24T00:36:53+00:00"
  }
}
```

8. Create a policy file named *policy-template.json* for the role (file provided in the repository):

```
{
  "Version": "2012-10-17",
  "Statement": [
    {
      "Sid": "DenyPBDelete", ❶
      "Effect": "Deny",
      "Action": "iam:DeleteRolePermissionsBoundary",
      "Resource": "*"
    },
    {
      "Sid": "IAMRead", ❷
      "Effect": "Allow",
      "Action": [
        "iam:Get*",
        "iam:List*"
      ],
      "Resource": "*"
    },
    {
      "Sid": "IAMPolicies", ❸
      "Effect": "Allow",
      "Action": [
        "iam:CreatePolicy",
        "iam:DeletePolicy",
        "iam:CreatePolicyVersion",
        "iam:DeletePolicyVersion",
        "iam:SetDefaultPolicyVersion"
      ],
      "Resource": "arn:aws:iam::AWS_ACCOUNT_ID:policy/AWSCookbook*"
    },
    {
      "Sid": "IAMRolesWithBoundary", ❹
      "Effect": "Allow",
      "Action": [
        "iam:CreateRole",
        "iam:DeleteRole",
        "iam:PutRolePolicy",
        "iam:DeleteRolePolicy",
        "iam:AttachRolePolicy",
        "iam:DetachRolePolicy"
      ],
      "Resource": [
        "arn:aws:iam::AWS_ACCOUNT_ID:role/AWSCookbook*"
      ],
      "Condition": {
        "StringEquals": {
          "iam:PermissionsBoundary": "arn:aws:iam::AWS_ACCOUNT_ID:policy/
AWSCookbook105PB"
        }
      }
    },
    {
      "Sid": "ServerlessFullAccess", ❺
```

```
    "Effect": "Allow",
     "Action": [
     "lambda:*",
     "logs:*",
     "dynamodb:*",
     "s3:*"
    ],
    "Resource": "*"
  },
  {
    "Sid": "PassRole", ❻
    "Effect": "Allow",
    "Action": "iam:PassRole",
    "Resource": "arn:aws:iam::AWS_ACCOUNT_ID:role/AWSCookbook*",
    "Condition": {
      "StringLikeIfExists": {
        "iam:PassedToService": "lambda.amazonaws.com"
      }
    }
  },
  {
    "Sid": "ProtectPB", ❼
    "Effect": "Deny",
    "Action": [
      "iam:CreatePolicyVersion",
      "iam:DeletePolicy",
      "iam:DeletePolicyVersion",
      "iam:SetDefaultPolicyVersion"
    ],
    "Resource": [
      "arn:aws:iam::AWS_ACCOUNT_ID:policy/AWSCookbook105PB",
      "arn:aws:iam::AWS_ACCOUNT_ID:policy/AWSCookbook105Policy"
    ]
  }
 ]
}
```

This custom IAM policy has several statements working together, which define certain permissions for the solution to the problem statement:

❶ DenyPBDelete: Explicitly deny the ability to delete permissions boundaries from roles.

❷ IAMRead: Allow read-only IAM access to developers to ensure that the IAM console works.

❸ IAMPolicies: Allow the creation of IAM policies but force a naming convention prefix AWSCookbook*.

❹ IAMRolesWithBoundary: Allow the creation and deletion of IAM roles only if they contain the permissions boundary referenced.

⑤ `ServerlessFullAccess`: Allow developers to have full access to the AWS Lambda, Amazon DynamoDB, Amazon CloudWatch logs, and Amazon S3 services.

⑥ `PassRole`: Allow developers to pass IAM roles to Lambda functions.

⑦ `ProtectPB`: Explicitly deny the ability to modify the permissions boundary that bound the roles they create.

9. Use the `sed` command to replace *AWS_ACCOUNT_ID* in the *policy-template.json* file and generate the *policy.json* file:

```
sed -e "s|AWS_ACCOUNT_ID|${AWS_ACCOUNT_ID}|g" \
    policy-template.json > policy.json
```

10. Create the policy for developer access:

```
aws iam create-policy --policy-name AWSCookbook105Policy \
    --policy-document file://policy.json
```

You should see output similar to the following:

```
{
  "Policy": {
    "PolicyName": "AWSCookbook105Policy",
    "PolicyId": "EXAMPLE",
    "Arn": "arn:aws:iam::11111111111:policy/AWSCookbook105Policy",
    "Path": "/",
    "DefaultVersionId": "v1",
    "AttachmentCount": 0,
    "PermissionsBoundaryUsageCount": 0,
    "IsAttachable": true,
    "CreateDate": "2021-09-24T00:37:13+00:00",
    "UpdateDate": "2021-09-24T00:37:13+00:00"
  }
}
```

11. Attach the policy to the role you created in step 2:

```
aws iam attach-role-policy --policy-arn \
    arn:aws:iam::$AWS_ACCOUNT_ID:policy/AWSCookbook105Policy \
    --role-name AWSCookbook105Role
```

Validation checks.   Assume the role you created and set the output to local variables for the AWS CLI:

```
creds=$(aws --output text sts assume-role --role-arn $ROLE_ARN \
    --role-session-name "AWSCookbook105" | \
    grep CREDENTIALS | cut -d " " -f2,4,5)
export AWS_ACCESS_KEY_ID=$(echo $creds | cut -d " " -f2)
export AWS_SECRET_ACCESS_KEY=$(echo $creds | cut -d " " -f4)
export AWS_SESSION_TOKEN=$(echo $creds | cut -d " " -f5)
```

Try to create an IAM role for a Lambda function, create an assume role policy for the Lambda service (*lambda-assume-role-policy.json*):

```json
{
  "Version": "2012-10-17",
  "Statement": [
    {
      "Effect": "Allow",
      "Principal": {
        "Service": "lambda.amazonaws.com"
      },
      "Action": "sts:AssumeRole"
    }
  ]
}
```

Create the role, specifying the permissions boundary, which conforms to the role-naming standard specified in the policy:

```
TEST_ROLE_1=$(aws iam create-role --role-name AWSCookbook105test1 \
    --assume-role-policy-document \
    file://lambda-assume-role-policy.json \
    --permissions-boundary \
    arn:aws:iam::$AWS_ACCOUNT_ID:policy/AWSCookbook105PB \
    --output text --query Role.Arn)
```

Attach the managed `AmazonDynamoDBFullAccess` policy to the role:

```
aws iam attach-role-policy --role-name AWSCookbook105test1 \
--policy-arn arn:aws:iam::aws:policy/AmazonDynamoDBFullAccess
```

Attach the managed `CloudWatchFullAccess` policy to the role:

```
aws iam attach-role-policy --role-name AWSCookbook105test1 \
--policy-arn arn:aws:iam::aws:policy/CloudWatchFullAccess
```

> Even though you attached `AmazonDynamoDBFullAccess` and `CloudWatchFullAccess` to the role, the effective permissions of the role are limited by the statements in the permissions boundary you created in step 3. Furthermore, even though you have `s3:GetObject` and `s3:PutObject` defined in the boundary, you have not defined these in the role policy, so the function will not be able to make these calls until you create a policy that allows these actions. When you attach this role to a Lambda function, the Lambda function can perform only the actions allowed in the intersection of the permissions boundary and the role policy (see Figure 1-7).

You can now create a Lambda function specifying this role (`AWSCookbook105test1`) as the execution role to validate the DynamoDB and CloudWatch Logs permissions granted to the function. You can also test the results with the IAM Policy Simulator.

You used an `AssumeRole` and set environment variables to override your local terminal AWS profile to perform these validation checks. To ensure that you revert back to your original authenticated session on the command line, perform the perform the cleanup steps provided at the top of the README file in the repository.

Cleanup

Follow the steps in this recipe's folder in the chapter code repository (*https:// github.com/AWSCookbook/Security*).

Be sure to delete your environment variables so that you can regain permissions needed for future recipes:

```
unset AWS_ACCESS_KEY_ID
unset AWS_SECRET_ACCESS_KEY
unset AWS_SESSION_TOKEN
```

Discussion

In your quest to implement a least privilege access model for users and applications within AWS, you need to enable developers to create IAM roles that their applications can assume when they need to interact with other AWS services. For example, an AWS Lambda function that needs to access an Amazon DynamoDB table would need a role created to be able to perform operations against the table. As your team scales, instead of your team members coming to you every time they need a role created for a specific purpose, you can enable (but control) them with permissions boundaries, without giving up too much IAM access. The `iam:PermissionsBoundary` condition in the policy that grants the `iam:CreateRole` ensures that the roles created must always include the permissions boundary attached.

Permissions boundaries act as a guardrail and limit privilege escalation. In other words, they limit the maximum effective permissions of an IAM principal created by a delegated administrator by defining what the roles created can do. As shown in Figure 1-7, they work in conjunction with the permissions policy (IAM policy) that is attached to an IAM principal (IAM user or role). This prevents the need to grant wide access to an administrator role, prevents privilege escalation, and helps you achieve least privilege access by allowing your team members to quickly iterate and create their own least-privileged roles for their applications.

In this recipe, you may have noticed that we used a naming convention of `AWSCook book*` on the roles and policies referenced in the permissions boundary policy, which ensures the delegated principals can create roles and policies within this convention. This means that developers can create resources, pass *only* these roles to services, and also keep a standard naming convention. This is an ideal practice when implementing permissions boundaries. You can develop a naming convention for different teams, applications, and services so that these can all coexist within the same account, yet have different boundaries applied to them based on their requirements, if necessary.

At minimum, you need to keep these four things in mind when building roles that implement permissions boundary guardrails to delegate IAM permissions to nonadministrators:

1. Allow the creation of IAM customer managed policies: your users can create any policy they wish; they do not have an effect until they are attached to an IAM principal.

2. Allow IAM role creation with a condition that a permissions boundary must be attached: force all roles created by your team members to include the permission boundary in the role creation.

3. Allow attachment of policies, but only to roles that have a permissions boundary: do not let users modify existing roles that they may have access to.

4. Allow `iam:PassRole` to AWS services that your users create roles for: your developers may need to create roles for Amazon EC2 and AWS Lambda, so give them the ability to pass only the roles they create to those services you define.

> Permissions boundaries are a powerful, advanced IAM concept that can be challenging to understand. We recommend checking out the talk (*https://oreil.ly/0Smmq*) by Brigid Johnson at AWS re:Inforce 2018 to see some real-world examples of IAM policies, roles, and permissions boundaries explained in a practical way.

Challenge

Extend the permissions boundary to allow roles created to publish to an SQS queue and SNS topic and adjust the policy for the role as well.

1.6 Connecting to EC2 Instances Using AWS SSM Session Manager

Problem

You have an EC2 instance in a private subnet and need to connect to the instance without using SSH over the internet.

Solution

Create an IAM role, attach the `AmazonSSMManagedInstanceCore` policy, create an EC2 instance profile, attach the IAM role you created to the instance profile, associate the

EC2 instance profile to an EC2 instance, and finally, run the `aws ssm start-session` command to connect to the instance. A logical flow of these steps is shown in Figure 1-8.

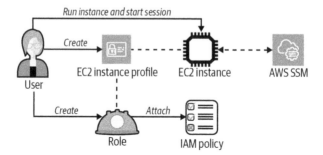

Figure 1-8. Using Session Manager to connect to an EC2 instance

Prerequisites

- Amazon Virtual Private Cloud (VPC) with isolated or private subnets and associated route tables
- Required VPC endpoints for AWS Systems Manager (*https://oreil.ly/qyNJR*)
- AWS CLI v2 with the Session Manager plugin installed (*https://oreil.ly/ejccM*)

Preparation

Follow the steps in this recipe's folder in the chapter code repository (*https://github.com/AWSCookbook/Security*).

Steps

1. Create a file named *assume-role-policy.json* with the following content (file provided in the repository):

    ```
    {
      "Version": "2012-10-17",
      "Statement": [
      {
        "Effect": "Allow",
        "Principal": {
          "Service": "ec2.amazonaws.com"
        },
        "Action": "sts:AssumeRole"
      }
      ]
    }
    ```

2. Create an IAM role with the statement in the provided *assume-role-policy.json* file using this command:

```
ROLE_ARN=$(aws iam create-role --role-name AWSCookbook106SSMRole \
    --assume-role-policy-document file://assume-role-policy.json \
    --output text --query Role.Arn)
```

3. Attach the `AmazonSSMManagedInstanceCore` managed policy to the role so that the role allows access to AWS Systems Manager:

```
aws iam attach-role-policy --role-name AWSCookbook106SSMRole \
    --policy-arn arn:aws:iam::aws:policy/AmazonSSMManagedInstanceCore
```

4. Create an instance profile:

```
aws iam create-instance-profile \
    --instance-profile-name AWSCookbook106InstanceProfile
```

You should see output similar to the following:

```
{
  "InstanceProfile": {
    "Path": "/",
    "InstanceProfileName": "AWSCookbook106InstanceProfile",
    "InstanceProfileId": "(RandomString",
    "Arn": "arn:aws:iam::111111111111:instance-profile/
AWSCookbook106InstanceProfile",
    "CreateDate": "2021-11-28T20:26:23+00:00",
    "Roles": []
  }
}
```

5. Add the role that you created to the instance profile:

```
aws iam add-role-to-instance-profile \
    --role-name AWSCookbook106SSMRole \
    --instance-profile-name AWSCookbook106InstanceProfile
```

> The EC2 instance profile contains a role that you create. The instance profile association with an instance allows it to define "who I am," and the role defines "what I am permitted to do." Both are required by IAM to allow an EC2 instance to communicate with other AWS services using the IAM service. You can get a list of instance profiles in your account by running the aws `iam list-instance-profiles` AWS CLI command.

6. Query SSM for the latest Amazon Linux 2 AMI ID available in your Region and save it as an environment variable:

```
AMI_ID=$(aws ssm get-parameters --names \
    /aws/service/ami-amazon-linux-latest/amzn2-ami-hvm-x86_64-gp2 \
    --query 'Parameters[0].[Value]' --output text)
```

7. Launch an instance in one of your subnets that references the instance profile you created and also uses a `Name` tag that helps you identify the instance in the console:

```
INSTANCE_ID=$(aws ec2 run-instances --image-id $AMI_ID \
    --count 1 \
    --instance-type t3.nano \
    --iam-instance-profile Name=AWSCookbook106InstanceProfile \
    --subnet-id $SUBNET_1 \
    --security-group-ids $INSTANCE_SG \
    --metadata-options \
HttpTokens=required,HttpPutResponseHopLimit=64,HttpEndpoint=enabled \
    --tag-specifications \
    'ResourceType=instance,Tags=[{Key=Name,Value=AWSCookbook106}]' \
    'ResourceType=volume,Tags=[{Key=Name,Value=AWSCookbook106}]' \
    --query Instances[0].InstanceId \
    --output text)
```

 EC2 instance metadata (*https://oreil.ly/DtodI*) is a feature you can use within your EC2 instance to access information about your EC2 instance over an HTTP endpoint from the instance itself. This is helpful for scripting and automation via user data (*https://oreil.ly/IMqFC*). You should always use the latest version of instance metadata. In step 7, you did this by specifying the `--metadata-options` flag and providing the `HttpTo kens=required` option that forces IMDSv2 (*https://oreil.ly/ KGC4n*).

Validation checks. Ensure your EC2 instance has registered with SSM. Use the following command to check the status. This command should return the instance ID:

```
aws ssm describe-instance-information \
    --filters Key=ResourceType,Values=EC2Instance \
    --query "InstanceInformationList[].InstanceId" --output text
```

Connect to the EC2 instance by using SSM Session Manager:

```
aws ssm start-session --target $INSTANCE_ID
```

You should now be connected to your instance and see a bash prompt. From the bash prompt, run a command to validate you are connected to your EC2 instance by querying the metadata service for an IMDSv2 token and using the token to query metadata for the instance profile associated with the instance:

```
TOKEN=`curl -X PUT "http://169.254.169.254/latest/api/token" -H "X-aws-ec2-metadata-
token-ttl-seconds: 21600"`
curl -H "X-aws-ec2-metadata-token: $TOKEN" http://169.254.169.254/latest/meta-
data/iam/info
```

You should see output similar to the following:

```
{
  "Code" : "Success",
  "LastUpdated" : "2021-09-23T16:03:25Z",
  "InstanceProfileArn" : "arn:aws:iam::111111111111:instance-profile/
AWSCookbook106InstanceProfile",
  "InstanceProfileId" : "AIPAZVTINAMEXAMPLE"
}
```

Exit the Session Manager session:

```
exit
```

Cleanup

Follow the steps in this recipe's folder in the chapter code repository (*https:// github.com/AWSCookbook/Security*).

Discussion

When you use AWS SSM Session Manager to connect to EC2 instances, you eliminate your dependency on Secure Shell (SSH) over the internet for command-line access to your instances. Once you configure Session Manager for your instances, you can instantly connect to a bash shell session on Linux or a PowerShell session for Windows systems.

> SSM can log all commands and their output during a session. You can set a preference to stop the logging of sensitive data (e.g., passwords) with this command:
>
> ```
> stty -echo; read passwd; stty echo;
> ```
>
> There is more information in an AWS article (*https://oreil.ly/QJcHr*) about logging session activity.

Session Manager works by communicating with the AWS Systems Manager (SSM) API endpoints within the AWS Region you are using over HTTPS (TCP port 443). The agent on your instance registers with the SSM service at boot time. No inbound security group rules are needed for Session Manager functionality. We recommend configuring VPC Endpoints for Session Manager (*https://oreil.ly/vNEZQ*) to avoid the need for internet traffic and the cost of Network Address Translation (NAT) gateways.

Here are some examples of the increased security posture Session Manager provides:

- No internet-facing TCP ports need to be allowed in security groups associated with instances.
- You can run instances in private (or isolated) subnets without exposing them directly to the internet and still access them for management duties.

- There is no need to create, associate, and manage SSH keys with instances.
- There is no need to manage user accounts and passwords on instances.
- You can delegate access to manage EC2 instances using IAM roles.

 Any tool like SSM that provides such powerful capabilities must be carefully audited. AWS provides information about locking down permissions (*https://oreil.ly/EQyPf*) for the SSM user, and more information about auditing session activity (*https://oreil.ly/aHzbf*).

Challenge

View the logs for a session and create an alert whenever the rm command is executed.

1.7 Encrypting EBS Volumes Using KMS Keys

Problem

You need an encryption key for encrypting EBS volumes attached to your EC2 instances in a Region, and you need to rotate the key automatically every 365 days.

Solution

Create a customer-managed KMS key (CMK), enable yearly rotation of the key, enable EC2 default encryption for EBS volumes in a Region, and specify the KMS key you created (shown in Figure 1-9).

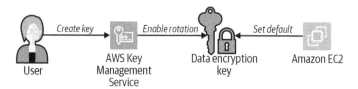

Figure 1-9. Create a customer-managed key, enable rotation, and set default encryption for EC2 using a customer-managed key

Steps

1. Create a customer-managed KMS key and store the key ARN as a local variable:
   ```
   KMS_KEY_ID=$(aws kms create-key --description "AWSCookbook107Key" \
       --output text --query KeyMetadata.KeyId)
   ```

2. Create a key alias to help you refer to the key in other steps:
   ```
   aws kms create-alias --alias-name alias/AWSCookbook107Key \
       --target-key-id $KMS_KEY_ID
   ```

3. Enable automated rotation of the symmetric key material every 365 days:

```
aws kms enable-key-rotation --key-id $KMS_KEY_ID
```

4. Enable EBS encryption by default for the EC2 service within your current Region:

```
aws ec2 enable-ebs-encryption-by-default
```

You should see output similar to the following:

```
{
    "EbsEncryptionByDefault": true
}
```

5. Update the default KMS key used for default EBS encryption to your customer-managed key that you created in step 1:

```
aws ec2 modify-ebs-default-kms-key-id \
    --kms-key-id alias/AWSCookbook107Key
```

You should see output similar to the following:

```
{
  "KmsKeyId": "arn:aws:kms:us-east-1:111111111111:key/1111111-aaaa-bbbb-222222222"
}
```

Validation checks. Use the AWS CLI to retrieve the default EBS encryption status for the EC2 service:

```
aws ec2 get-ebs-encryption-by-default
```

You should see output similar to the following:

```
{
  "EbsEncryptionByDefault": true
}
```

Retrieve the KMS key ID used for default encryption:

```
aws ec2 get-ebs-default-kms-key-id
```

You should see output similar to the following:

```
{
  "KmsKeyId": "arn:aws:kms:us-east-1:1111111111:key/1111111-aaaa-3333-222222222c64b"
}
```

Check the automatic rotation status of the key you created:

```
aws kms get-key-rotation-status --key-id $KMS_KEY_ID
```

You should see output similar to the following:

```
{
  "KeyRotationEnabled": true
}
```

Cleanup

Follow the steps in this recipe's folder in the chapter code repository (*https://github.com/AWSCookbook/Security*).

Discussion

When you are faced with the challenge of ensuring that all of your newly created EBS volumes are encrypted, the ebs-encryption-by-default option comes to the rescue. With this setting enabled, every EC2 instance you launch will by default have its EBS volumes encrypted with the specified KMS key. If you do not specify a KMS key, a default AWS-managed aws/ebs KMS key is created and used. If you need to manage the lifecycle of the key or have a requirement specifying that you or your organization must manage the key, customer-managed keys should be used.

Automatic key rotation (*https://oreil.ly/ofr4y*) on the KMS service simplifies your approach to key rotation and key lifecycle management.

KMS is a flexible service you can use to implement a variety of data encryption strategies. It supports key policies that you can use to control who has access to the key. These key policies layer on top of your existing IAM policy strategy for added security. You can use KMS keys to encrypt many different types of data at rest within your AWS account, for example:

- Amazon S3
- Amazon EC2 EBS volumes
- Amazon RDS databases and clusters
- Amazon DynamoDB tables
- Amazon EFS volumes
- Amazon FSx file shares
- And many more

Challenge 1

Change the key policy on the KMS key to allow access to only your IAM principal and the EC2 service.

Challenge 2

Create an EBS volume and verify that it is encrypted by using the aws ec2 describe-volumes command (*https://oreil.ly/UyOQA*).

1.8 Storing, Encrypting, and Accessing Passwords Using Secrets Manager

Problem

You need to give your EC2 instance the ability to securely store and retrieve a database password for your application.

Solution

Create a password, store the password in Secrets Manager, create an IAM Policy with access to the secret, and grant an EC2 instance profile access to the secret, as shown in Figure 1-10.

Figure 1-10. Create a secret and retrieve it via the EC2 instance

Prerequisites

- VPC with isolated subnets and associated route tables.
- EC2 instance deployed. You will need the ability to connect to this for testing.

Preparation

Follow the steps in this recipe's folder in the chapter code repository.

Steps

1. Create a secret using the AWS CLI:
   ```
   RANDOM_STRING=$(aws secretsmanager get-random-password \
       --password-length 32 --require-each-included-type \
       --output text \
       --query RandomPassword)
   ```

2. Store it as a new secret in Secrets Manager:
   ```
   SECRET_ARN=$(aws secretsmanager \
       create-secret --name AWSCookbook108/Secret1 \
       --description "AWSCookbook108 Secret 1" \
       --secret-string $RANDOM_STRING \
   ```

```
    --output text \
    --query ARN)
```

3. Create a file called *secret-access-policy-template.json* that references the secret you created. (file provided in the repository):

```
{
  "Version": "2012-10-17",
  "Statement": [
    {
      "Effect": "Allow",
      "Action": [
        "secretsmanager:GetResourcePolicy",
        "secretsmanager:GetSecretValue",
        "secretsmanager:DescribeSecret",
        "secretsmanager:ListSecretVersionIds"
      ],
      "Resource": [
        "SECRET_ARN"
      ]
    },
    {
      "Effect": "Allow",
      "Action": "secretsmanager:ListSecrets",
      "Resource": "*"
    }
  ]
}
```

4. Use the `sed` command to replace *SECRET_ARN* in the *secret-access-policy-template.json* file and generate the *secret-access-policy.json* file:

```
sed -e "s|SECRET_ARN|$SECRET_ARN|g" \
    secret-access-policy-template.json > secret-access-policy.json
```

5. Create the IAM policy for secret access:

```
aws iam create-policy --policy-name AWSCookbook108SecretAccess \
    --policy-document file://secret-access-policy.json
```

You should see output similar to the following:

```
{
  "Policy": {
    "PolicyName": "AWSCookbook108SecretAccess",
    "PolicyId": "(Random String)",
    "Arn": "arn:aws:iam::1111111111:policy/AWSCookbook108SecretAccess",
    "Path": "/",
    "DefaultVersionId": "v1",
    "AttachmentCount": 0,
    "PermissionsBoundaryUsageCount": 0,
    "IsAttachable": true,
    "CreateDate": "2021-11-28T21:25:23+00:00",
    "UpdateDate": "2021-11-28T21:25:23+00:00"
  }
}
```

6. Grant an EC2 instance ability to access the secret by adding the IAM policy you created to the EC2 instance profile's currently attached IAM role:

```
aws iam attach-role-policy --policy-arn \
    arn:aws:iam::$AWS_ACCOUNT_ID:policy/AWSCookbook108SecretAccess \
    --role-name $ROLE_NAME
```

Validation checks. Connect to the EC2 instance:

```
aws ssm start-session --target $INSTANCE_ID
```

Set and export your default region:

```
export AWS_DEFAULT_REGION=us-east-1
```

Retrieve the secret from Secrets Manager from the EC2:

```
aws secretsmanager get-secret-value --secret-id AWSCookbook108/Secret1
```

You should see output similar to the following:

```
{
    "Name": "AWSCookbook108/Secret1",
    "VersionId": "<string>",
    "SecretString": "<secret value>",
    "VersionStages": [
        "AWSCURRENT"
    ],
    "CreatedDate": 1638221015.646,
    "ARN": "arn:aws:secretsmanager:us-east-1:111111111111:secret:AWSCookbook108/
Secret1-<suffix>"
}</suffix>
```

Exit the Session Manager session:

```
exit
```

Cleanup

Follow the steps in this recipe's folder in the chapter code repository (*https:// github.com/AWSCookbook/Security*).

Discussion

Securely creating, storing, and managing the lifecycle of secrets, like API keys and database passwords, is a fundamental component to a strong security posture in the cloud. You can use Secrets Manager to implement a secrets management strategy that supports your security strategy. You can control who has access to what secrets using IAM policies to ensure the secrets you manage are accessible by only the necessary security principals.

Since your EC2 instance uses an instance profile, you do not need to store any hard-coded credentials on the instance in order for it to access the secret. The access is granted via the IAM policy attached to the instance profile. Each time you (or your application) access the secret from the EC2 instance, temporary session credentials are obtained from the STS service to allow the `get-secret-value` API call to retrieve the secret. The AWS CLI automates this process of token retrieval when an EC2 instance profile is attached to your instance. You can also use the AWS SDK within your applications to achieve this functionality.

Some additional benefits to using Secrets Manager include the following:

- Encrypting secrets with KMS keys that you create and manage
- Auditing access to secrets through CloudTrail
- Automating secret rotation using Lambda
- Granting access to other users, roles, and services like EC2 and Lambda
- Replicating secrets to another Region for high availability and disaster recovery purposes

Challenge

Configure a Lambda function to access the secret securely with an IAM role.

1.9 Blocking Public Access for an S3 Bucket

Problem

You have been alerted by your organization's security team that an S3 bucket has been incorrectly configured and you need to block public access to it.

Solution

Apply the Amazon S3 Block Public Access feature to your bucket, and then check the status with the Access Analyzer (see Figure 1-11).

AWS provides information on what is considered "public" in an article on S3 storage (*https://oreil.ly/h6Ozf*).

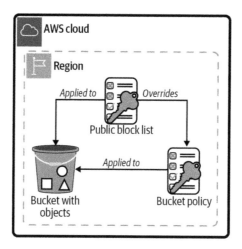

Figure 1-11. Blocking public access to an S3 bucket

Prerequisite

- S3 bucket with publicly available object(s)

Preparation

Follow the steps in this recipe's folder in the chapter code repository (*https://github.com/AWSCookbook/Security*).

Steps

1. Create an Access Analyzer to use for validation of access:

```
ANALYZER_ARN=$(aws accessanalyzer create-analyzer \
    --analyzer-name awscookbook109\
    --type ACCOUNT \
    --output text --query arn)
```

2. Perform a scan of your S3 bucket with the Access Analyzer:

```
aws accessanalyzer start-resource-scan \
    --analyzer-arn $ANALYZER_ARN \
    --resource-arn arn:aws:s3:::awscookbook109-$RANDOM_STRING
```

3. Get the results of the Access Analyzer scan (it may take about 30 seconds for the scan results to become available):

```
aws accessanalyzer get-analyzed-resource \
    --analyzer-arn $ANALYZER_ARN \
    --resource-arn arn:aws:s3:::awscookbook109-$RANDOM_STRING
```

You should see output similar to the following (note the `isPublic` value):

```
{
  "resource": {
  "actions": [
```

```
    "s3:GetObject",
    "s3:GetObjectVersion"
  ],
  "analyzedAt": "2021-06-26T17:42:00.861000+00:00",
  "createdAt": "2021-06-26T17:42:00.861000+00:00",
  "isPublic": true,
  "resourceArn": "arn:aws:s3:::awscookbook109-<<string>>",
  "resourceOwnerAccount": "111111111111",
  "resourceType": "AWS::S3::Bucket",
  "sharedVia": [
    "POLICY"
  ],
  "status": "ACTIVE",
  "updatedAt": "2021-06-26T17:42:00.861000+00:00"
  }
}
```

4. Set the public access block for your bucket:

```
aws s3api put-public-access-block \
    --bucket awscookbook109-$RANDOM_STRING \
    --public-access-block-configuration \
"BlockPublicAcls=true,IgnorePublicAcls=true,BlockPublicPolicy=true,RestrictPublic
Buckets=true"
```

> See the AWS article (*https://oreil.ly/3jRmO*) on the available
> PublicAccessBlock configuration properties.

Validation checks. Perform a scan of your S3 bucket:

```
aws accessanalyzer start-resource-scan \
    --analyzer-arn $ANALYZER_ARN \
    --resource-arn arn:aws:s3:::awscookbook109-$RANDOM_STRING
```

Get the results of the Access Analyzer scan:

```
aws accessanalyzer get-analyzed-resource \
    --analyzer-arn $ANALYZER_ARN \
    --resource-arn arn:aws:s3:::awscookbook109-$RANDOM_STRING
```

You should see output similar to the following:

```
{
  "resource": {
  "analyzedAt": "2021-06-26T17:46:24.906000+00:00",
  "isPublic": false,
  "resourceArn": "arn:aws:s3:::awscookbook109-<<string>>",
  "resourceOwnerAccount": "111111111111",
  "resourceType": "AWS::S3::Bucket"
  }
}
```

Cleanup

Follow the steps in this recipe's folder in the chapter code repository (*https:// github.com/AWSCookbook/Security*).

Discussion

One of the best things you can do to ensure data security in your AWS account is to always make certain that you apply the right security controls to your data. If you mark an object as public in your S3 bucket, it is accessible to anyone on the internet, since S3 serves objects using HTTP. One of the most common security misconfigurations that users make in the cloud is marking object(s) as public when that is not intended or required. To protect against misconfiguration of S3 objects, enabling `BlockPublicAccess` for your buckets is a great thing to do from a security standpoint.

You can also set public block settings at your account level, which would include all S3 buckets in your account:

```
aws s3control put-public-access-block \
    --public-access-block-configuration \

BlockPublicAcls=true,IgnorePublicAcls=true,BlockPublicPolicy
=true,RestrictPublicBuckets=true \
    --account-id $AWS_ACCOUNT_ID
```

You can serve S3 content to internet users via HTTP and HTTPS while keeping your bucket private. Content delivery networking (CDN), like Amazon CloudFront, provides more secure, efficient, and cost-effective ways to achieve global static website hosting and still use S3 as your object source. To see an example of a CloudFront configuration that serves static content from an S3 bucket, see Recipe 1.10.

Challenge

Deploy a VPC endpoint for S3 within your VPC and create a bucket policy to restrict access to your S3 bucket through this endpoint only.

1.10 Serving Web Content Securely from S3 with CloudFront

Problem

You have nonpublic web content in S3 and want to configure CloudFront to serve the content.

Solution

Create a CloudFront distribution and set the origin to your S3 bucket. Then configure an origin access identity (OAI) to require the bucket to be accessible only from
CloudFront (see Figure 1-12).

Figure 1-12. CloudFront and S3

Prerequisite

- S3 bucket with static web content

Preparation

Follow the steps in this recipe's folder in the chapter code repository (*https://
github.com/AWSCookbook/Security*).

Steps

1. Create a CloudFront OAI to reference in an S3 bucket policy:

   ```
   OAI=$(aws cloudfront create-cloud-front-origin-access-identity \
       --cloud-front-origin-access-identity-config \
       CallerReference="awscookbook",Comment="AWSCookbook OAI" \
       --query CloudFrontOriginAccessIdentity.Id --output text)
   ```

2. Use the `sed` command to replace the values in the *distribution-config-
   template.json* file with your CloudFront OAI and S3 bucket name:

   ```
   sed -e "s/CLOUDFRONT_OAI/${OAI}/g" \
       -e "s|S3_BUCKET_NAME|awscookbook110-$RANDOM_STRING|g" \
       distribution-template.json > distribution.json
   ```

3. Create a CloudFront distribution that uses the distribution configuration JSON
   file you just created:

   ```
   DISTRIBUTION_ID=$(aws cloudfront create-distribution \
       --distribution-config file://distribution.json \
       --query Distribution.Id --output text)
   ```

4. The distribution will take a few minutes to create; use this command to check the
   status. Wait until the status reaches "Deployed":

   ```
   aws cloudfront get-distribution --id $DISTRIBUTION_ID \
       --output text --query Distribution.Status
   ```

5. Configure the S3 bucket policy to allow only requests from CloudFront by using a bucket policy like this (we have provided *bucket-policy-template.json* in the repository):

```
{
  "Version": "2012-10-17",
  "Id": "PolicyForCloudFrontPrivateContent",
  "Statement": [
    {
      "Effect": "Allow",
      "Principal": {
        "AWS": "arn:aws:iam::cloudfront:user/CloudFront Origin Access Identity
CLOUDFRONT_OAI"
      },
      "Action": "s3:GetObject",
      "Resource": "arn:aws:s3:::S3_BUCKET_NAME/*"
    }
  ]
}
```

6. Use the `sed` command to replace the values in the *bucket-policy-template.json* file with the CloudFront OAI and S3 bucket name:

```
sed -e "s/CLOUDFRONT_OAI/${OAI}/g" \
    -e "s|S3_BUCKET_NAME|awscookbook110-$RANDOM_STRING|g" \
    bucket-policy-template.json > bucket-policy.json
```

7. Apply the bucket policy to the S3 bucket with your static web content:

```
aws s3api put-bucket-policy --bucket awscookbook110-$RANDOM_STRING \
    --policy file://bucket-policy.json
```

8. Get the `DOMAIN_NAME` of the distribution you created:

```
DOMAIN_NAME=$(aws cloudfront get-distribution --id $DISTRIBUTION_ID \
    --query Distribution.DomainName --output text)
```

Validation checks.   Try to access the S3 bucket directly using HTTPS to verify that the bucket does not serve content directly:

```
curl https://awscookbook110-$RANDOM_STRING.s3.$AWS_REGION.amazonaws.com/index.html
```

You should see output similar to the following:

```
$ curl https://awscookbook110-$RANDOM_STRING.s3.$AWS_REGION.amazonaws.com/index.html
<?xml version="1.0" encoding="UTF-8"?>
<Error><Code>AccessDenied</Code><Message>Access
Denied</Message><RequestId>0AKQD0EFJC9ZHPCC</
RequestId><HostId>gfld4qKp9A93G8ee7VPBFrXBZV1HE3jiOb3bNB54fP
EPTihit/OyFh7hF2Nu4+Muv6JEc0ebLL4=</HostId></Error>
110-Optimizing-S3-with-CloudFront:$
```

Use `curl` to observe that your *index.html* file is served from the private S3 bucket through CloudFront:

```
curl $DOMAIN_NAME
```

You should see output similar to the following:

```
$ curl $DOMAIN_NAME
AWSCookbook
$
```

Cleanup

Follow the steps in this recipe's folder in the chapter code repository (*https://github.com/AWSCookbook/Security*).

Discussion

This configuration allows you to keep the S3 bucket private and allows only the CloudFront distribution to be able to access objects in the bucket. You created an origin access identity (*https://oreil.ly/aABzJ*) and defined a bucket policy to allow only CloudFront access to your S3 content. This gives you a solid foundation to keep your S3 buckets secure with the additional protection of the CloudFront global CDN.

The protection that a CDN gives from a distributed-denial-of-service (DDoS) attack (*https://oreil.ly/mtHSB*) is worth noting, as the end user requests to your content are directed to a point of presence on the CloudFront network with the lowest latency. This also protects you from the costs of having a DDoS attack against static content hosted in an S3 bucket, as it is generally less expensive to serve requests out of CloudFront rather than S3 directly.

By default, CloudFront comes with an HTTPS certificate on the default hostname for your distribution that you use to secure traffic. With CloudFront, you can associate your own custom domain name, attach a custom certificate from Amazon Certificate Manager (ACM), redirect to HTTPS from HTTP, force HTTPS, customize cache behavior, invoke Lambda functions (Lambda @Edge), and more.

Challenge

Add a geo restriction (*https://oreil.ly/FMGj0*) to your CloudFront distribution.

CHAPTER 2

Networking

2.0 Introduction

Many exciting topics, like computer vision, Internet of Things (IoT), and AI-enabled chat bots, dominate headlines. This causes traditional core technologies to be forgotten. While it's great to have many new capabilities at your fingertips, it is important to realize that these technologies would not be possible without a strong foundation of reliable and secure connectivity. Data processing is useful only if the results are reliably delivered and accessible over a network. Containers are a fantastic application deployment method, but they provide the best experience for users when they are networked together.

Networking services and features within AWS are the backbone to almost all of the big services we cover in this book. AWS has many great features for you to connect what you want, where you want, and how you want. Gaining a better understanding of networking will allow you to have a better grasp of the cloud and therefore to be more comfortable using it.

Keeping up with new networking innovations at AWS requires continuous learning. Each year at AWS re:Invent (*https://rein vent.awsevents.com*), many network services, features, and approaches are discussed.

Two suggested viewings of great networking talks from AWS re:Invent are Eric Brandwine's "Another Day, Another Billion Packets" (*https://oreil.ly/oB1BN*) from 2015 and the annual "From One to Many: Evolving VPC Design" (*https://oreil.ly/leKi9*) from 2019.

In this chapter, you will learn about essential cloud networking services and features. We will focus only on recipes that are realistic for you to accomplish in your personal account. Some advanced operations (e.g., AWS Direct Connect setup) are too dependent on external factors, so we left them out in order to focus on more easily accessible recipes and outcomes. While some recipes in this chapter may seem simple or short, they allow us to discuss important topics and concepts that are crucial to get right.

Workstation Configuration

Follow the "General workstation setup steps for CLI recipes" on page xvii to validate your configuration and set up the required environment variables. Then, clone the chapter code repository:

```
git clone https://github.com/AWSCookbook/Networking
```

2.1 Defining Your Private Virtual Network in the Cloud by Creating an Amazon VPC

Problem

You need a network foundation to host cloud resources.

Solution

You will create an Amazon Virtual Private Cloud (VPC) and configure a Classless Inter-Domain Routing (CIDR) block (*https://oreil.ly/2GrP7*) for it, as shown in Figure 2-1.

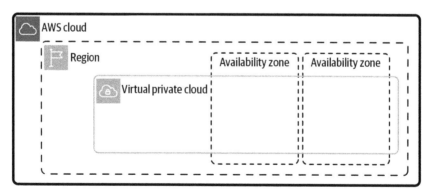

Figure 2-1. VPC deployed in a Region

Steps

1. Create a VPC with an IPv4 CIDR block. We will use 10.10.0.0/16 as the address range, but you can modify it based on your needs:

```
VPC_ID=$(aws ec2 create-vpc --cidr-block 10.10.0.0/16 \
    --tag-specifications
'ResourceType=vpc,Tags=[{Key=Name,Value=AWSCookbook201}]' \
    --output text --query Vpc.VpcId)
```

 When you are creating a VPC, the documentation (*https://oreil.ly/uIfsH*) states that the largest block size for VPC IPv4 (*https://oreil.ly/M0D9Y*) CIDRs is a /16 netmask (65,536 IP addresses). The smallest is a /28 netmask (16 IP addresses).

Validation checks.   Use this command to verify that the VPC's state is `available`:

```
aws ec2 describe-vpcs --vpc-ids $VPC_ID
```

You should see output similar to the following:

```
{
  "Vpcs": [
  {
    "CidrBlock": "10.10.0.0/16",
    "DhcpOptionsId": "dopt-<<snip>>",
    "State": "available",
    "VpcId": "vpc-<<snip>>",
    "OwnerId": "111111111111",
    "InstanceTenancy": "default",
    "CidrBlockAssociationSet": [
      {
        "AssociationId": "vpc-cidr-assoc-<<snip>>",
        "CidrBlock": "10.10.0.0/16",
        "CidrBlockState": {
        "State": "associated"
        }
      }
    ],
    "IsDefault": false,
<<snip>>
  ...
```

Cleanup

Follow the steps in this recipe's folder in the chapter code repository (*https://github.com/AWSCookbook/Networking*).

Discussion

Here are two important reasons for carefully selecting CIDR block(s) for your VPC:

- Once a CIDR block is associated with a VPC, it can't be modified (although it can be extended) (*https://oreil.ly/xUB24*). If you wish to modify a CIDR block, it (and all resources within it) will need to be deleted and re-created.
- If a VPC is connected to other networks by peering (see Recipe 2.11) or gateways (e.g., Transit and VPN), having overlapping IP ranges will cause unwanted problems.

You can add IPv4 space to the VPC by using the `aws ec2 associate-vpc-cidr-block` command to specify the additional IPv4 space. When IP space becomes scarce from usage and under-provisioning, it's good to know that you don't need to dedicate a large block to a VPC, especially if you aren't sure if all of it will be utilized.

Here is an example of associating an additional IPv4 CIDR block to your VPC:

```
aws ec2 associate-vpc-cidr-block \
    --cidr-block 10.11.0.0/16 \
    --vpc-id $VPC_ID
```

In addition to IPv4, VPC also supports IPv6 (*https://oreil.ly/sBL99*). You can configure an Amazon-provided IPv6 CIDR block by specifying the `--amazon-provided-ipv6-cidr-block` option. Here is an example of creating a VPC with an IPv6 CIDR block:

```
aws ec2 create-vpc --cidr-block 10.10.0.0/16 \
    --amazon-provided-ipv6-cidr-block \
    --tag-specifications
'ResourceType=vpc,Tags=[{Key=Name,Value=AWSCookbook201-IPv6}]'
```

A VPC is a Regional construct in AWS. A *Region* is a geographical area, and *Availability Zones* are physical data centers that reside within a Region. Regions span all Availability Zones (AZs), which are groups of isolated physical data centers. The number of AZs per Region varies, but all Regions have at least three. For the most up-to-date information about AWS Regions and AZs, see this article on "Regions and Availability Zones" (*https://oreil.ly/tJuIg*).

Per the VPC user guide (*https://oreil.ly/Z4MTP*), the initial quota (*https://oreil.ly/wcJPH*) of IPv4 CIDR blocks per VPC is 5. This can be raised to 50. The allowable number of IPv6 CIDR blocks per VPC is 1.

Challenge

Create another VPC with a different CIDR range.

2.2 Creating a Network Tier with Subnets and a Route Table in a VPC

Problem

You have a VPC and need to create a network layout consisting of individual IP spaces for segmentation and redundancy.

Solution

Create a route table within your VPC. Create two subnets in separate Availability Zones in a VPC. Associate the route table with the subnets (see Figure 2-2).

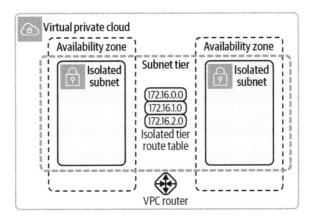

Figure 2-2. Isolated subnet tier and route table

Prerequisite

- A VPC

Preparation

Follow the steps in this recipe's folder in the chapter code repository (*https://github.com/AWSCookbook/Networking*).

Steps

1. Create a route table. This will allow you to create customized traffic routes for subnets associated with it:

```
ROUTE_TABLE_ID=$(aws ec2 create-route-table --vpc-id $VPC_ID \
    --tag-specifications \
    'ResourceType=route-table,Tags=[{Key=Name,Value=AWSCookbook202}]' \
    --output text --query RouteTable.RouteTableId)
```

2. Create two subnets, one in each AZ. This will define the address spaces for you to create resources for your VPC:

```
SUBNET_ID_1=$(aws ec2 create-subnet --vpc-id $VPC_ID \
    --cidr-block 10.10.0.0/24 --availability-zone ${AWS_REGION}a \
    --tag-specifications \
    'ResourceType=subnet,Tags=[{Key=Name,Value=AWSCookbook202a}]' \
    --output text --query Subnet.SubnetId)

SUBNET_ID_2=$(aws ec2 create-subnet --vpc-id $VPC_ID \
    --cidr-block 10.10.1.0/24 --availability-zone ${AWS_REGION}b \
    --tag-specifications \
    'ResourceType=subnet,Tags=[{Key=Name,Value=AWSCookbook202b}]' \
    --output text --query Subnet.SubnetId)
```

 In the previous commands, the --availability-zone parameter uses an environment variable for your Region appended with lowercase a or b characters to indicate which logical AZ (e.g., us-east-1a) to provision each subnet. AWS states that these names are randomized per account to balance resources across AZs.

If you are using multiple AWS accounts and want to find Availability Zone IDs for a Region that are consistent, run this command:

```
aws ec2 describe-availability-zones --region $AWS_REGION
```

3. Associate the route table with the two subnets:

```
aws ec2 associate-route-table \
    --route-table-id $ROUTE_TABLE_ID --subnet-id $SUBNET_ID_1

aws ec2 associate-route-table \
    --route-table-id $ROUTE_TABLE_ID --subnet-id $SUBNET_ID_2
```

4. For each command in step 3, you should see output similar to the following:

```
{
  "AssociationId": "rtbassoc-<<snip>>",
  "AssociationState": {
  "State": "associated"
  }
}
```

Validation checks.   Retrieve the configuration of the subnets you created and verify that they are in the same VPC but different AZs:

```
aws ec2 describe-subnets --subnet-ids $SUBNET_ID_1
aws ec2 describe-subnets --subnet-ids $SUBNET_ID_2
```

For each `describe-subnets` command, you should see output similar to this:

```
{
  "Subnets": [
  {
    "AvailabilityZone": "us-east-1a",
    "AvailabilityZoneId": "use1-az6",
    "AvailableIpAddressCount": 251,
    "CidrBlock": "10.10.0.0/24",
    "DefaultForAz": false,
    "MapPublicIpOnLaunch": false,
    "MapCustomerOwnedIpOnLaunch": false,
    "State": "available",
    "SubnetId": "subnet-<<snip>>",
    "VpcId": "vpc-<<snip>>",
    "OwnerId": "111111111111",
    "AssignIpv6AddressOnCreation": false,
    "Ipv6CidrBlockAssociationSet": [],
<<snip>>
...
```

Validate that the route table you created is associated with the two subnets:

```
aws ec2 describe-route-tables --route-table-ids $ROUTE_TABLE_ID
```

You should see output similar to the following:

```
{
  "RouteTables": [
  {
    "Associations": [
      {
        "Main": false,
        "RouteTableAssociationId": "rtbassoc-<<snip>>",
        "RouteTableId": "rtb-<<snip>>",
        "SubnetId": "subnet-<<snip>>",
        "AssociationState": {
        "State": "associated"
        }
      },
      {
        "Main": false,
        "RouteTableAssociationId": "rtbassoc-<<snip>>",
        "RouteTableId": "rtb-<<snip>>",
        "SubnetId": "subnet-<<snip>>",
        "AssociationState": {
        "State": "associated"
        }
      }
    }
<<snip>>
...
```

Cleanup

Follow the steps in this recipe's folder in the chapter code repository (*https://github.com/AWSCookbook/Networking*).

Discussion

When designing a subnet strategy, you should choose subnet sizes that fit your current needs and account for your application's future growth. Subnets are used (*https:// oreil.ly/KULJn*) for elastic network interface (ENI) placement for AWS resources. This means that a particular ENI lives within a single AZ.

> You may run into a case where routes overlap. AWS provides information on how priority is determined (*https://oreil.ly/j1RWe*).

AWS reserves the first four and last IP addresses of every subnet's CIDR block for features and functionality when you create a subnet. These are not available for your use. Per the documentation (*https://oreil.ly/qbkcf*), these are the reserved addresses in the case of your example:

.0   Network address.
.1   Reserved by AWS for the VPC router.
.2   Reserved by AWS for the IP address of the DNS server. This is always set to the VPC network range plus two.
.3   Reserved by AWS for future use.
.255 Network broadcast address. Broadcast in a VPC is not supported.

A subnet has one route table associated with it. Route tables can be associated with one or more subnets and direct traffic to a destination of your choosing (more on this with the NAT gateway, internet gateway, and transit gateway recipes later). Entries within route tables are called *routes* and are defined as pairs of Destinations and Targets. When you created the route table, a default local route that handles intra-VPC traffic was automatically added for you. You have the ability to create custom routes that fit your needs. For a complete list of targets available to use within route tables, see this support document (*https://oreil.ly/oKVq1*).

> ENIs receive an IP address from an AWS managed DHCP server within your VPC. The DHCP options set is automatically configured with defaults for assigning addresses within the subnets you define. For more information about DHCP option sets, and how to create your own DHCP option sets see this support document (*https://oreil.ly/OsebX*).

When creating a VPC in a Region, it is a best practice to spread subnets across AZs in that network tier. The number of AZs differs per Region, but most have at least three. An example of this in practice would be that if you had a public tier and an isolated tier spread over two AZs, you would have a total of four subnets: 2 tiers × 2 subnets per tier (one per AZ); see Figure 2-3.

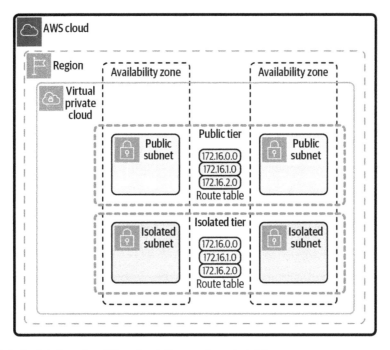

Figure 2-3. Isolated and public subnet tiers and route tables

Challenge

Create a second route table and associate it with $SUBNET_ID_2. Configuring route tables for each AZ is a common pattern.

2.3 Connecting Your VPC to the Internet Using an Internet Gateway

Problem

You have an existing EC2 instance in a subnet of a VPC. You need to provide the ability for this instance to directly reach clients on the internet.

Solution

You will create an internet gateway and attach it to your VPC. Next you will modify the route table associated with the subnet where the EC2 instance lives. You will add a route that sends traffic from the subnets to the internet gateway. Finally, create an Elastic IP (EIP) and associate it with the instance, as shown in Figure 2-4.

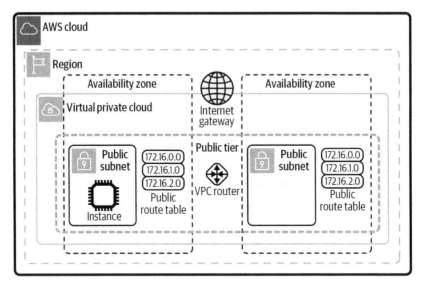

Figure 2-4. Public subnet tier, internet gateway, and route table

Prerequisites

- VPC and subnets created in two AZs and associated route tables.
- EC2 instance deployed. You will need the ability to connect to this for testing.

Preparation

Follow the steps in this recipe's folder in the chapter code repository (*https://github.com/AWSCookbook/Networking*).

Steps

1. Create an internet gateway (IGW):

    ```
    INET_GATEWAY_ID=$(aws ec2 create-internet-gateway \
        --tag-specifications \
    'ResourceType=internet-gateway,Tags=[{Key=Name,Value=AWSCookbook202}]' \
        --output text --query InternetGateway.InternetGatewayId)
    ```

2. Attach the internet gateway to the existing VPC:

    ```
    aws ec2 attach-internet-gateway \
        --internet-gateway-id $INET_GATEWAY_ID --vpc-id $VPC_ID
    ```

3. In each route table of your VPC, create a route that sets the default route destination to the internet gateway:

```
aws ec2 create-route --route-table-id $ROUTE_TABLE_ID_1 \
    --destination-cidr-block 0.0.0.0/0 --gateway-id $INET_GATEWAY_ID

aws ec2 create-route --route-table-id $ROUTE_TABLE_ID_2 \
    --destination-cidr-block 0.0.0.0/0 --gateway-id $INET_GATEWAY_ID
```

For each command in step 3, you should see output similar to the following:

```
{
  "Return": true
}
```

4. Create an EIP:

```
ALLOCATION_ID=$(aws ec2 allocate-address --domain vpc \
    --output text --query AllocationId)
```

 AWS defines an Elastic IP address (EIP) (*https://oreil.ly/ FCrvT*) as "a static IPv4 address designed for dynamic cloud computing. An EIP address is allocated to your AWS account and is yours until you release it."

5. Associate the EIP with the existing EC2 instance:

```
aws ec2 associate-address \
    --instance-id $INSTANCE_ID --allocation-id $ALLOCATION_ID
```

You should see output similar to the following:

```
{
  "AssociationId": "eipassoc-<<snip>>"
}
```

Validation checks. Connect to the EC2 instance using SSM Session Manager (see Recipe 1.6):

```
aws ssm start-session --target $INSTANCE_ID
```

Ping a host on the internet to test internet connectivity:

```
ping -c 4 homestarrunner.com
```

You should see output similar to the following:

```
sh-4.2$ ping -c 4 homestarrunner.com
PING homestarrunner.com (72.10.33.178) 56(84) bytes of data.
64 bytes from homestarrunner.com (72.10.33.178): icmp_seq=1 ttl=49 time=2.12 ms
64 bytes from homestarrunner.com (72.10.33.178): icmp_seq=2 ttl=49 time=2.04 ms
64 bytes from homestarrunner.com (72.10.33.178): icmp_seq=3 ttl=49 time=2.05 ms
64 bytes from homestarrunner.com (72.10.33.178): icmp_seq=4 ttl=49 time=2.08 ms
--- homestarrunner.com ping statistics ---
4 packets transmitted, 4 received, 0% packet loss, time 3002ms
rtt min/avg/max/mdev = 2.045/2.078/2.127/0.045 ms
sh-4.2$
```

The public IP is not part of the OS configuration. If you want to retrieve the public IP from the instance's metadata (*https://oreil.ly/lmZ1U*), you can use this command:

```
curl http://169.254.169.254/latest/meta-data/public-ipv4
```

Exit the Session Manager session:

```
exit
```

Clean up

Follow the steps in this recipe's folder in the chapter code repository (*https://github.com/AWSCookbook/Networking*).

Discussion

The route that you created in your route table entry sends all nonlocal traffic to the IGW that provides your VPC internet connectivity. Because you were working with an existing running EC2 instance, you needed to create an Elastic IP and associated it with the instance. These steps enabled internet communication to the instance without having to interact with it. There is an option to enable auto-assignment (*https://oreil.ly/disUG*) of public IPv4 addresses for newly launched instances in a subnet. However, if you utilize auto-assignment, the public IPs will change after each instance reboot. EIPs associated with an instance will not change after reboots.

 Route tables give priority to the most specific route. AWS also allows you to create routes that are more specific than the default local route. This allows you to create very controlled network flows. More information about route priority can be found in an AWS discussion (*https://oreil.ly/DKpNO*).

The security group associated with your instance does not allow inbound access. If you would like to allow inbound internet access to an instance in a public subnet, you will have to configure a security group ingress rule for this.

A subnet that has a route of 0.0.0.0/0 associated with an IGW is considered a public subnet. It is considered a security best practice to place instances only in this type of tier that require inbound access from the public internet. End-user-facing load balancers are commonly placed in public subnets. A public subnet would not be an ideal choice for an application server or a database. In these cases, you can create a private tier or an isolated tier to fit your needs with the appropriate routing and use a NAT gateway to direct that subnet traffic to the internet gateway only when outbound internet access is required.

Challenge

Install a web server on the EC2 instance, modify the security group, and connect to the instance from your workstation. See Recipe 2.7 for an example of how to configure internet access for instances in private subnets using a load balancer.

2.4 Using a NAT Gateway for Outbound Internet Access from Private Subnets

Problem

You have public subnets in your VPC that have a route to an internet gateway. You want to leverage this setup to provide outbound-only internet access for an instance in private subnets.

Solution

Create a NAT gateway in one of the public subnets. Then create an Elastic IP and associate it with the NAT gateway. In the route table associated with the private subnets, add a route for internet-bound traffic that targets the NAT gateway (see Figure 2-5).

Prerequisites

- VPC with public subnets in two AZs and associated route tables.
- Isolated subnets created in two AZs (we will turn these into the private subnets) and associated route tables.
- Two EC2 instances deployed in the isolated subnets. You will need the ability to connect to these for testing.

Preparation

Follow the steps in this recipe's folder in the chapter code repository (*https://github.com/AWSCookbook/Networking*).

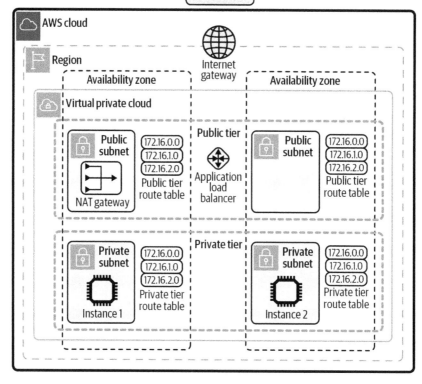

Figure 2-5. Internet access for private subnets provided by NAT gateways

Steps

1. Create an Elastic IP to be used with the NAT gateway:

```
ALLOCATION_ID=$(aws ec2 allocate-address --domain vpc \
    --output text --query AllocationId)
```

2. Create a NAT gateway within the public subnet of AZ1:

```
NAT_GATEWAY_ID=$(aws ec2 create-nat-gateway \
    --subnet-id $VPC_PUBLIC_SUBNET_1 \
    --allocation-id $ALLOCATION_ID \
    --output text --query NatGateway.NatGatewayId)
```

3. This will take a few moments for the state to become available; check the status:

```
aws ec2 describe-nat-gateways \
    --nat-gateway-ids $NAT_GATEWAY_ID \
    --output text --query NatGateways[0].State
```

4. Add a default route for 0.0.0.0/0 with a destination of the NAT gateway to both of the private tier's route tables. This default route sends all traffic not matching a more specific route to the destination specified:

```
aws ec2 create-route --route-table-id $PRIVATE_RT_ID_1 \
    --destination-cidr-block 0.0.0.0/0 \
    --nat-gateway-id $NAT_GATEWAY_ID

aws ec2 create-route --route-table-id $PRIVATE_RT_ID_2 \
    --destination-cidr-block 0.0.0.0/0 \
    --nat-gateway-id $NAT_GATEWAY_ID
```

For each command in step 4, you should see output similar to the following:

```
{
    "Return": true
}
```

Validation checks.   Connect to EC2 instance 1 by using SSM Session Manager (see Recipe 1.6):

```
aws ssm start-session --target $INSTANCE_ID_1
```

Test internet access with a ping:

```
ping -c 4 homestarrunner.com
```

You should see output similar to the following:

```
sh-4.2$ ping -c 4 homestarrunner.com

PING homestarrunner.com (72.10.33.178) 56(84) bytes of data.
64 bytes from homestarrunner.com (72.10.33.178): icmp_seq=1 ttl=47 time=2.95 ms
64 bytes from homestarrunner.com (72.10.33.178): icmp_seq=2 ttl=47 time=2.16 ms
64 bytes from homestarrunner.com (72.10.33.178): icmp_seq=3 ttl=47 time=2.13 ms
64 bytes from homestarrunner.com (72.10.33.178): icmp_seq=4 ttl=47 time=2.13 ms

--- homestarrunner.com ping statistics ---
4 packets transmitted, 4 received, 0% packet loss, time 3003ms
rtt min/avg/max/mdev = 2.134/2.348/2.958/0.356 ms
sh-4.2$
```

Exit the Session Manager session:

```
exit
```

(Optional) Repeat the validation steps for EC2 instance 2.

Cleanup

Follow the steps in this recipe's folder in the chapter code repository (*https://github.com/AWSCookbook/Networking*).

Discussion

This architecture gives you a subnet tier that allows outbound access but does not permit direct inbound internet access to resources within it. One way to allow internet resources inbound access to services running on resources in private subnets is to use a load balancer in the public subnets. We'll look more at that type of configuration in Recipe 2.7.

The EIP associated with your NAT gateway becomes the external IP address for all communication that goes through it. For example, if a vendor needed to add your IP to an allow list, the NAT gateway EIP would be the "source" IP address provided to the vendor. Your EIP will remain the same as long as you keep it provisioned within your account.

> If you created a VPC with IPv6 capability, you can also create an egress-only internet gateway to allow outbound internet access for private subnets, as discussed in an AWS article (*https://oreil.ly/RxlYN*).

This NAT gateway was provisioned within one AZ in your VPC. While this is a cost-effective way to achieve outbound internet access for your private subnets, for production and mission-critical applications, you should consider provisioning NAT gateways in each AZ to provide resiliency and reduce the amount of cross-AZ traffic. This would also require creating route tables for each of your private subnets so that you can direct the 0.0.0.0/0 traffic to the NAT gateway in that particular subnet's AZ. See the challenge for this recipe.

> If you have custom requirements or would like more granular control of your outbound routing for your NAT implementation, you can create a NAT instance. For a comparison of NAT gateways and NAT instances, see this support document (*https://oreil.ly/roLbq*).

Challenge

Create a second NAT gateway in the public subnet in AZ2. Then modify the default route in the route table associated with the private subnet in AZ2. Change the destination to the newly created NAT gateway.

2.5 Granting Dynamic Access by Referencing Security Groups

Problem

You have an application group that currently consists of two instances and need to allow Secure Shell (SSH) between them. This needs to be configured in a way to allow for future growth of the number of instances securely and easily.

Solution

A common misconception is that by merely associating the same security group to ENIs for multiple EC2 instances, it will allow communication between them (see Figure 2-6).

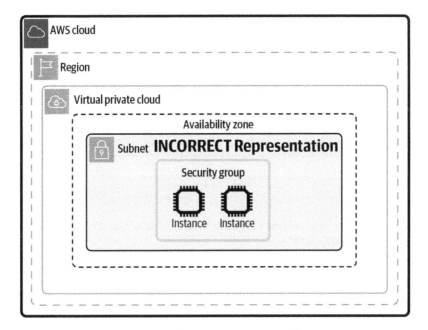

Figure 2-6. Incorrect representation of two instances using the same security group

In this recipe, we will create a security group and an associate each to the ENIs of two EC2 instances. Finally, we will create an ingress rule that authorizes the security group to reach itself on TCP port 22 (see Figure 2-7).

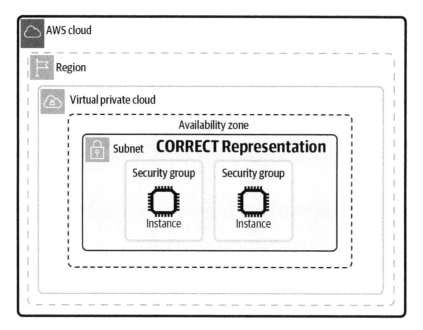

Figure 2-7. Correct visualization of the ENIs of two instances using the same security group

Prerequisites

- VPC with a subnet and associated route table.
- Two EC2 instances deployed in the subnet. You will need the ability to connect to these for testing.

Preparation

Follow the steps in this recipe's folder in the chapter code repository (*https://github.com/AWSCookbook/Networking*).

Steps

1. Create a new security group for the EC2 instances:

```
SG_ID=$(aws ec2 create-security-group \
    --group-name AWSCookbook205Sg \
    --description "Instance Security Group" --vpc-id $VPC_ID \
    --output text --query GroupId)
```

2. Attach the security group to instances 1 and 2:

```
aws ec2 modify-instance-attribute --instance-id $INSTANCE_ID_1 \
    --groups $SG_ID
```

```
aws ec2 modify-instance-attribute --instance-id $INSTANCE_ID_2 \
    --groups $SG_ID
```

 You used the modify-instance-attribute (*https://oreil.ly/GT2KH*) command to attach a new security group to the ENIs of your EC2 instances. To list the security groups associated with the ENI of an EC2 instance, you can view them in the EC2 console under the Security tab of the instance details or use this command (replacing *$INSTANCE_ID_1* with your own instance ID):

```
aws ec2 describe-security-groups --group-ids \
    $(aws ec2 describe-instances --instance-id
$INSTANCE_ID_1 \
    --query
"Reservations[].Instances[].SecurityGroups[].GroupId[]"
\
    --output text) --output text
```

3. Add an ingress rule to the security group that allows access on TCP port 22 from itself:

```
aws ec2 authorize-security-group-ingress \
    --protocol tcp --port 22 \
    --source-group $SG_ID \
    --group-id $SG_ID \
```

 You can and should create descriptions for all your security group rules to indicate the intended functionality of the authorization.

You should see output similar to the following:

```
{
  "Return": true,
  "SecurityGroupRules": [
  {
    "SecurityGroupRuleId": "sgr-<<snip>>",
    "GroupId": "sg-<<snip>>",
    "GroupOwnerId": "111111111111",
    "IsEgress": false,
    "IpProtocol": "tcp",
    "FromPort": 22,
    "ToPort": 22,
    "ReferencedGroupInfo": {
      "GroupId": "sg-<<snip>>"
    }
  }
  ]
}
```

This type of security group rule is called a *self-referencing* rule. It allows access to the specific port from traffic originating from ENIs (not a static range of IPs) that have this same security group attached to them.

Validation checks.   List the IP address for instance 2:

```
aws ec2 describe-instances --instance-ids $INSTANCE_ID_2 \
    --output text \
    --query Reservations[0].Instances[0].PrivateIpAddress
```

Connect to your instance 1 by using SSM Session Manager (see Recipe 1.6):

```
aws ssm start-session --target $INSTANCE_ID_1
```

Install the *Ncat* utility:

```
sudo yum -y install nc
```

Test SSH connectivity to instance 2 (use instance 2's IP that you listed previously):

```
nc -vz $INSTANCE_IP_2 22
```

You should see output similar to the following:

```
Ncat: Version 7.50 ( https://nmap.org/ncat )
Ncat: Connected to 10.10.0.48:22.
Ncat: 0 bytes sent, 0 bytes received in 0.01 seconds.
sh-4.2$
```

Exit the Session Manager session:

```
exit
```

(Optional) Repeat the validation steps from instance 2 to instance 1.

Cleanup

Follow the steps in this recipe's folder in the chapter code repository (*https:// github.com/AWSCookbook/Networking*).

Discussion

The on-demand nature of the cloud (e.g., autoscaling) presents an opportunity for elasticity. Network security mechanisms, like security group references, are suitable for that. Traditionally, network architects might authorize CIDR ranges within firewall configurations. This type of authorization is generally referred to as *static references*. This legacy practice doesn't scale dynamically, as you may add or remove instances from your workloads.

A security group (*https://oreil.ly/rYohM*) acts as a stateful virtual firewall for ENIs. The default behavior for security groups is to implicitly block all ingress while allowing all egress. You can associate multiple security groups with an ENI. There is an initial quota (*https://oreil.ly/FR5J1*) of 5 security groups per ENI and 60 rules (inbound or outbound) per security group.

You can also specify CIDR notation for authorizations. For example, for an authorization intended to allow RDP access from your New York branch office, you would use the following:

```
aws ec2 authorize-security-group-ingress \
    --group-id sg-1234567890abcdef0 \
    --ip-permissions
    IpProtocol=tcp,FromPort=3389,ToPort=3389,IpRanges='[{CidrIp=XXX.XXX.XXX.XXX/
24,Description="RDP access from NY office"}]'
```

> Remember that security groups cannot be deleted if the following conditions are present:
>
> - They are currently attached to an ENI.
> - They are referenced by other security groups (including themselves).

Challenge

Create a third EC2 instance; use the same security group. Test access to and from it. (Hint: in the repository.)

2.6 Using VPC Reachability Analyzer to Verify and Troubleshoot Network Paths

Problem

You have two EC2 instances deployed in isolated subnets. You need to troubleshoot SSH connectivity between them.

Solution

You will create, analyze, and describe network insights by using the VPC Reachability Analyzer. Based on the results, you will add a rule to the security group of instance 2 that allows the SSH port (TCP port 22) from instance 1's security group. Finally, you will rerun the VPC Reachability Analyzer and view the updated results (see Figure 2-8).

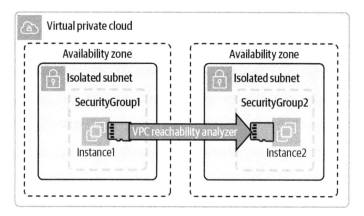

Figure 2-8. VPC Reachability Analyzer

Prerequisites

- VPC with isolated subnets in two AZs and associated route tables.
- Two EC2 instances deployed in the isolated subnets. You will need the ability to connect to these for testing.

Preparation

Follow the steps in this recipe's folder in the chapter code repository (*https://github.com/AWSCookbook/Networking*).

Steps

1. Create a network insights path specifying both of the EC2 instances you deployed and TCP port 22:

    ```
    INSIGHTS_PATH_ID=$(aws ec2 create-network-insights-path \
        --source $INSTANCE_ID_1 --destination-port 22 \
        --destination $INSTANCE_ID_2 --protocol tcp \
        --output text --query NetworkInsightsPath.NetworkInsightsPathId)
    ```

2. Start the network insights analysis between the two instances using the `INSIGHTS_PATH_ID` created in the previous step:

    ```
    ANALYSIS_ID_1=$(aws ec2 start-network-insights-analysis \
        --network-insights-path-id $INSIGHTS_PATH_ID --output text \
        --query NetworkInsightsAnalysis.NetworkInsightsAnalysisId)
    ```

3. Wait a few seconds until the analysis is done running and then view the results:

    ```
    aws ec2 describe-network-insights-analyses \
        --network-insights-analysis-ids $ANALYSIS_ID_1
    ```

    You should see output similar to the following (note the `NetworkPathFound` and `ExplanationCode` fields):

```json
{
  "NetworkInsightsAnalyses": [
    {
      "NetworkInsightsAnalysisId": "nia-<<snip>>",
      "NetworkInsightsAnalysisArn": "arn:aws:ec2:us-east-1:111111111111:network-
insights-analysis/nia-<<snip>>",
      "NetworkInsightsPathId": "nip-<<snip>>",
      "StartDate": "2020-12-22T02:12:36.836000+00:00",
      "Status": "succeeded",
      "NetworkPathFound": false,
      "Explanations": [
        {
          "Direction": "ingress",
          "ExplanationCode": "ENI_SG_RULES_MISMATCH",
          "NetworkInterface": {
            "Id": "eni-<<snip>>",
            "Arn": "arn:aws:ec2:us-east-1:11111111111:network-interface/eni-
<<snip>>"
          },
```

4. Update the security group attached to instance 2. Add a rule to allow access from instance 1's security group to TCP port 22 (SSH):

```
aws ec2 authorize-security-group-ingress \
    --protocol tcp --port 22 \
    --source-group $INSTANCE_SG_ID_1 \
    --group-id $INSTANCE_SG_ID_2
```

You should see output similar to the following:

```json
{
  "Return": true,
  "SecurityGroupRules": [
  {
    "SecurityGroupRuleId": "sgr-<<snip>>",
    "GroupId": "sg-<<snip>>",
    "GroupOwnerId": "111111111111",
    "IsEgress": false,
    "IpProtocol": "tcp",
    "FromPort": 22,
    "ToPort": 22,
    "ReferencedGroupInfo": {
      "GroupId": "sg-<<snip>>"
    }
  }
  ]
}
```

5. Rerun the network insights analysis. Use the same INSIGHTS_PATH_ID as you did previously:

```
ANALYSIS_ID_2=$(aws ec2 start-network-insights-analysis \
    --network-insights-path-id $INSIGHTS_PATH_ID --output text \
    --query NetworkInsightsAnalysis.NetworkInsightsAnalysisId)
```

6. Show the results of the new analysis:

```
aws ec2 describe-network-insights-analyses \
    --network-insights-analysis-ids $ANALYSIS_ID_2
```

You should see output similar to the following (note the `NetworkPathFound` field):

```
{
  "NetworkInsightsAnalyses": [
    {
      "NetworkInsightsAnalysisId": "nia-<<snip>>",
      "NetworkInsightsAnalysisArn": "arn:aws:ec2:us-east-1:111111111111:network-
insights-analysis/nia-<<snip>>",
      "NetworkInsightsPathId": "nip-<<snip>>",
      "StartDate": "2021-02-21T23:52:15.565000+00:00",
      "Status": "succeeded",
      "NetworkPathFound": true,
      "ForwardPathComponents": [
        {
          "SequenceNumber": 1,
          "Component": {
          "Id": "i-<<snip>>",
  ...
```

Validation checks.   List the IP address for instance 2:

```
aws ec2 describe-instances --instance-ids $INSTANCE_ID_2 \
    --output text \
    --query Reservations[0].Instances[0].PrivateIpAddress
```

Connect to your EC2 instance by using SSM Session Manager (see Recipe 1.6):

```
aws ssm start-session --target $INSTANCE_ID_1
```

Install the *Ncat* utility:

```
sudo yum -y install nc
```

Test SSH connectivity to instance 2 (use instance 2's IP that you listed previously):

```
nc -vz $INSTANCE_IP_2 22
```

You should see output similar to the following:

```
Ncat: Version 7.50 ( https://nmap.org/ncat )
Ncat: Connected to 10.10.0.48:22.
Ncat: 0 bytes sent, 0 bytes received in 0.01 seconds.
sh-4.2$
```

Exit the Session Manager session:

```
exit
```

Cleanup

Follow the steps in this recipe's folder in the chapter code repository (*https://github.com/AWSCookbook/Networking*).

Discussion

A network insights path is a definition of the connectivity you want to test. Initially, there wasn't SSH connectivity between the instances because the security group on the destination (instance 2) did not allow access. After you updated the security group associated with instance 2 and reran an analysis, you were able to verify successful connectivity. Using the VPC Reachability Analyzer (*https://oreil.ly/szPNC*) is an efficient capability for network troubleshooting and validating configuration in a "serverless" manner. It does not require you to provision infrastructure to analyze, verify, and troubleshoot network connectivity.

> VPC reachability has broad support of sources and destinations for resources within your VPCs. For a complete list of supported sources and destinations, see this support document (*https://oreil.ly/boPoh*).

VPC Reachability Analyzer provides explanation codes that describe the result of a network path analysis. In this recipe, you observed the code ENI_SG_RULES_MISMATCH that indicates that the security groups are not allowing traffic between the source and destination. The complete list of explanation codes is available in this documentation (*https://oreil.ly/v6o18*).

Challenge

Add an internet gateway to your VPC and test access to that from an instance.

2.7 Redirecting HTTP Traffic to HTTPS with an Application Load Balancer

Problem

You have a containerized application running in a private subnet. Users on the internet need to access this application. To help secure the application, you would like to redirect all requests from HTTP to HTTPS.

Solution

Create an Application Load Balancer (ALB). Next, create listeners on the ALB for ports 80 and 443, target groups for your containerized application, and listener rules. Configure the listener rules to send traffic to your target group, as shown in Figure 2-9. Finally, configure an action to redirect with an HTTP 301 response code, port 80 (HTTP) to port 443 (HTTPS) while preserving the URL in the request (see Figure 2-10).

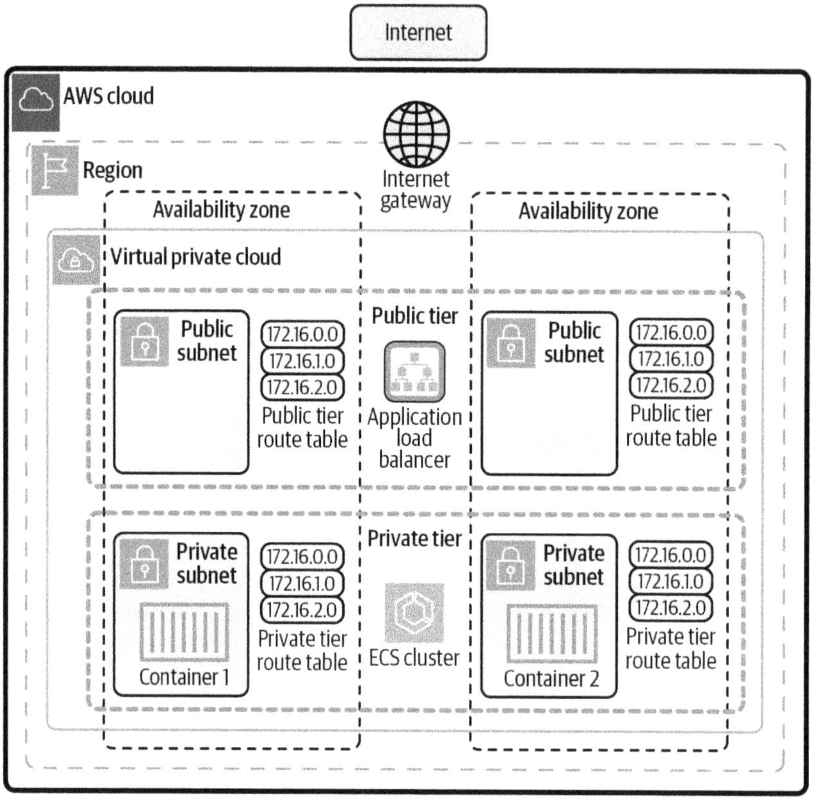

Figure 2-9. VPC with ALB serving internet traffic to containers in private subnets

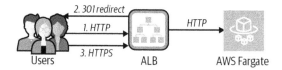

Figure 2-10. Redirecting HTTP to HTTPs with an ALB

Prerequisites

- VPC with public subnets in two AZs and associated route tables.
- Private subnets created in two AZs and associated route tables.
- An ECS cluster and container definition exposing a web application on port 80.
- A Fargate service that runs tasks on the ECS cluster.
- OpenSSL. (You can install this using `brew install openssl` or `yum install openssl`.)

Preparation

Follow the steps in this recipe's folder in the chapter code repository (*https://github.com/AWSCookbook/Networking*).

Steps

1. Create a new private key to be used for the certificate:

   ```
   openssl genrsa 2048 > my-private-key.pem
   ```

   You should see output similar to the following:

   ```
   Generating RSA private key, 2048 bit long modulus
   ..........................................................+++
   ...............................................................+++
   e is 65537 (0x10001)
   ```

2. Generate a self-signed certificate using OpenSSL CLI:

   ```
   openssl req -new -x509 -nodes -sha256 -days 365 \
       -key my-private-key.pem -outform PEM -out my-certificate.pem
   ```

   You should see output similar to the following:

   ```
   You are about to be asked to enter information that will be incorporated
   into your certificate request.
   What you are about to enter is what is called a Distinguished Name or a DN.
   There are quite a few fields but you can leave some blank
   For some fields there will be a default value,
   If you enter '.', the field will be left blank.
   -----
   Country Name (2 letter code) []:US
   State or Province Name (full name) []:Pennsylvania
   Locality Name (eg, city) []:Scranton
   Organization Name (eg, company) []:AWS Cookbook Inc
   Organizational Unit Name (eg, section) []:Cloud Team
   Common Name (eg, fully qualified host name) []:mytest.com
   Email Address []:you@youremail.com
   ```

    You are using a self-signed certificate for this recipe, which will throw a warning when you access the Load Balancer DNS name in most browsers. You can generate a trusted certificate for your own DNS record by using AWS Certificate Manager (ACM) (*https://oreil.ly/Sa88c*).

3. Upload the generated certificate into IAM:

   ```
   CERT_ARN=$(aws iam upload-server-certificate \
       --server-certificate-name AWSCookbook207 \
       --certificate-body file://my-certificate.pem \
       --private-key file://my-private-key.pem \
       --query ServerCertificateMetadata.Arn --output text)
   ```

4. Create a security group to use with the ALB that you will create later:

```
ALB_SG_ID=$(aws ec2 create-security-group --group-name Cookbook207SG \
    --description "ALB Security Group" --vpc-id $VPC_ID \
    --output text --query GroupId)
```

5. Add rules to the security group to allow HTTP and HTTPS traffic from the world:

```
aws ec2 authorize-security-group-ingress \
    --protocol tcp --port 443 \
    --cidr '0.0.0.0/0' \
    --group-id $ALB_SG_ID

aws ec2 authorize-security-group-ingress \
    --protocol tcp --port 80 \
    --cidr '0.0.0.0/0' \
    --group-id $ALB_SG_ID
```

For each command in step 5, you should see output similar to the following:

```
{
  "Return": true,
  "SecurityGroupRules": [
  {
    "SecurityGroupRuleId": "sgr-<<snip>>",
    "GroupId": "sg-<<snip>>",
    "GroupOwnerId": "111111111111",
    "IsEgress": false,
    "IpProtocol": "tcp",
    "FromPort": 80,
    "ToPort": 80,
    "CidrIpv4": "0.0.0.0/0"
  }
  ]
}
```

6. Authorize the container's security group to allow ingress traffic from the ALB:

```
aws ec2 authorize-security-group-ingress \
    --protocol tcp --port 80 \
    --source-group $ALB_SG_ID \
    --group-id $APP_SG_ID
```

7. Create an ALB across the public subnets and assign it the previously created security group:

```
LOAD_BALANCER_ARN=$(aws elbv2 create-load-balancer \
    --name aws-cookbook207-alb \
    --subnets $VPC_PUBLIC_SUBNETS --security-groups $ALB_SG_ID \
    --scheme internet-facing \
    --output text --query LoadBalancers[0].LoadBalancerArn)
```

8. Create a target group for the Load Balancer:

```
TARGET_GROUP=$(aws elbv2 create-target-group \
    --name aws-cookbook207-tg --vpc-id $VPC_ID \
    --protocol HTTP --port 80 --target-type ip \
    --query "TargetGroups[0].TargetGroupArn" \
    --output text)
```

9. Get the IP of the container that is running your application:

```
TASK_ARN=$(aws ecs list-tasks --cluster $ECS_CLUSTER_NAME \
    --output text --query taskArns)
CONTAINER_IP=$(aws ecs describe-tasks --cluster $ECS_CLUSTER_NAME \
    --task $TASK_ARN --output text \
    --query tasks[0].attachments[0].details[4] | cut -f 2)
```

10. Register a container with the target group:

```
aws elbv2 register-targets --targets Id=$CONTAINER_IP \
    --target-group-arn $TARGET_GROUP
```

> For this recipe, you register an IP address of an ECS task within an ECS service with the load balancer that you created. You can optionally associate an ECS service directly with an Application Load Balancer on ECS service creation. For more information, see this documentation (*https://oreil.ly/wF1si*).

11. Create an HTTPS listener on the ALB that uses the certificate you imported and forwards traffic to your target group:

```
HTTPS_LISTENER_ARN=$(aws elbv2 create-listener \
    --load-balancer-arn $LOAD_BALANCER_ARN \
    --protocol HTTPS --port 443 \
    --certificates CertificateArn=$CERT_ARN \
    --default-actions Type=forward,TargetGroupArn=$TARGET_GROUP \
    --output text --query Listeners[0].ListenerArn)
```

12. Add a rule for the listener on port 443 to forward traffic to the target group that you created:

```
aws elbv2 create-rule \
    --listener-arn $HTTPS_LISTENER_ARN \
    --priority 10 \
    --conditions '{"Field":"path-pattern","PathPatternConfig":{"Values":["/*"]}}' \
    --actions Type=forward,TargetGroupArn=$TARGET_GROUP
```

You should see output similar to the following:

```
{
  "Rules": [
  {
    "RuleArn": "arn:aws:elasticloadbalancing:us-east-1:111111111111:listener-
rule/app/aws-cookbook207-alb/<<snip>>",
    "Priority": "10",
    "Conditions": [
      {
        "Field": "path-pattern",
        "Values": [
          "/*"
        ],
        "PathPatternConfig": {
        "Values": [
          "/*"
        ]
        }
```

```
        }
      ],
      "Actions": [
        {
          "Type": "forward",
  ...
```

13. Create a redirect response for all HTTP traffic that sends a 301 response to the browser while preserving the full URL for the HTTPS redirect:

```
aws elbv2 create-listener --load-balancer-arn $LOAD_BALANCER_ARN \
    --protocol HTTP --port 80 \
    --default-actions \
"Type=redirect,RedirectConfig={Protocol=HTTPS,Port=443,Host='#{host}',Query='#{qu
ery}',Path='/#{path}',
StatusCode=HTTP_301}"
```

You should see output similar to the following:

```
{
  "Listeners": [
    {
      "ListenerArn": "arn:aws:elasticloadbalancing:us-
east-1:111111111111:listener/app/aws-cookbook207-alb/<<snip>>",
      "LoadBalancerArn": "arn:aws:elasticloadbalancing:us-
east-1:111111111111:loadbalancer/app/aws-cookbook207-alb/<<snip>>",
      "Port": 80,
      "Protocol": "HTTP",
      "DefaultActions": [
        {
          "Type": "redirect",
          "RedirectConfig": {
          "Protocol": "HTTPS",
          "Port": "443",
          "Host": "#{host}",
          "Path": "/#{path}",
          "Query": "#{query}",
          "StatusCode": "HTTP_301"
          }
        }
  ...
```

14. Verify the health of the targets:

```
aws elbv2 describe-target-health --target-group-arn $TARGET_GROUP \
    --query TargetHealthDescriptions[*].TargetHealth.State
```

You should see output similar to this:

```
[
  "healthy"
]
```

Validation checks. Get the URL of the load balancer so that you can test it:

```
LOAD_BALANCER_DNS=$(aws elbv2 describe-load-balancers \
    --names aws-cookbook207-alb \
    --output text --query LoadBalancers[0].DNSName)
```

Display the URL and test it in your browser. You should notice that you end up at an HTTPS URL. You will most likely receive a warning from your browser because of the self-signed cert:

```
echo $LOAD_BALANCER_DNS
```

Or test it from the command line.

cURL the Load Balancer DNS over HTTP and observe the 301 code:

```
curl -v http://$LOAD_BALANCER_DNS
```

cURL the Load Balancer DNS and specify to follow the redirect to HTTPS:

```
curl -vkL http://$LOAD_BALANCER_DNS
```

Cleanup

Follow the steps in this recipe's folder in the chapter code repository (*https://github.com/AWSCookbook/Networking*).

Discussion

When you added a 301 redirect rule for the port 80 listener, this allowed the ALB to instruct clients to follow the redirect to port 443 so that users of your application will be automatically redirected to HTTPS. The redirect rule also preserves the URL path in the original request.

Application Load Balancers operate on Layer 7 of the OSI model. The ALB documentation (*https://oreil.ly/bJZsg*) lists the available target types of EC2 instances, IP addresses, and Lambda functions. You can create internet-facing ALBs (when your VPC has an internet gateway attached) and internal ALBs for usage within your internal network only. The ALB provisions elastic network interfaces that have IP addresses within your chosen subnets to communicate with your services. ALBs continuously run health checks for members of your associated target groups that allow the ALB to detect healthy components of your application to route traffic to. ALBs are also a great layer to add in front of your applications for increased security since you can allow the targets to be accessed by only the load balancer—not by clients directly.

AWS offers multiple types of load balancers for specific use cases. You should choose the load balancer that best fits your needs. For example, for high-performance Layer 4 load balancing with static IP address capability, you might consider Network Load Balancers, and for network virtual appliances (NVAs) like virtual firewalls and security appliances, you might consider Gateway Load Balancers. For more information on and a comparison of the types of load balancers available in AWS, see the support document (*https://oreil.ly/8G9xc*).

Challenge

Update the SSL certificate with a new one.

2.8 Simplifying Management of CIDRs in Security Groups with Prefix Lists

Problem

You have two applications hosted in public subnets. The applications are hosted on instances with specific access requirements for each application. During normal operation, these applications need to be accessed from virtual desktops in another Region. However, you need to reach them from your home PC for a short period for testing.

Solution

Using the AWS-provided IP address ranges list, create a managed prefix list that contains a list of CIDR ranges for WorkSpaces gateways in us-west-2 and associate it with each security group. Update the prefix list with your home IP for testing and then optionally remove it (see Figure 2-11).

Prerequisites

- VPC with public subnets in two AZs and associated route tables
- Two EC2 instances in each public subnet running a web server on port 80
- Two security groups, one associated with each EC2 instance

Preparation

Follow the steps in this recipe's folder in the chapter code repository (*https:// github.com/AWSCookbook/Networking*).

Figure 2-11. Two applications in public subnets protected by security groups

Steps

1. Download the AWS IP address ranges JSON file:

```
curl -o ip-ranges.json https://ip-ranges.amazonaws.com/ip-ranges.json
```

> You will need to install the *jq* utility if your workstation doesn't already have it; for example, `brew install jq`.

2. Generate a list of the CIDR ranges for Amazon WorkSpaces gateways in us-west-2:

```
jq -r '.prefixes[] | select(.region=="us-west-2") |
select(.service=="WORKSPACES_GATEWAYS") | .ip_prefix' < ip-ranges.json
```

You can find more information on AWS IP address ranges in their documentation (*https://oreil.ly/iQrPY*).

3. Use the IP ranges for Amazon WorkSpaces from *ip-ranges.json* to create a managed prefix list:

```
PREFIX_LIST_ID=$(aws ec2 create-managed-prefix-list \
    --address-family IPv4 \
    --max-entries 15 \
    --prefix-list-name allowed-us-east-1-cidrs \
    --output text --query "PrefixList.PrefixListId" \
    --entries
    Cidr=44.234.54.0/23,Description=workspaces-us-west-2-cidr1
Cidr=54.244.46.0/23,Description=workspaces-us-west-2-cidr2)
```

At this point, your workstation should not be able to reach either of the instances. If you try one of these commands, you will receive a "Connection timed out" error:

```
curl -m 2 $INSTANCE_IP_1
curl -m 2 $INSTANCE_IP_2
```

4. Get your workstation's public IPv4 address:

```
MY_IP_4=$(curl myip4.com | tr -d ' ')
```

5. Update your managed prefix list and add your workstation's public IPv4 address (see Figure 2-12):

```
aws ec2 modify-managed-prefix-list \
    --prefix-list-id $PREFIX_LIST_ID \
    --current-version 1 \
    --add-entries Cidr=${MY_IP_4}/32,Description=my-workstation-ip
```

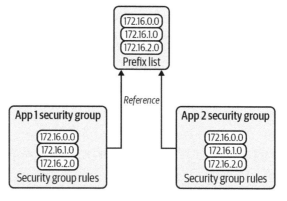

Figure 2-12. Security group rules referencing a prefix list

There is an AWS-managed prefix list (*https://oreil.ly/wcdzB*) for S3.

You should see output similar to the following:

```
{
  "PrefixList": {
    "PrefixListId": "pl-013217b85144872d2",
    "AddressFamily": "IPv4",
    "State": "modify-in-progress",
    "PrefixListArn": "arn:aws:ec2:us-east-1:111111111111:prefix-list/
pl-013217b85144872d2",
    "PrefixListName": "allowed-us-east-1-cidrs",
    "MaxEntries": 10,
    "Version": 1,
    "OwnerId": "111111111111"
  }
}
```

6. For each application's security group, add an inbound rule that allows TCP port 80 access from the prefix list:

```
aws ec2 authorize-security-group-ingress \
    --group-id $INSTANCE_SG_1 --ip-permissions \
IpProtocol=tcp,FromPort=80,ToPort=80,PrefixListIds="[{Description=http-from-
prefix-list,PrefixListId=$PREFIX_LIST_ID}]"
```

```
aws ec2 authorize-security-group-ingress \
    --group-id $INSTANCE_SG_2 --ip-permissions \
IpProtocol=tcp,FromPort=80,ToPort=80,PrefixListIds="[{Description=http-from-
prefix-list,PrefixListId=$PREFIX_LIST_ID}]"
```

 Find out where your managed list is used. This command is helpful for auditing where prefix lists are used throughout your AWS environments:

```
aws ec2 get-managed-prefix-list-associations \
    --prefix-list-id $PREFIX_LIST_ID
```

Validation checks. Test access to both instances from your workstation's PC:

```
curl -m 2 $INSTANCE_IP_1
```

```
curl -m 2 $INSTANCE_IP_2
```

Cleanup

Follow the steps in this recipe's folder in the chapter code repository (*https://github.com/AWSCookbook/Networking*).

Discussion

If you need to update the list of CIDR blocks allowing ingress communication to your instances, you can simply update the prefix list instead of the security group. This helps reduce the amount of maintenance overhead if you need to use this type of authorization across many security groups; you need to update the prefix list in only a single location rather than modify every security group authorization that requires this network security configuration. You can also use prefix lists for egress security group authorizations.

Prefix lists can be associated with route tables; they are also useful for blackholing traffic (prohibiting access to a specific list of IP addresses and CIDR blocks) and can also simplify your route table configuration. For example, you could maintain a prefix list of branch office CIDR ranges and use them to implement your routing and security group authorizations, simplifying your management for network flow and security configuration. An example of associating a prefix list with a route looks like this:

```
aws ec2 create-route --route-table-id $Sub1RouteTableID \
    --destination-prefix-list-id $PREFIX_LIST_ID \
    --instance-id $INSTANCE_ID
```

Prefix lists also provide a powerful versioning mechanism (*https://oreil.ly/KgSne*), allowing you to quickly roll back to previous known working states. If, for example, you updated a prefix list and found that the change broke some existing functionality, you can roll back to a previous version of a prefix list to restore previous functionality while you investigate the root cause of the error. If you decide to roll back to a previous version for some reason, first describe the prefix list to get the current version number:

```
aws ec2 describe-prefix-lists --prefix-list-ids $PREFIX_LIST_ID
```

Challenge

Revert the active version of the prefix list so that your workstation IP is removed and you can no longer access either application. (Hint: in the repository.)

2.9 Controlling Network Access to S3 from Your VPC Using VPC Endpoints

Problem

Resources within your VPC should be able to access only a specific S3 bucket. Also, this S3 traffic should not traverse the internet for security reasons and to keep bandwidth costs low.

Solution

You will create a gateway VPC endpoint for S3, associate it with a route table, and customize its policy document (see Figure 2-13).

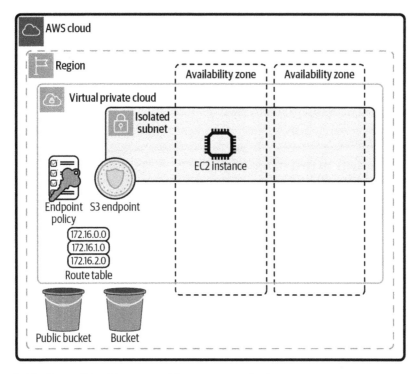

Figure 2-13. Controlling S3 access with gateway endpoints

Prerequisites

- VPC with isolated subnets in two AZs and associated route tables
- One EC2 instance in a public subnet that you can access for testing
- An existing S3 bucket that you want to limit access to

Preparation

Follow the steps in this recipe's folder in the chapter code repository (*https:// github.com/AWSCookbook/Networking*).

Steps

1. Create a gateway endpoint in your VPC and associate the endpoint with the isolated route tables:

```
END_POINT_ID=$(aws ec2 create-vpc-endpoint \
    --vpc-id $VPC_ID \
    --service-name com.amazonaws.$AWS_REGION.s3 \
    --route-table-ids $RT_ID_1 $RT_ID_2 \
    --query VpcEndpoint.VpcEndpointId --output text)
```

2. Create a template endpoint policy file called *policy.json* with the following content (included in the repository). This is used to limit access to only the S3 bucket that you created in the preparation steps:

```
{
  "Statement": [
    {
      "Sid": "RestrictToOneBucket",
      "Principal": "*",
      "Action": [
        "s3:GetObject",
        "s3:PutObject"
      ],
      "Effect": "Allow",
      "Resource": ["arn:aws:s3:::S3BucketName",
                   "arn:aws:s3:::S3BucketName/*"]
    }
  ]
}
```

3. Insert your S3_BUCKET_NAME in the *policy-template.json* file:

```
sed -e "s/S3BucketName/${BUCKET_NAME}/g" \
    policy-template.json > policy.json
```

4. Modify the endpoint's policy document. Endpoint policies limit or restrict the resources that can be accessed through the VPC endpoint:

```
aws ec2 modify-vpc-endpoint \
    --policy-document file://policy.json \
    --vpc-endpoint-id $END_POINT_ID
```

Validation checks. Output the name of your S3 Bucket so that you can refer to it when you are connected to your EC2 Instance:

```
echo $BUCKET_NAME
```

Connect to the EC2 instance by using SSM Session Manager (see Recipe 1.6):

```
aws ssm start-session --target $INSTANCE_ID
```

Set the Region by grabbing the value from the instance's metadata:

```
export AWS_DEFAULT_REGION=$(curl \
--silent http://169.254.169.254/latest/dynamic/instance-identity/document \
| awk -F'"' ' /region/ {print $4}')
```

Retrieve the allowed S3 bucket name:

```
BUCKET=$(aws ssm get-parameters \
    --names "Cookbook209S3Bucket" \
    --query "Parameters[*].Value" --output text)
```

Test access by trying to copy a file from your S3 bucket:

```
aws s3 cp s3://${BUCKET_NAME}/test_file /home/ssm-user/
```

You should see output similar to the following:

```
download: s3://cdk-aws-cookbook-209-awscookbookrecipe20979239201-115xoj77fgxoh/
test_file to ./test_file
```

 The following command is attempting to list a public S3 bucket. However, because of the endpoint policy we have configured, it is expected that this will fail.

Try to list the contents of a *public* S3 bucket associated with the OpenStreetMap Foundation Public Dataset Initiative:

```
aws s3 ls s3://osm-pds/
```

You should see output similar to the following:

```
An error occurred (AccessDenied) when calling the ListObjectsV2 operation: Access
Denied
```

Exit the Session Manager session:

```
exit
```

Cleanup

Follow the steps in this recipe's folder in the chapter code repository (*https://github.com/AWSCookbook/Networking*).

Discussion

Using an endpoint policy is a useful security implementation to restrict access to S3 buckets. This applies not only to S3 buckets owned by your account but also to all S3 buckets globally on AWS.

 Recently, AWS announced support for S3 interface endpoints (*https://oreil.ly/mBBsN*). However, it is worth noting that while these are great for some use cases (e.g., when you want to control traffic with security groups), they are not ideal for this problem because of the costs associated with interface endpoints (*https://oreil.ly/1WUGl*).

Per the VPC User Guide (*https://oreil.ly/LAWFo*), Gateway VPC endpoints are free and used within your VPC's route tables to keep traffic bound for AWS services within the AWS backbone network without traversing the network. This allows you to create VPCs that do not need internet gateways for applications that do not require them but need access to other AWS services like S3 and DynamoDB. All traffic bound for these services will be directed by the route table to the VPC endpoint rather than the public internet route, since the VPC endpoint route table entry is more specific than the default 0.0.0.0/0 route.

S3 VPC endpoint policies leverage JSON policy documents that can be as fine-grained as your needs require. You can use conditionals, source IP addresses, VPC endpoint IDs, S3 bucket names, and more. For more information on the policy elements available, see the support document (*https://oreil.ly/M8q8J*).

Challenge

Modify the bucket policy for the S3 bucket to allow access only from the VPC endpoint that you created. For some tips on this, check out the S3 User Guide (*https://oreil.ly/tEajj*).

2.10 Enabling Transitive Cross-VPC Connections Using Transit Gateway

Problem

You need to implement transitive routing across all of your VPCs and share internet egress from a shared services VPC to your other VPCs to reduce the number of NAT gateways you have to deploy.

Solution

Deploy an AWS transit gateway (TGW) and configure transit gateway VPC attachments for all of your VPCs. Update your VPC route tables of each VPC to send all nonlocal traffic to the transit gateway and enable sharing of the NAT gateway in your shared services VPC for all of your spoke VPCs (see Figure 2-14).

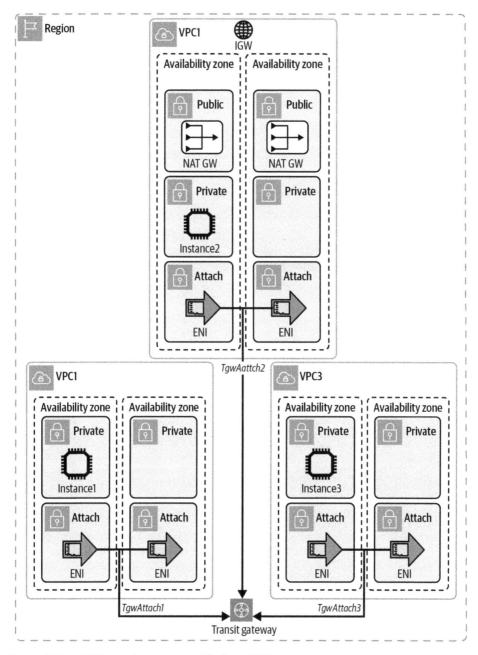

Figure 2-14. AWS transit gateway with three VPCs

The default initial quota of VPCs per Region per account is five (*https://oreil.ly/T4WD8*). This solution will deploy three VPCs. If you already have more than two VPCs, you can decide among four choices: deploy to a different Region, delete any existing VPCs that are no longer needed, use a test account, or request a quota increase (*https://oreil.ly/cFRs5*).

Prerequisites

- Three VPCs in the same Region with private and isolated subnet tiers
- Internet gateway attached to a VPC (VPC2 in our example)
  — NAT gateway deployed in public subnets

Preparation

Follow the steps in this recipe's folder in the chapter code repository (*https://github.com/AWSCookbook/Networking*).

Steps

1. Create a transit gateway:
   ```
   TGW_ID=$(aws ec2 create-transit-gateway \
       --description AWSCookbook210 \
       --
   options=AmazonSideAsn=65010,AutoAcceptSharedAttachments=enable,DefaultRouteTableA
   ssociation=enable,\
       DefaultRouteTablePropagation=enable,VpnEcmpSupport=enable,DnsSupport=enable \
       --output text --query TransitGateway.TransitGatewayId)
   ```

2. Wait until the transit gateway's state has reached available. This may take several minutes:
   ```
   aws ec2 describe-transit-gateways \
       --transit-gateway-ids $TGW_ID \
       --output text --query TransitGateways[0].State
   ```

3. Create a transit gateway attachment for VPC1:
   ```
   TGW_ATTACH_1=$(aws ec2 create-transit-gateway-vpc-attachment \
       --transit-gateway-id $TGW_ID \
       --vpc-id $VPC_ID_1 \
       --subnet-ids $ATTACHMENT_SUBNETS_VPC_1 \
       --query TransitGatewayVpcAttachment.TransitGatewayAttachmentId \
       --output text)
   ```

4. Create a transit gateway attachment for VPC2:
   ```
   TGW_ATTACH_2=$(aws ec2 create-transit-gateway-vpc-attachment \
       --transit-gateway-id $TGW_ID \
       --vpc-id $VPC_ID_2 \
       --subnet-ids $ATTACHMENT_SUBNETS_VPC_2 \
       --query TransitGatewayVpcAttachment.TransitGatewayAttachmentId \
       --output text)
   ```

5. Create a transit gateway attachment for VPC3:

```
TGW_ATTACH_3=$(aws ec2 create-transit-gateway-vpc-attachment \
    --transit-gateway-id $TGW_ID \
    --vpc-id $VPC_ID_3 \
    --subnet-ids $ATTACHMENT_SUBNETS_VPC_3 \
    --query TransitGatewayVpcAttachment.TransitGatewayAttachmentId \
    --output text)
```

6. Add routes for all private subnets in VPCs 1 and 3 to target the TGW for destinations of 0.0.0.0/0. This enables consolidated internet egress through the NAT gateway in VPC2 and transitive routing to other VPCs:

```
aws ec2 create-route --route-table-id $VPC_1_RT_ID_1 \
    --destination-cidr-block 0.0.0.0/0 \
    --transit-gateway-id $TGW_ID

aws ec2 create-route --route-table-id $VPC_1_RT_ID_2 \
    --destination-cidr-block 0.0.0.0/0 \
    --transit-gateway-id $TGW_ID

aws ec2 create-route --route-table-id $VPC_3_RT_ID_1 \
    --destination-cidr-block 0.0.0.0/0 \
    --transit-gateway-id $TGW_ID

aws ec2 create-route --route-table-id $VPC_3_RT_ID_2 \
    --destination-cidr-block 0.0.0.0/0 \
    --transit-gateway-id $TGW_ID
```

7. Now add a route to your 10.10.0.0/24 supernet (*https://oreil.ly/AVrM7*) in the route tables associated with the private subnets of VPC2, pointing its destination to the transit gateway. This is more specific than the 0.0.0.0/0 destination that is already present and therefore takes higher priority in routing decisions. This directs traffic bound for VPCs 1, 2, and 3 to the TGW:

```
aws ec2 create-route --route-table-id $VPC_2_RT_ID_1 \
    --destination-cidr-block 10.10.0.0/24 \
    --transit-gateway-id $TGW_ID

aws ec2 create-route --route-table-id $VPC_2_RT_ID_2 \
    --destination-cidr-block 10.10.0.0/24 \
    --transit-gateway-id $TGW_ID
```

8. Query for the NAT gateways in use; we'll need these to add routes to them for internet traffic:

```
NAT_GW_ID_1=$(aws ec2 describe-nat-gateways \
    --filter "Name=subnet-id,Values=$VPC_2_PUBLIC_SUBNET_ID_1" \
    --output text --query NatGateways[*].NatGatewayId)

NAT_GW_ID_2=$(aws ec2 describe-nat-gateways \
    --filter "Name=subnet-id,Values=$VPC_2_PUBLIC_SUBNET_ID_2" \
    --output text --query NatGateways[*].NatGatewayId)
```

9. Add a route for the attachment subnet in VPC2 to direct internet traffic to the NAT gateway:

```
aws ec2 create-route --route-table-id $VPC_2_ATTACH_RT_ID_1 \
    --destination-cidr-block 0.0.0.0/0 \
    --nat-gateway-id $NAT_GW_ID_1

aws ec2 create-route --route-table-id $VPC_2_ATTACH_RT_ID_2 \
    --destination-cidr-block 0.0.0.0/0 \
    --nat-gateway-id $NAT_GW_ID_2
```

10. Add a static route to the route tables associated with the public subnet in VPC2. This enables communication back to the TGW to allow sharing the NAT gateway with all attached VPCs:

```
aws ec2 create-route --route-table-id $VPC_2_PUBLIC_RT_ID_1 \
    --destination-cidr-block 10.10.0.0/24 \
    --transit-gateway-id $TGW_ID

aws ec2 create-route --route-table-id $VPC_2_PUBLIC_RT_ID_2 \
    --destination-cidr-block 10.10.0.0/24 \
    --transit-gateway-id $TGW_ID
```

11. Add a static route for the private subnets in VPC2 to allow communication back to the TGW attachments from VPC2 private subnets:

```
aws ec2 create-route --route-table-id $VPC_2_RT_ID_1 \
    --destination-cidr-block 10.10.0.0/24 \
    --transit-gateway-id $TGW_ID

aws ec2 create-route --route-table-id $VPC_2_RT_ID_2 \
    --destination-cidr-block 10.10.0.0/24 \
    --transit-gateway-id $TGW_ID
```

12. Get the transit route table ID:

```
TRAN_GW_RT=$(aws ec2 describe-transit-gateways \
    --transit-gateway-ids $TGW_ID --output text \
    --query TransitGateways[0].Options.AssociationDefaultRouteTableId)
```

13. Add a static route in the transit gateway route table for VPC2 (with the NAT gateways) to send all internet traffic over this path:

```
aws ec2 create-transit-gateway-route \
  --destination-cidr-block 0.0.0.0/0 \
  --transit-gateway-route-table-id $TRAN_GW_RT \
  --transit-gateway-attachment-id $TGW_ATTACH_2
```

Validation checks. Ensure your EC2 Instance 1 has registered with SSM. To check the status use the following command, which should return the instance ID:

```
aws ssm describe-instance-information \
    --filters Key=ResourceType,Values=EC2Instance \
    --query "InstanceInformationList[].InstanceId" --output text
```

Connect to your EC2 instance by using SSM Session Manager:

```
aws ssm start-session --target $INSTANCE_ID_1
```

Test internet access:

```
ping -c 4 aws.amazon.com
```

You should see output similar to the following:

```
PING dr49lng3n1n2s.cloudfront.net (99.86.187.73) 56(84) bytes of data.
64 bytes from server-99-86-187-73.iad79.r.cloudfront.net (99.86.187.73): icmp_seq=1
ttl=238 time=3.44 ms
64 bytes from server-99-86-187-73.iad79.r.cloudfront.net (99.86.187.73): icmp_seq=2
ttl=238 time=1.41 ms
64 bytes from server-99-86-187-73.iad79.r.cloudfront.net (99.86.187.73): icmp_seq=3
ttl=238 time=1.43 ms
64 bytes from server-99-86-187-73.iad79.r.cloudfront.net (99.86.187.73): icmp_seq=4
ttl=238 time=1.44 ms

--- dr49lng3n1n2s.cloudfront.net ping statistics ---
4 packets transmitted, 4 received, 0% packet loss, time 3004ms
rtt min/avg/max/mdev = 1.411/1.934/3.449/0.875 ms
sh-4.2$
```

Exit the Session Manager session:

```
exit
```

Challenge 1

You can limit which VPCs can access the internet through the NAT gateway in VPC2 by modifying the route tables. Try adding a more specific route of 10.10.0.0/24 instead of the 0.0.0.0/0 destination for VPC3 to see how you can customize the internet egress sharing.

Challenge 2

You may not want to allow VPC1 and VPC3 to be able to communicate with each other. Try adding a new transit gateway route table, updating the attachments to accomplish this.

Challenge 3

In the solution, you deployed three VPCs each of /26 subnet size within the 10.10.0.0/24 supernet. There is room for an additional /26 subnet. Try adding an additional VPC with a /26 CIDR with subnets and route tables; then attach it to the transit gateway.

Cleanup

Follow the steps in this recipe's folder in the chapter code repository (*https://github.com/AWSCookbook/Networking*).

Discussion

Transit gateways (*https://oreil.ly/VKW2V*) allow you to quickly implement a multi-VPC *hub-and-spoke* network topology for your network in AWS. You may have had to use many peering connections to achieve similar results or used third-party software on instances in a transit VPC architecture (*https://oreil.ly/LUxIm*). Transit gateway also supports cross-region peering of transit gateways (*https://oreil.ly/kD1pI*) and cross-account sharing via Resource Access Manager (RAM) (*https://oreil.ly/qovsS*).

When you attached your VPCs to the transit gateway, you used subnets in each AZ for resiliency. You also used dedicated "attachment" subnets for the VPC attachments. You can attach the transit gateway to any subnet(s) within your VPC. Using a dedicated subnet for these attachments gives you flexibility to granularly define subnets you choose to route to the TGW. That is, if you attached the private subnet, it would always have a route to the TGW; this might not be intended based on your use case. In your case, you configured routes for your private subnets to send all traffic to the transit gateway which enabled sharing of the NAT gateway and internet gateway; this results in cost savings over having to deploy multiple NAT gateways (e.g., one for each VPC).

You can connect your on-premises network or any virtual network directly to a transit gateway, as it acts as a hub for all of your AWS network traffic (*https://oreil.ly/13s7R*). You can connect IPsec VPNs, Direct Connect (DX), and third-party network appliances to the transit gateway to extend your AWS network to non-AWS networks. This also allows you to consolidate VPN connections and/or Direct Connect connections by connecting one directly to the transit gateway to access all of your VPCs in a Region. Border Gateway Protocol (BGP) is supported by TGW (*https://oreil.ly/pbqwP*) over these types of network extensions for dynamic route updates in both directions.

Challenge

Create a fourth VPC and attach your TGW to subnets in it. Allow it to use the existing NAT gateway to reach the internet.

2.11 Peering Two VPCs Together for Inter-VPC Network Communication

Problem

You need to enable two instances in separate VPCs to communicate with each other in a simple and cost-effective manner.

Solution

Request a peering connection between two VPCs, accept the peering connection, update the route tables for each VPC subnet, and finally test the connection from one instance to another (see Figure 2-15).

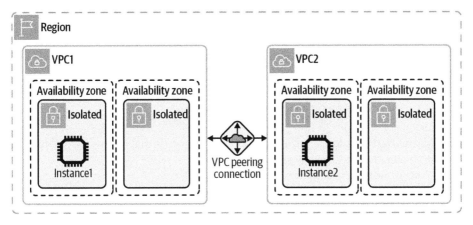

Figure 2-15. Communication between instances in peered VPCs

Prerequisites

- Two VPCs, each with isolated subnets in two AZs and associated route tables
- In each VPC, one EC2 instance that you can access for testing

Preparation

Follow the steps in this recipe's folder in the chapter code repository (*https://github.com/AWSCookbook/Networking*).

Steps

1. Create a VPC peering connection to connect VPC1 to VPC2:

```
VPC_PEERING_CONNECTION_ID=$(aws ec2 create-vpc-peering-connection \
    --vpc-id $VPC_ID_1 --peer-vpc-id $VPC_ID_2 --output text \
    --query VpcPeeringConnection.VpcPeeringConnectionId)
```

2. Accept the peering connection:

```
aws ec2 accept-vpc-peering-connection \
    --vpc-peering-connection-id $VPC_PEERING_CONNECTION_ID
```

 VPC peering connections can be established from one AWS account to a different AWS account. If you choose to peer VPCs across AWS accounts, you need to ensure you have the correct IAM configuration (*https://oreil.ly/pWmDE*) to create and accept the peering connection within each account.

3. In the route tables associated with each subnet, add a route to direct traffic destined for the peered VPC's CIDR range to the VPC_PEERING_CONNECTION_ID:

```
aws ec2 create-route --route-table-id $VPC_SUBNET_RT_ID_1 \
    --destination-cidr-block $VPC_CIDR_2 \
    --vpc-peering-connection-id $VPC_PEERING_CONNECTION_ID

aws ec2 create-route --route-table-id $VPC_SUBNET_RT_ID_2 \
    --destination-cidr-block $VPC_CIDR_1 \
    --vpc-peering-connection-id $VPC_PEERING_CONNECTION_ID
```

4. Add an ingress rule to instance 2's security group that allows ICMPv4 access from instance 1's security group:

```
aws ec2 authorize-security-group-ingress \
    --protocol icmp --port -1 \
    --source-group $INSTANCE_SG_1 \
    --group-id $INSTANCE_SG_2
```

Validation checks. Get instance 2's IP:

```
aws ec2 describe-instances --instance-ids $INSTANCE_ID_2\
    --output text \
    --query Reservations[0].Instances[0].PrivateIpAddress
```

Ensure your EC2 instance 1 has registered with SSM. Use this command to check the status:

```
aws ssm describe-instance-information \
    --filters Key=ResourceType,Values=EC2Instance \
    --query "InstanceInformationList[].InstanceId" --output text
```

Connect to your EC2 instance by using SSM Session Manager:

```
aws ssm start-session --target $INSTANCE_ID_1
```

Ping instance 2 from instance 1:

```
ping -c 4 <<INSTANCE_IP_2>>

Output:
PING 10.20.0.242 (10.20.0.242) 56(84) bytes of data.
64 bytes from 10.20.0.242: icmp_seq=1 ttl=255 time=0.232 ms
64 bytes from 10.20.0.242: icmp_seq=2 ttl=255 time=0.300 ms
64 bytes from 10.20.0.242: icmp_seq=3 ttl=255 time=0.186 ms
64 bytes from 10.20.0.242: icmp_seq=4 ttl=255 time=0.183 ms

--- 10.20.0.242 ping statistics ---
4 packets transmitted, 4 received, 0% packet loss, time 3059ms
rtt min/avg/max/mdev = 0.183/0.225/0.300/0.048 ms
```

Exit the Session Manager session:

```
exit
```

You can search for a security group ID in the VPC console to show all security groups that reference others. You can also run the aws ec2 describe-security-group-references (*https://oreil.ly/BRCsd*) CLI command to accomplish this. This is helpful in gaining insight into which security groups reference others. You can reference security groups in peered VPCs owned by other AWS accounts but not located in other Regions (*https://oreil.ly/BxIDv*).

Cleanup

Follow the steps in this recipe's folder in the chapter code repository (*https://github.com/AWSCookbook/Networking*).

Discussion

VPC peering connections are nontransitive. Each VPC needs to peer with every other VPC that they need to communicate with. This type of connection is ideal (*https://oreil.ly/0sJeK*) when you might have a VPC hosting shared services that other VPCs need to access, while not having the "spoke" VPCs communicate with one another.

In addition to the peering connections, you need to configure the route tables associated with the VPC subnets to send traffic destined for the peered VPC's CIDR to the peering connection (PCX). In other words, to enable VPC1 to be able to communicate with VPC2, the destination route must be present in VPC1 and the return route also must be present in VPC2.

If you were to add a third VPC to this recipe, and you needed all VPCs to be able to communicate with one another, you would need to peer that third VPC with the previous two and update all of the VPC route tables accordingly to allow for all of the VPCs to have communication with one another. As you continue to add more VPCs to a network architecture like this, you may notice that the number of peering connections and route table updates required begin to increase exponentially. Because of this, transit gateway is a better choice for transitive VPC communication using transit gateway route tables.

You can use VPC peering cross-account if needed, and you can also reference security groups in peered VPCs (*https://oreil.ly/53awx*) in a similar way of referencing security groups within a single VPC. This allows you to use the same type of strategy with how you manage security groups across your AWS environment when using VPC peering (*https://oreil.ly/ce4M8*).

Connecting VPCs together requires nonoverlapping CIDR ranges (*https://oreil.ly/3j1KN*) in order for routing to work normally. The VPC route tables must include a specific route directing traffic destined for the peered VPC to the peering connection.

Challenge

VPC peering connections can be established across AWS Regions (*https://oreil.ly/PAKmf*). Connect a VPC in another Region to the VPC you deployed in the Region used for the recipe.

CHAPTER 3
Storage

3.0 Introduction

Many industries have put a heavy emphasis on cloud data storage technologies to help facilitate increasing demands of data. Many options are available for data storage to suit your needs, with seemingly infinite scale. Even with many new storage options available in the cloud, Amazon S3 remains a powerful, fundamental building block for so many use cases. It is amazing to think that it was released more than 15 years ago (*https://oreil.ly/nfIGt*). Over time, many features have been added and new storage services launched. Multiple storage options are available to meet security requirements (e.g., key management service [KMS] encryption) while reducing costs (e.g., S3 Intelligent-Tiering). Ensuring that data is secured and available is a challenge that all developers and architects face.

The storage services available on AWS allow for integration with other AWS services to provide ways for developers and application architects who integrate with many AWS services. These services can also be used to replace legacy storage systems (*https://oreil.ly/qSEnc*) you run and operate with on-premises environments. For example:

- S3 can be used to automatically invoke Lambda functions on object operations like upload.

- EFS can be used with EC2 to replace existing shared file systems provided by Network File System (NFS) servers.

- FSx for Windows (*https://aws.amazon.com/fsx/windows*) can be used to replace Windows-based file servers for your EC2 workloads.

- EBS replaces Fibre Channel and Internet Small Computer Systems Interface (iSCSI) targets by providing block devices, and it offers many throughput options to meet performance requirements.

In this chapter, you will use some of these services so that you can start building intelligent, scalable, and secure systems that have the potential to minimize costs and operational overhead.

Workstation Configuration

Follow the "General workstation setup steps for CLI recipes" on page xvii to validate your configuration and set up the required environment variables. Then, clone the chapter code repository:

```
git clone https://github.com/AWSCookbook/Storage
```

3.1 Using S3 Lifecycle Policies to Reduce Storage Costs

Problem

You need to transition infrequently accessed objects to a more cost-effective storage tier without impacting performance or adding operational overhead.

Solution

Create an S3 Lifecycle rule to transition objects to the S3 Infrequent Access (IA) storage class after a predefined time period of 30 days. Then apply this Lifecycle policy to your S3 bucket (see Figure 3-1).

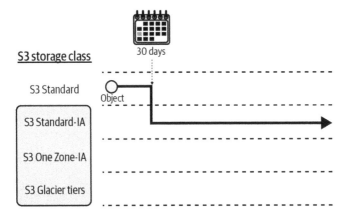

Figure 3-1. S3 Lifecycle rule configuration

Prerequisite

- An S3 bucket

Preparation

Follow the steps in this recipe's folder in the chapter code repository (*https://github.com/AWSCookbook/Storage*).

Steps

1. Create a *lifecycle-rule.json* file (provided in the repository) to use as the Lifecycle policy that you will apply to your S3 bucket:

```
{
  "Rules": [
    {
      "ID": "Move all objects to Infrequent Access",
      "Prefix": "",
      "Status": "Enabled",
      "Transitions": [
        {
          "Date": "2015-11-10T00:00:00.000Z",
          "Days": 30,
          "StorageClass": "INFREQUENTLY_ACCESSED"
        }
      ]
    }
  ]
}
```

2. Apply the Lifecycle rule configuration:

```
aws s3api put-bucket-lifecycle-configuration \
    --bucket awscookbook301-$RANDOM_STRING \
    --lifecycle-configuration file://lifecycle-rule.json
```

> A Lifecycle rule helps automate the transition to a different storage class for some or all objects within a bucket (prefixes, tags, and object names can all be used as filters for Lifecycle rules). For a complete list of Lifecycle rule capabilities, see the documentation (*https://oreil.ly/2sUzK*).

Validation checks.   Get the Lifecycle configuration for your bucket:

```
aws s3api get-bucket-lifecycle-configuration \
    --bucket awscookbook301-$RANDOM_STRING
```

(Optional) Copy an object to the bucket:

```
aws s3 cp book_cover.png s3://awscookbook301-$RANDOM_STRING
```

Check the storage class for the object:

```
aws s3api list-objects-v2 --bucket awscookbook301-$RANDOM_STRING
```

You should see output similar to the following:

```
{
  "Contents": [
  {
    "Key": "book_cover.png",
    "LastModified": "2021-06-16T02:30:06+00:00",
    "ETag": "\"d...9\"",
    "Size": 255549,
    "StorageClass": "STANDARD"
  }
  ]
}
```

You will see after 30 days that the storage class for the object is `STANDARD_IA` after running the same command.

 "Days" in the Transition action must be greater than or equal to 30 for `StorageClass STANDARD_IA`. Other storage tiers allow for shorter transition times to meet your requirements. For a list of all of the storage classes available with transition times for Lifecycle rules, see the support document (*https://oreil.ly/6jPLh*).

Cleanup

Follow the steps in this recipe's folder in the chapter code repository (*https://github.com/AWSCookbook/Storage*).

Discussion

When you upload objects to an S3 bucket, if you do not specify the storage class, the default Standard storage class is used. Amazon S3 has multiple storage classes available that can be more cost-effective for long-term storage while also suiting your performance and resiliency requirements. If you cannot change your application to specify storage tiers for object uploads, Lifecycle rules can help automate the transition to your desired storage class. Lifecycle rules can be applied to some or all objects within a bucket with a filter.

As the name may imply, S3 Infrequent Access is a storage class that provides reduced cost (compared to the S3 Standard storage class (*https://oreil.ly/ZDWtF*)) for data stored for objects that you rarely access. This provides the same level of redundancy for your data within a Region for a reduced cost, but the cost associated with accessing objects is slightly higher. If your data access patterns are unpredictable, and you would still like to optimize your S3 storage for cost, performance, and resiliency, take a look at S3 Intelligent-Tiering in the next recipe.

Challenge 1

Configure the Lifecycle rule to apply only to objects based on object-level tags.

Challenge 2

Configure the Lifecycle rule to transition objects to a Deep Archive.

3.2 Using S3 Intelligent-Tiering Archive Policies to Automatically Archive S3 Objects

Problem

You need to automatically transition infrequently accessed objects to a different archive storage class without impacting performance or adding operational overhead.

Solution

Create a policy to automate the archival of S3 objects to the S3 Glacier archive based on access patterns for objects that are more than 90 days old. Apply it to your S3 bucket, as shown in Figure 3-2.

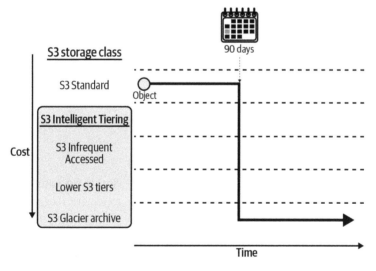

Figure 3-2. S3 Intelligent-Tiering archive

Prerequisite

• An S3 bucket

Preparation

Follow the steps in this recipe's folder in the chapter code repository (*https://github.com/AWSCookbook/Storage*).

Steps

1. Create a file named *tiering.json* for the configuration (file provided in the repository):

```
{
  "Id": "awscookbook302",
  "Status": "Enabled",
  "Tierings": [
    {
      "Days": 90,
      "AccessTier": "ARCHIVE_ACCESS"
    }
  ]
}
```

2. Apply the Intelligent-Tiering configuration:

```
aws s3api put-bucket-intelligent-tiering-configuration \
    --bucket awscookbook302-$RANDOM_STRING \
    --id awscookbook302 \
    --intelligent-tiering-configuration "$(cat tiering.json)"
```

 Ensure that your use case and applications can support the increased retrieval time associated with the S3 Glacier archive storage tier. You can configure your application to use an expedited retrieval mechanism supported by S3 Glacier archive to decrease the retrieval time but increase cost. For a complete list of archive times and how to configure expedited access, please refer to the support document (*https://oreil.ly/tru0v*).

Validation checks.   Get the configuration of Intelligent-Tiering for your bucket:

```
aws s3api get-bucket-intelligent-tiering-configuration \
    --bucket awscookbook302-$RANDOM_STRING \
    --id awscookbook302
```

Copy an object to the bucket:

```
aws s3 cp ./book_cover.png s3://awscookbook302-$RANDOM_STRING
```

Check the storage class for the object:

```
aws s3api list-objects-v2 --bucket awscookbook302-$RANDOM_STRING
```

Cleanup

Follow the steps in this recipe's folder in the chapter code repository (*https://github.com/AWSCookbook/Networking*).

Discussion

An S3 Intelligent-Tiering archive provides an automatic mechanism to transition "cool" (less frequently accessed) objects to an S3 Glacier archive (*https://aws.amazon.com/s3/glacier*). You can define the length of time required for an object to transition to the archive (between 90 and 730 days). This feature helps with meeting long-term retention requirements that you may have for compliance. The storage tiers available within S3 Intelligent-Tiering map directly to S3 tiers:

Frequent Access
  Optimized for frequent access (S3 Standard)

Infrequent Access
  Optimized for infrequent access (S3 Standard-IA)

Archive Access
  Archive purposes (S3 Glacier)

Deep Archive Access
  Long-term retention purposes (S3 Glacier Deep Archive)

This archive configuration is separate from the main S3 Intelligent-Tiering tier configuration that you place on objects, as this is a bucket-specific configuration. In the previous recipe, you configured a Lifecycle rule to configure all objects within a bucket to transition to the S3 Intelligent-Tiering storage tier. This recipe adds additional configuration to transition objects to S3 archive tiers based on your configuration. You can use either of these methods separately or both concurrently to meet your own requirements.

 S3 tiers are object-specific, which differs from the Intelligent-Tiering archive being bucket-specific. You can filter an archive configuration to apply only to certain prefixes, object tags, and object names if you wish to include or exclude objects in a configuration. For more information, see the support document (*https://oreil.ly/WIpqW*).

Challenge 1

Configure the Intelligent-Tiering archive to send objects that are older than one year to the Glacier Deep Archive tier.

Challenge 2

Configure the Intelligent-Tiering archive to use object-level tags and configure an object with a tag that matches your configuration.

3.3 Replicating S3 Buckets to Meet Recovery Point Objectives

Problem

Your company's data security policy mandates that objects be replicated within the same Region to meet a recovery point objective of 15 minutes.

Solution

First, create source and destination S3 buckets with versioning enabled. Then create an IAM role and attach an IAM policy that allows S3 to copy objects from the source to the destination bucket. Finally, create an S3 replication policy that references the IAM role, and apply that policy to the source bucket, as shown in Figure 3-3.

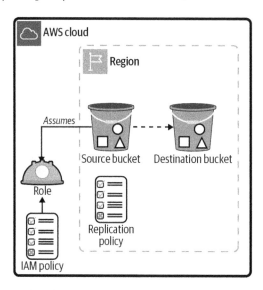

Figure 3-3. S3 bucket replication

Prerequisite

- An S3 bucket with versioning enabled that you will use as your source

Preparation

Follow the steps in this recipe's folder in the chapter code repository (*https://github.com/AWSCookbook/Networking*).

Steps

1. Create the destination S3 bucket:

   ```
   aws s3api create-bucket --bucket awscookbook303-dst-$RANDOM_STRING
   ```

2. Enable versioning for the destination S3 bucket:

   ```
   aws s3api put-bucket-versioning \
       --bucket awscookbook303-dst-$RANDOM_STRING \
       --versioning-configuration Status=Enabled
   ```

3. Create a file named *s3-assume-role-policy.json* with the following content (file provided in the repository):

   ```
   {
     "Version": "2012-10-17",
     "Statement": [
     {
       "Effect": "Allow",
       "Principal": {
         "Service": "s3.amazonaws.com"
       },
       "Action": "sts:AssumeRole"
     }
     ]
   }
   ```

4. Create an IAM role using the statement in the provided *assume-role-policy.json* file using this command:

   ```
   ROLE_ARN=$(aws iam create-role --role-name AWSCookbook303S3Role \
       --assume-role-policy-document file://s3-assume-role-policy.json \
       --output text --query Role.Arn)
   ```

5. Create a file named *s3-perms-policy-template.json* with the following content (file provided in the repository) to allow S3 replication access to your source and destination buckets:

   ```
   {
     "Version":"2012-10-17",
     "Statement":[
     {
       "Effect":"Allow",
       "Action":[
       "s3:GetObjectVersionForReplication",
       "s3:GetObjectVersionAcl",
       "s3:GetObjectVersionTagging"
       ],
   ```

```
        "Resource":[
        "arn:aws:s3:::SRCBUCKET/*"
        ]
    },
    {
        "Effect":"Allow",
        "Action":[
        "s3:ListBucket",
        "s3:GetReplicationConfiguration"
        ],
        "Resource":[
            "arn:aws:s3:::SRCBUCKET"
            ]
    },
    {
        "Effect":"Allow",
        "Action":[
        "s3:ReplicateObject",
        "s3:ReplicateDelete",
        "s3:ReplicateTags",
        "s3:GetObjectVersionTagging"
        ],
        "Resource":"arn:aws:s3:::DSTBUCKET/*"
    }
    ]
}
```

6. Replace the values for *DSTBUCKET* and *SRCBUCKET* in the file and save it as *s3-perms-policy.json*:

```
sed -e "s/DSTBUCKET/awscookbook303-dst-${RANDOM_STRING}/g" \
    -e "s|SRCBUCKET|awscookbook303-src-${RANDOM_STRING}|g" \
    s3-perms-policy-template.json > s3-perms-policy.json
```

7. Attach the policy to the role you just created:

```
aws iam put-role-policy \
    --role-name AWSCookbook303S3Role \
    --policy-document file://s3-perms-policy.json \
    --policy-name S3ReplicationPolicy
```

8. Create a file named *s3-replication-template.json* with the following content to configure a replication time of 15 minutes to your destination bucket:

```
{
  "Rules": [
  {
    "Status": "Enabled",
    "Filter": {
      "Prefix": ""
    },
    "Destination": {
      "Bucket": "arn:aws:s3:::DSTBUCKET",
      "Metrics": {
        "Status": "Enabled",
        "EventThreshold": {
        "Minutes": 15
        }
```

```
          },
          "ReplicationTime": {
            "Status": "Enabled",
            "Time": {
            "Minutes": 15
            }
          }
        },
        "DeleteMarkerReplication": {
          "Status": "Disabled"
        },
        "Priority": 1
      }
    ],
    "Role": "ROLEARN"
  }
```

9. Replace the values for *DSTBUCKET* and *ROLEARN* in the file and save it as *s3-replication.json*:

```
sed -e "s|ROLEARN|${ROLE_ARN}|g" \
    -e "s|DSTBUCKET|awscookbook303-dst-${RANDOM_STRING}|g" \
    s3-replication-template.json > s3-replication.json
```

10. Configure the replication policy for the source S3 bucket:

```
aws s3api put-bucket-replication \
    --replication-configuration file://s3-replication.json \
    --bucket awscookbook303-src-${RANDOM_STRING}
```

Validation checks.   View the replication configuration for the source bucket:

```
aws s3api get-bucket-replication \
    --bucket awscookbook303-src-${RANDOM_STRING}
```

Copy an object to the source bucket:

```
aws s3 cp ./book_cover.png s3://awscookbook303-src-$RANDOM_STRING
```

View the replication status for the file that you uploaded to the source bucket:

```
aws s3api head-object --bucket awscookbook303-src-${RANDOM_STRING} \
    --key book_cover.png
```

You should see output similar to the following:

```
{
  "AcceptRanges": "bytes",
  "LastModified": "2021-06-20T00:17:25+00:00",
  "ContentLength": 255549,
  "ETag": "\"d<<>>d\"",
  "VersionId": "I<>>X",
  "ContentType": "image/png",
  "Metadata": {},
  "ReplicationStatus": "PENDING"
}
```

View the replication status after 15 minutes and confirm that `ReplicationStatus` is `COMPLETED`, similar to the following:

```
{
    "AcceptRanges":"bytes",
    "ContentType":"image/png",
    "LastModified":"2021-06-20T00:17:41+00:00",
    "ContentLength":255549,
    "ReplicationStatus":"COMPLETED",
    "VersionId":"I<>>X",
    "ETag":\"d<<>>d\"",
    "Metadata":{}
}
```

You can also view the replication metrics (*https://oreil.ly/jlcu1*) in the AWS Console.

Cleanup

Follow the steps in this recipe's folder in the chapter code repository (*https://github.com/AWSCookbook/Storage*).

Discussion

If you are an engineer, developer, or architect working on AWS, there is a good chance you will end up using S3. You may have to implement some sort of replication on S3 for your applications; S3 offers two types of replication (*https://oreil.ly/oxTcA*) to meet your specific needs: Same-Region Replication (SRR) and Cross-Region Replication (CRR). The replication time is a configurable parameter of S3 Replication Time Control (S3 RTC) and is documented to meet a 15-minute recovery point objective (RPO) backed by a service level agreement (SLA) (*https://aws.amazon.com/s3/sla-rtc*).

SRR uses an IAM role, a source and destination bucket, and a replication configuration that references the role and buckets. You use SRR in this recipe to configure a one-way replication; you can use SRR to facilitate many types of use cases:

- Log aggregation to a central bucket for indexing
- Replication of data between production and test environments
- Data redundancy while retaining object metadata
- Designing redundancy around data-sovereignty and compliance requirements
- Backup and archival purposes

CRR uses a similar IAM role, a source and destination bucket, and a replication configuration that references the role and buckets. You can use CRR to extend the possibilities of what SRR enables:

- Meet requirements for data storage and archival across Regions
- Locate similar datasets closer to your regional compute and access needs to reduce latency

> S3 buckets that have versioning add markers to objects that you have deleted. Both types of S3 replication are able to replicate delete markers to your target bucket if you choose. For more information, see the support document (*https://oreil.ly/2sIL5*).

Challenge 1

Create an S3 bucket in another Region and replicate the source bucket to that as well.

Challenge 2

You can replicate specific paths and prefixes using a filter. Apply a filter so that only objects under a certain prefix (e.g., `protected/`) are replicated.

3.4 Observing S3 Storage and Access Metrics Using Storage Lens

Problem

You need to gain observability into the usage patterns of your S3 buckets.

Solution

Configure S3 Storage Lens to provide observability and analytics about your S3 usage, as shown in Figure 3-4.

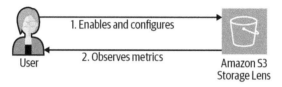

Figure 3-4. Configuring S3 Storage Lens for S3 observability

Prerequisite

- S3 bucket

Preparation

Follow the steps in this recipe's folder in the chapter code repository (*https://github.com/AWSCookbook/Storage*).

Steps

 Per the documentation (*https://oreil.ly/Je1u0*): You can't use your account's *root* user credentials to view Amazon S3 Storage Lens dashboards.

1. From the S3 console, select S3 Storage Lens from the navigation pane on the left.

2. Click "Create dashboard."

 All AWS accounts have a default dashboard associated with them that shows the free metrics available through S3 Storage Lens. Enabling advanced metrics gives you deeper insights into your S3 usage and also provides cost-savings recommendations you can take action on to optimize for cost. You can use the default dashboard and/or create your own. The rest of these steps will show you how to create your own.

3. Give your dashboard a name, as shown in Figure 3-5.

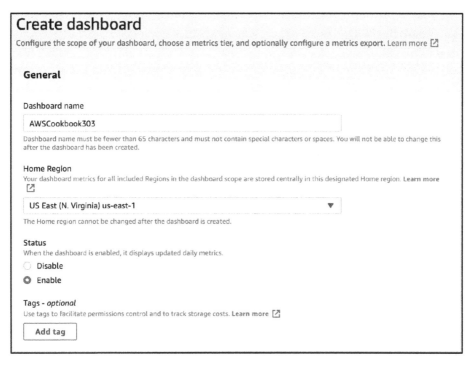

Figure 3-5. S3 Storage Lens dashboard creation

4. Include all of your buckets and Regions (use the default values) for the "Dashboard scope" (see Figure 3-6).

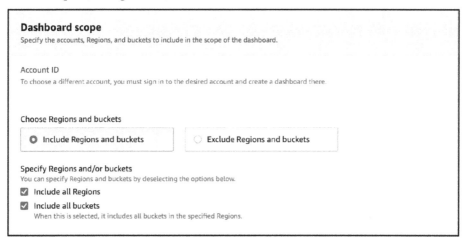

Figure 3-6. Dashboard scope

5. Enable "Advanced metrics and recommendations," keeping the default values, as shown in Figure 3-7.

Metrics selection - *optional*
Choose additional metrics and functionality.

Metrics selection

○ Free metrics
Include usage metrics aggregated at the bucket level with 14-day data retention. Learn more ⤷

◉ Advanced metrics and recommendations
Include usage metrics aggregated by prefix, activity metrics aggregated by bucket, 15-month data retention, and recommendations. Storage Lens metrics pricing ⤷

Activity metrics and prefix aggregations

☑ Enable activity metrics
Additional metrics to help you track requests and errors for objects included in this specified scope.

☐ Enable prefix aggregation
Generate insights based on top prefixes.

▶ **View metrics included for this dashboard (29)**

Figure 3-7. Selecting advanced metrics

6. Choose the defaults for Export settings (no export).

You can enable an automated export to periodically export your metrics to CSV and Apache Parquet formats and send them to an S3 bucket of your choice to run your own reports and visualizations.

7. Click "Create dashboard," and then view your dashboard from the dashboard selection.

It may take up to 48 hours for advanced metrics to begin accumulating for your usage and access patterns. In the meantime, you can view the default dashboard for the free metrics associated with your S3 usage for all of your buckets in your account.

Validation checks. Open the Storage Lens and view the dashboard that you configured. You should see metrics that correspond to your S3 usage. A sample is shown in Figure 3-8.

Snapshot for Sep 7, 2021
A glossary of metrics is available. Learn more ☑

24.1 TB	99.6 M	260.2 KB	35	1
Total storage	Object count	Avg. object size	Active buckets	Accounts

Metrics				% change comparison		
Summary	Cost efficiency	Data protection		**Day/day**	Week/week	Month/month

Metric name	Total for Sep 7, 2021	% change	30-day trend
Total storage	24.1 TB	0.01%	
Object count	99.6 M	0.03%	
Avg. object size	260.2 KB	-0.03%	
Active buckets	35	0%	
Accounts	1	0%	

Figure 3-8. Sample S3 Storage Lens dashboard

 You can drill down into "Cost efficiency" and "Data protection" metrics from the dashboard. After some time, you will be able to view historical data that allows you to take action on moving your objects to storage tiers that meet your needs for data access patterns and availability requirements.

Cleanup

Follow the steps in this recipe's folder in the chapter code repository (*https:// github.com/AWSCookbook/Storage*).

Discussion

S3 was one of the first AWS services, and as a result, many customers have been using S3 for a very long time. As customer storage usage grew exponentially, the ability to analyze what is being stored became a clear, desired capability. S3 Storage Lens gives you the ability to "see" into your S3 usage for your AWS accounts. Analyzing bucket usage, observing storage costs, and discovering anomalies (e.g., undeleted multipart upload fragments) are just a few of the many use cases S3 Storage Lens provides.

With Storage Lens, you can discover where your objects are being stored with a visual dashboard backed by a powerful analytics engine so that you can make adjustments to optimize for cost without impacting performance. You can also enable advanced metrics (*https://oreil.ly/6XLUt*) on your dashboard to gain deeper insights and cost-savings recommendations for your S3 buckets.

S3 Storage Lens uses metrics to help you visualize your usage and activity. There are free metrics available and advanced metrics that also give you recommendations on your usage. For more information about the different types of metrics and their associated costs, see the support document (*https://oreil.ly/HQcLH*).

Challenge 1

Use Storage Lens findings to observe metrics and set an alert to continuously monitor your usage.

Challenge 2

Create a new storage lens configuration that looks at only specific buckets.

3.5 Configuring Application-Specific Access to S3 Buckets with S3 Access Points

Problem

You have an S3 bucket and two applications. You need to grant read/write access to one of your applications and read-only access to another application. You do not want to use S3 bucket policies, as you expect to have to add additional applications with fine-grained security requirements in the future.

Solution

Create two S3 access points and apply a policy granting the `S3:PutObject` and `S3:GetObject` actions to one of the access points and `S3:GetObject` to the other access point. Then, configure your application to use the respective access point DNS name (see Figure 3-9).

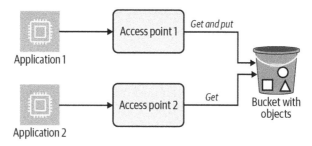

Figure 3-9. S3 access points for two applications using the same S3 bucket

Prerequisites

- VPC with isolated subnets created in two AZs and associated route tables.
- Two EC2 instances deployed. You will need the ability to connect to test access.
- S3 bucket.

Preparation

Follow the steps in this recipe's folder in the chapter code repository (*https://github.com/AWSCookbook/Storage*).

Steps

1. In your VPC, create an access point for Application 1:

   ```
   aws s3control create-access-point --name cookbook305-app-1 \
       --account-id $AWS_ACCOUNT_ID \
       --bucket $BUCKET_NAME --vpc-configuration VpcId=$VPC_ID
   ```

2. In your VPC, create an access point for Application 2:

   ```
   aws s3control create-access-point --name cookbook305-app-2 \
       --account-id $AWS_ACCOUNT_ID \
       --bucket $BUCKET_NAME --vpc-configuration VpcId=$VPC_ID
   ```

3. Create a file named *app-1-policy-template.json* with the access point policy for Application 1 to read/write with the following content (file provided in the repository):

   ```
   {
     "Version":"2012-10-17",
     "Statement": [
     {
       "Effect": "Allow",
       "Principal": {
         "AWS": "EC2_INSTANCE_PROFILE"
       },
       "Action": [ACTIONS],
       "Resource": "arn:aws:s3:AWS_REGION:AWS_ACCOUNT_ID:accesspoint/
   ACCESS_POINT_NAME/object/*"
     }]
   }
   ```

4. Use the `sed` command to replace the values in *app-policy-template.json* with your *EC2_INSTANCE_PROFILE*, *AWS_REGION*, *AWS_ACCOUNT_ID*, *ACCESS_POINT_NAME*, and *ACTIONS* values for Application 1:

   ```
   sed -e "s/AWS_REGION/${AWS_REGION}/g" \
       -e "s|EC2_INSTANCE_PROFILE|${INSTANCE_ROLE_1}|g" \
       -e "s|AWS_ACCOUNT_ID|${AWS_ACCOUNT_ID}|g" \
       -e "s|ACCESS_POINT_NAME|cookbook305-app-1|g" \
       -e "s|ACTIONS|\"s3:GetObject\",\"s3:PutObject\"|g" \
       app-policy-template.json > app-1-policy.json
   ```

5. Put the policy you created on the access point for Application 1:

```
aws s3control put-access-point-policy --account-id $AWS_ACCOUNT_ID \
    --name cookbook305-app-1 --policy file://app-1-policy.json
```

6. Use the sed command to replace the values in *app-policy-template.json* with your *EC2_INSTANCE_PROFILE*, *AWS_REGION*, *AWS_ACCOUNT_ID*, *ACCESS_POINT_NAME*, and *ACTIONS* values for Application 2:

```
sed -e "s/AWS_REGION/${AWS_REGION}/g" \
    -e "s|EC2_INSTANCE_PROFILE|${INSTANCE_ROLE_2}|g" \
    -e "s|AWS_ACCOUNT_ID|${AWS_ACCOUNT_ID}|g" \
    -e "s|ACCESS_POINT_NAME|cookbook305-app-2|g" \
    -e "s|ACTIONS|\"s3:GetObject\"|g" \
    app-policy-template.json > app-2-policy.json
```

7. Put the policy you created on the access point for Application 2:

```
aws s3control put-access-point-policy --account-id $AWS_ACCOUNT_ID \
    --name cookbook305-app-2 --policy file://app-2-policy.json
```

 You can use specific access points with AWS SDK and CLI in a similar way. For example, the bucket name becomes the following for SDK usage: *https://[access_point_name]-[accountID].s3-accesspoint.[region].amazonaws.com* for URLs and `arn:aws:s3:[region]:[accountID]:[access_point_name]` as "bucket name" for CLI usage.

Here is a CLI example:

```
aws s3api get-object --key object.zip \
    --bucket \
    arn:aws:s3:us-east-1:111111111111:access_point_name object.zip
```

8. Follow this guide to modifying the bucket policy (*https://oreil.ly/kqXrN*) so that you delegate control to the access points.

Validation checks. Connect to the EC2 instance 1 by using SSM Session Manager (see Recipe 1.6):

```
aws ssm start-session --target $INSTANCE_ID_1
```

Set your AWS account ID from the instance's metadata:

```
export AWS_ACCOUNT_ID=$(curl --silent http://169.254.169.254/latest/dynamic/instance-
identity/document \
| awk -F'"' ' /accountId/ {print $4}')
```

Set the Region by grabbing the value from the instance's metadata:

```
export AWS_DEFAULT_REGION=$(curl --silent http://169.254.169.254/latest/dynamic/
instance-identity/document \
| awk -F'"' ' /region/ {print $4}')
```

Try to get an object from the S3 access point for Application 1:

```
aws s3api get-object --key Recipe305Test.txt \
    --bucket arn:aws:s3:$AWS_DEFAULT_REGION:$AWS_ACCOUNT_ID:accesspoint/cookbook305-
app-1 \
    /tmp/Recipe305Test.txt
```

Write an object to the S3 access point for Application 1:

```
aws s3api put-object \
    --bucket arn:aws:s3:$AWS_DEFAULT_REGION:$AWS_ACCOUNT_ID:accesspoint/cookbook305-
app-1 \
--key motd.txt --body /etc/motd
```

 These two commands work for Application 1 because you configured read/write access for this access point.

Disconnect from EC2 instance 1:

```
exit
```

Connect to the EC2 instance 2 using SSM Session Manager (see Recipe 1.6):

```
aws ssm start-session --target $INSTANCE_ID_2
```

Set your AWS account ID from the instance's metadata:

```
export AWS_ACCOUNT_ID=$(curl --silent http://169.254.169.254/latest/dynamic/instance-
identity/document \
| awk -F'"' ' /accountId/ {print $4}')
```

Set the Region by grabbing the value from the instance's metadata:

```
export AWS_DEFAULT_REGION=$(curl --silent http://169.254.169.254/latest/dynamic/
instance-identity/document \
| awk -F'"' ' /region/ {print $4}')
```

Try to get an object from the S3 bucket:

```
aws s3api get-object --key Recipe305Test.txt \
    --bucket \
arn:aws:s3:$AWS_DEFAULT_REGION:$AWS_ACCOUNT_ID:accesspoint/cookbook305-app-2 \
    /tmp/Recipe305Test.txt
```

Try to put an object to the S3 bucket:

```
aws s3api put-object \
    --bucket arn:aws:s3:$AWS_DEFAULT_REGION:$AWS_ACCOUNT_ID:accesspoint/cookbook305-
app-2 \
--key motd2.txt --body /etc/motd
```

The first command works, and the second command fails, for Application 2 because you configured read-only access for this access point.

Disconnect from EC2 instance 2:

```
exit
```

Cleanup

Follow the steps in this recipe's folder in the chapter code repository (*https:// github.com/AWSCookbook/Storage*).

Discussion

S3 access points allow you to grant fine-grained access to specific principals, and they can be easier to manage than S3 bucket policies. In this recipe, you created two access points with different kinds of allowed actions and associated the access points with specific roles using access point IAM policies. You verified that only specific actions were granted to your EC2 instances when they were being used with the CLI and S3 access point.

To help you meet your security requirements, access points use IAM policies (*https:// oreil.ly/T6Wdq*) in a similar way that you use for other AWS services. You can also configure S3 Block Public Access on access points to ensure that no public access is ever granted by mistake to your S3 buckets (see Recipe 1.9). There is no additional cost for S3 access points.

Challenge

Configure a third access point and specify access to a specific object or prefix only.

3.6 Using Amazon S3 Bucket Keys with KMS to Encrypt Objects

Problem

You need to encrypt S3 objects at rest with a Key Management Service (KMS) customer-managed key (CMK) and ensure that all objects within the bucket are encrypted with the KMS key in a cost-effective manner.

Solution

Create a KMS customer-managed key, configure your S3 bucket to use S3 bucket keys referencing your AWS KMS CMK, and configure an S3 bucket policy requiring KMS to be used for all S3:PutObject operations (see Figure 3-10).

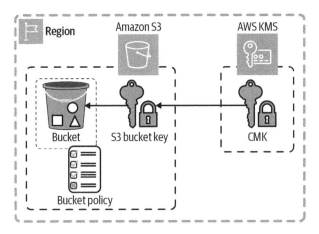

Figure 3-10. Encrypting objects in S3

Prerequisite

- An S3 bucket

Preparation

Follow the steps in this recipe's folder in the chapter code repository (*https://github.com/AWSCookbook/Storage*).

Steps

1. Create a KMS key to use for your S3 bucket and store the key ID in an environment variable:

   ```
   KEY_ID=$(aws kms create-key \
       --tags TagKey=Name,TagValue=AWSCookbook306Key \
       --description "AWSCookbook S3 CMK" \
       --query KeyMetadata.KeyId \
       --output text)
   ```

2. Create an alias to reference your key:

   ```
   aws kms create-alias \
       --alias-name alias/awscookbook306 \
       --target-key-id $KEY_ID
   ```

3. Configure the S3 bucket to use an S3 bucket key specifying your KMS key ID:

```
aws s3api put-bucket-encryption \
    --bucket awscookbook306-$RANDOM_STRING \
    --server-side-encryption-configuration '{
      "Rules": [
        {
          "ApplyServerSideEncryptionByDefault": {
            "SSEAlgorithm": "aws:kms",
            "KMSMasterKeyID": "${KEY_ID}"
          },
          "BucketKeyEnabled": true
        }
      ]
    }'
```

4. Create a bucket policy template for the bucket to force encryption of all objects:

```
{
  "Version":"2012-10-17",
  "Id":"PutObjectPolicy",
  "Statement":[{
    "Sid":"DenyUnEncryptedObjectUploads",
    "Effect":"Deny",
    "Principal":"*",
    "Action":"s3:PutObject",
    "Resource":"arn:aws:s3:::BUCKET_NAME/*",
    "Condition":{
      "StringNotEquals":{
        "s3:x-amz-server-side-encryption":"aws:kms"
      }
    }
  }
  ]
}
```

5. Use the **sed** command to replace the value in *bucket-policy-template.json* with your *BUCKET_NAME*:

```
sed -e "s|BUCKET_NAME|awscookbook306-${RANDOM_STRING}|g" \
    bucket-policy-template.json > bucket-policy.json
```

6. Apply the bucket policy to force encryption on all uploads:

```
aws s3api put-bucket-policy --bucket awscookbook306-$RANDOM_STRING \
    --policy file://bucket-policy.json
```

Validation checks.   Upload an object to the S3 bucket with encryption from the command line. You will see a successful upload:

```
aws s3 cp ./book_cover.png s3://awscookbook306-$RANDOM_STRING \
    --sse aws:kms --sse-kms-key-id $KEY_ID
```

Now, upload an object to the S3 bucket without encryption. You will notice that you receive a KMS.NotFoundException error on the command line. This indicates that the bucket policy you configured is working properly:

```
aws s3 cp ./book_cover.png s3://awscookbook306-$RANDOM_STRING
```

Cleanup

Follow the steps in this recipe's folder in the chapter code repository (*https://github.com/AWSCookbook/Storage*).

Discussion

When applying encryption to your S3 bucket, you could have chosen to use an AWS-managed CMK that Amazon S3 creates in your AWS account and manages for you. Like the customer-managed CMK, your AWS managed CMK is unique to your AWS account and Region. Only Amazon S3 has permission to use this CMK on your behalf. You can create, rotate, and disable auditable customer-managed CMKs from the AWS KMS Console. The S3 documentation (*https://oreil.ly/oGBG0*) provides a comprehensive explanation of the differences between the types of encryption supported on S3.

When you encrypt your data, your data is protected, but you have to protect your encryption key. *Envelope encryption* (*https://oreil.ly/gK0o0*) is the practice of encrypting plaintext data with a data key, and then encrypting the data key under another key, as shown in Figure 3-11.

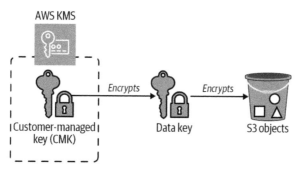

Figure 3-11. S3 encryption process with KMS

Challenge

To validate that you can rotate your keys without impacting your data, put an object into your bucket, trigger a rotation of the KMS CMK, and then get the object back out of the S3 bucket and confirm it can decrypt properly (see this AWS article for a hint (*https://oreil.ly/RVAFZ*)).

3.7 Creating and Restoring EC2 Backups to Another Region Using AWS Backup

Problem

You need to create a backup of an instance and restore it in another Region (*https://oreil.ly/j3pWr*).

Solution

Create an on-demand backup with AWS Backup for your EC2 instance and restore the backup from the vault by using the AWS Console, as shown in Figure 3-12.

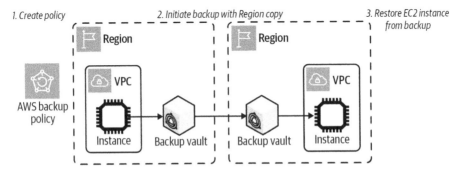

Figure 3-12. Creating and restoring EC2 backups

Prerequisites

- VPC with isolated subnets created in two AZs and associated route tables
- EC2 instance deployed

Preparation

Follow the steps in this recipe's folder in the chapter code repository (*https://github.com/AWSCookbook/Storage*).

Steps

1. Navigate to the AWS Backup console and select "Protected resources" from the lefthand navigation pane.

2. Click the "Create an on-demand backup" and select your EC2 instance, choose defaults, and click "Create on-demand backup" (see Figure 3-13).

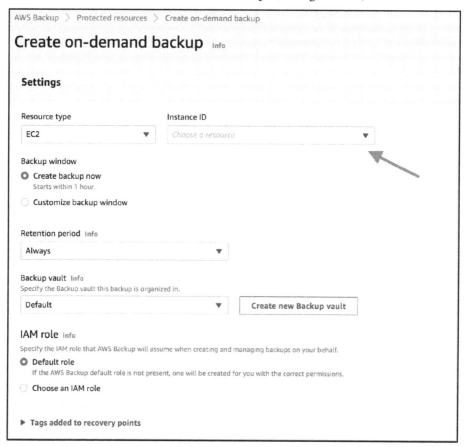

Figure 3-13. Creating on-demand backup

 AWS Backup will create a role for its purposes that uses the AWS Backup Managed Policy to perform the required actions for backups. You can also create your own custom role if you require. For more information, see this AWS document (*https://oreil.ly/WirFO*).

The backup starts in the backup jobs view, as shown in Figure 3-14.

Figure 3-14. View of backup job running

3. Wait for the backup to complete in your account (this may take a few moments to reach the Completed status shown in Figure 3-15).

Figure 3-15. View of backup job completed

4. Select the Default Backup vault for your current Region and view your image backup that you just completed.

5. Click the backup recovery point that you just created and choose Copy, as shown in Figure 3-16.

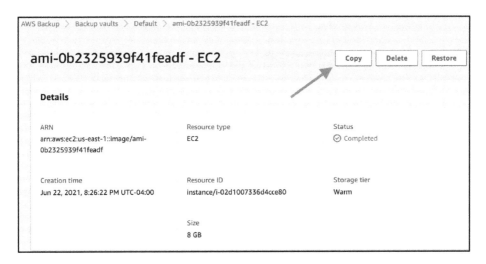

Figure 3-16. Copy recovery point

6. Select your destination Region, keep all defaults, and click Copy (shown in Figure 3-17). You will see the copy job enter Running status, as shown in Figure 3-18.

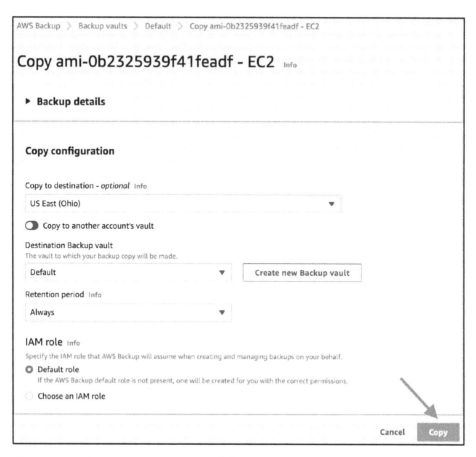

Figure 3-17. Copy recovery point to a different AWS Region

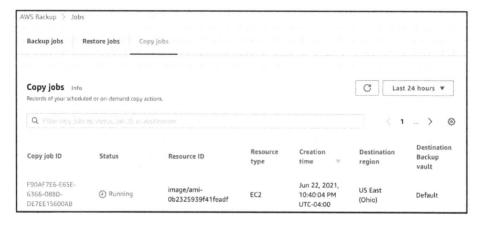

Figure 3-18. Copy recovery point running

7. After the copy job has completed in a few minutes, in the AWS Console, select the destination Region from the drop-down Region selector (top right of the AWS console).

8. Select your default Backup vault and choose the backup you wish to restore, as shown in Figure 3-19.

Figure 3-19. Restore recovery point

9. Under "Network settings," select your instance type and VPC for your restore, and click "Restore backup." An example of inputs is shown in Figure 3-20.

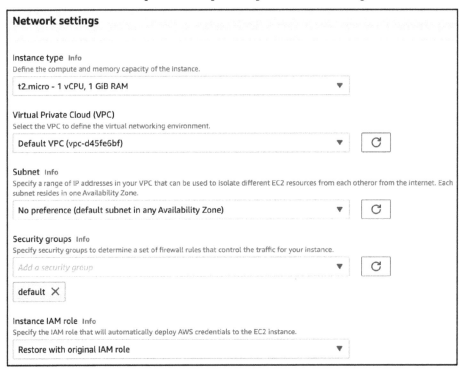

Figure 3-20. Network settings for backup restoration

---

10. You can monitor the progress of the restore under the "Restore jobs" tab of the Jobs section in the console, shown in Figure 3-21.

Figure 3-21. Recovery point restore job running

Validation checks. Browse to the EC2 console to view your running instance in your destination Region. This EC2 instance is a copy of your original instance.

Cleanup

Follow the steps in this recipe's folder in the chapter code repository (*https://github.com/AWSCookbook/Storage*).

Discussion

AWS Backup (*https://aws.amazon.com/backup/faqs*) lets you manage and monitor the backups across the AWS services you use, from a single place. You can back up many AWS services (*https://oreil.ly/KHpPB*) and set backup policies for cloud resources in the AWS services that you use. You can also copy backups cross-Region within your account (or to other AWS accounts), which is what you explored in this recipe. EBS snapshots (*https://oreil.ly/BYWAl*) are an essential component of a backup strategy on AWS if you use the EC2 service to run instances with persistent data on them that you would like to protect. You can take snapshots of EBS volumes manually, write your own automation, automate them with Data Lifecycle Manager (*https://oreil.ly/eXbT7*), or use AWS Backup.

When you use AWS Backup to back up an EC2 instance, the service stores backups in a backup vault (*https://oreil.ly/OnzyN*) of your choice (a default backup vault is created if you do not have one), handles the process of building an Amazon Machine

Image (AMI) which contains all of the configuration parameters, backed-up attached EBS volumes, and metadata. The service stores the entire bundle within the backup vault. This allows you to simply launch an EC2 instance from the AMI that was generated by the AWS Backup service to reduce the recovery time objective (RTO) associated with restoring an instance from a backup within your primary Region or another Region of your choice.

Challenge

Configure an Automated Backup of the EC2 instance on a weekly schedule using backup plans (*https://oreil.ly/uguyM*), which copies the backed-up instances to a vault within another Region.

3.8 Restoring a File from an EBS Snapshot

Problem

You need to restore a file from an EBS snapshot that you have taken from a volume in your account.

Solution

Create a volume from a snapshot, mount the volume from an EC2 instance, and copy the file to your instance volume (see Figure 3-22).

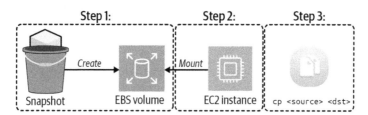

Figure 3-22. Process flow for file restore from a snapshot

Prerequisites

- VPC with isolated subnets created in two AZs and associated route tables.
- EC2 instance deployed. You will need the ability to connect to mount the EBS snapshot and restore a file.

Preparation

Follow the steps in this recipe's folder in the chapter code repository (*https://github.com/AWSCookbook/Storage*).

Steps

1. Find the EBS volume attached to your EC2 instance:

   ```
   ORIG_VOLUME_ID=$(aws ec2 describe-volumes \
       --filters Name=attachment.instance-id,Values=$INSTANCE_ID \
       --output text \
       --query Volumes[0].Attachments[0].VolumeId)
   ```

2. Take a snapshot of the EBS volume (this will take a moment to complete):

   ```
   SNAPSHOT_ID=$(aws ec2 create-snapshot \
       --volume-id $ORIG_VOLUME_ID \
       --output text --query SnapshotId)
   ```

3. Create a volume from the snapshot and save the VOLUME_ID as an environment variable:

   ```
   SNAP_VOLUME_ID=$(aws ec2 create-volume \
       --snapshot-id $SNAPSHOT_ID \
       --size 8 \
       --volume-type gp2 \
       --availability-zone us-east-1a \
       --output text --query VolumeId)
   ```

Validation checks.   Attach the volume to the EC2 instance as /dev/sdf:

```
aws ec2 attach-volume --volume-id $SNAP_VOLUME_ID \
    --instance-id $INSTANCE_ID --device /dev/sdf
```

Wait until the volume's state has reached Attached:

```
aws ec2 describe-volumes \
    --volume-ids $SNAP_VOLUME_ID
```

Connect to the EC2 instance using SSM Session Manager (see Recipe 1.6):

```
aws ssm start-session --target $INSTANCE_ID
```

Run the lsblk command to see volumes, and note the volume name that you attached (you will use this volume name in the subsequent step to mount the volume):

```
lsblk
```

You should see output similar to this:

```
NAME            MAJ:MIN RM SIZE RO TYPE MOUNTPOINT
nvme0n1         259:0    0   8G  0 disk
├─nvme0n1p1     259:1    0   8G  0 part /
└─nvme0n1p128   259:2    0   1M  0 part
nvme1n1         259:3    0   8G  0 disk
├─nvme1n1p1     259:4    0   8G  0 part
└─nvme1n1p128   259:5    0   1M  0 part
```

Create a folder to mount the attached disk:

```
sudo mkdir /mnt/restore
```

Mount the volume you attached to the folder you created:

```
sudo mount -t xfs -o nouuid /dev/nvme1n1p1 /mnt/restore
```

> The XFS file uses universally unique identifiers (UUIDs) to identify filesystems. By default, a safety mechanism is in place in the mount command to prevent you from mounting the same filesystem twice. Since you created a block-level snapshot and created a volume from it, the mount command you used requires overriding this check to allow mounting a volume with the same UUID using the -o nouuid parameter. For more information, consult the man page for mount.

Copy the file(s) you need from the mounted volume to the local filesystem:

```
sudo cp /mnt/restore/home/ec2-user/.bash_profile \
    /tmp/.bash_profile.restored
```

Unmount the volume:

```
sudo umount /dev/nvme1n1p1
```

Log out of the EC2 instance:

```
exit
```

Cleanup

Follow the steps in this recipe's folder in the chapter code repository (*https://github.com/AWSCookbook/Storage*).

Discussion

EBS snapshots (*https://oreil.ly/0DwtK*) are an important part of a backup strategy within the EC2 service. If you run EC2 instances, snapshots enable you to restore an instance to a point in time when the snapshot was created. You can also create an EBS volume from a snapshot and attach it to a running instance, which you accomplished in this recipe. This is useful for site reliability engineering (SRE) teams, operations teams, and users who need to restore single files to a point in time to meet their needs.

> EBS snapshots allow you to take snapshots of EBS volumes manually, write your own automation (like a Lambda function on a schedule), automate with Data Lifecycle Manager, or use AWS Backup (see Recipe 3.7) for a more comprehensive solution to backing up and restoring EC2 instances.

Challenge

Create an AMI (*https://oreil.ly/8KFje*) from the snapshot you create and launch a new instance from the newly created AMI.

3.9 Replicating Data Between EFS and S3 with DataSync

Problem

You need to replicate files from Amazon S3 to Amazon EFS.

Solution

Configure AWS DataSync with an S3 source and EFS target; then create a DataSync task and start the replication task, as shown in Figure 3-23.

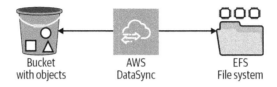

Figure 3-23. Replicating S3 Bucket and EFS file system with DataSync

Prerequisites

- An S3 bucket and EFS file system.
- VPC with isolated subnets created in two AZs and associated route tables.
- EC2 instance deployed with EFS file system attached. You will need the ability to connect to it for testing.

Preparation

Follow the steps in this recipe's folder in the chapter code repository (*https://github.com/AWSCookbook/Storage*).

Steps

1. Create an IAM role using the statement in the provided *assume-role-policy.json* file with this command:

    ```
    S3_ROLE_ARN=$(aws iam create-role --role-name AWSCookbookS3LocationRole \
        --assume-role-policy-document file://assume-role-policy.json \
        --output text --query Role.Arn)
    ```

2. Attach the AmazonS3ReadOnlyAccess IAM managed policy to the IAM role:

    ```
    aws iam attach-role-policy --role-name AWSCookbookS3LocationRole \
        --policy-arn arn:aws:iam::aws:policy/AmazonS3ReadOnlyAccess
    ```

3. Create a DataSync S3 location:

```
S3_LOCATION_ARN=$(aws datasync create-location-s3 \
    --s3-bucket-arn $BUCKET_ARN \
    --s3-config BucketAccessRoleArn=$S3_ROLE_ARN \
    --output text --query LocationArn)
```

4. Create an IAM role using the statement in the provided *assume-role-policy.json* file with this command:

```
EFS_ROLE_ARN=$(aws iam create-role --role-name AWSCookbookEFSLocationRole \
    --assume-role-policy-document file://assume-role-policy.json \
    --output text --query Role.Arn)
```

5. Attach the `AmazonElasticFileSystemClientReadWriteAccess` IAM managed policy to the IAM role:

```
aws iam attach-role-policy --role-name AWSCookbookEFSLocationRole \
    --policy-arn arn:aws:iam::aws:policy/AmazonElasticFileSystemClientFullAccess
```

6. Get the ARN of the EFS file system:

```
EFS_FILE_SYSTEM_ARN=$(aws efs describe-file-systems \
    --file-system-id $EFS_ID \
    --output text --query FileSystems[0].FileSystemArn)
```

7. Get the ARN of the subnet:

```
SUBNET_ARN=$(aws ec2 describe-subnets \
    --subnet-ids $ISOLATED_SUBNET_1 \
    --output text --query Subnets[0].SubnetArn)
```

8. Get the ARN of the security group:

```
SG_ARN=arn:aws:ec2:$AWS_REGION:$AWS_ACCOUNT_ID:security-group/$EFS_SG
```

9. Create a DataSync EFS location:

```
EFS_LOCATION_ARN=$(aws datasync create-location-efs \
    --efs-filesystem-arn $EFS_FILE_SYSTEM_ARN \
    --ec2-config SubnetArn=$SUBNET_ARN,SecurityGroupArns=[$SG_ARN] \
    --output text)
```

10. Create a DataSync task:

```
TASK_ARN=$(aws datasync create-task \
    --source-location-arn $S3_LOCATION_ARN \
    --destination-location-arn $EFS_LOCATION_ARN \
    --output text --query TaskArn)
```

11. Execute the task:

```
aws datasync start-task-execution \
    --task-arn $TASK_ARN
```

12. Ensure the task has completed after a few seconds:

```
aws datasync list-task-executions \
    --task-arn $TASK_ARN
```

Validation checks. Ensure your EC2 instance 1 has registered with SSM. Use this command to check the status. This command should return the instance ID:

```
aws ssm describe-instance-information \
    --filters Key=ResourceType,Values=EC2Instance \
    --query "InstanceInformationList[].InstanceId" --output text
```

Connect to your EC2 instance using SSM Session Manager:

```
aws ssm start-session --target $INSTANCE_ID
```

The EC2 instance has the EFS volume mounted at */mnt/efs*. You can browse to the directory and view that the *S3-Test-Content.txt* file has been replicated from your S3 bucket to your EFS volume, as shown in the sample output:

```
sh-4.2$ cd /mnt/efs

sh-4.2$ ls

sh-4.2$ ls -al

total 12
drwxr-xr-x 3 nfsnobody nfsnobody 6144 Jan  1  1970 .
drwxr-xr-x 3 root      root        17 Sep 10 02:07 ..
drwx------ 2 root      root      6144 Sep 10 03:27 .aws-datasync
-rwxr-xr-x 1 nfsnobody nfsnobody   30 Jan  1  1970 S3-Test-Content.txt
```

Exit the Session Manager session:

```
exit
```

Cleanup

Follow the steps in this recipe's folder in the chapter code repository (*https://github.com/AWSCookbook/Storage*).

Discussion

You can use AWS DataSync (*https://aws.amazon.com/datasync*) for both on-demand and ongoing/automated file synchronization tasks across a variety of AWS services. DataSync preserves metadata for copied items and checks file integrity during the synchronization task, supporting retries if needed. This is useful if you are a developer or cloud engineer looking to move data among a variety of sources and targets without provisioning any infrastructure or writing your own scripts to accomplish the same task. In this recipe, you used it to synchronize data between S3 and EFS hosted in your AWS account, but you can also use it to synchronize data among your non-AWS servers if you have a VPN connection, Direct Connect, or among other AWS accounts using VPC peering or a transit gateway.

 At the time of this writing, the minimum automated sync schedule interval you can set is one hour. You can find other details about DataSync in the user documentation (*https://oreil.ly/dVnun*).

Like many AWS services, DataSync uses IAM roles to perform actions against S3 and EFS for you. You granted DataSync the ability to interact with S3 and EFS. DataSync provisions network interfaces in your VPC to connect to your EFS file shares and uses the AWS APIs to interact with S3. It encrypts traffic in transit using TLS and also supports encryption at rest using KMS should your security and compliance requirements mandate encryption at rest.

Challenge 1

Set up a DataSync task that excludes filenames in a certain folder (e.g., *private-folder*).

Challenge 2

Set up a scheduled DataSync task to replicate data from S3 to EFS on an hourly schedule.

CHAPTER 4

Databases

4.0 Introduction

You have a myriad of choices for using databases with AWS. Installing and running a database on EC2 provides you with the most choices of database engines and custom configurations, but brings about challenges like patching, backups, configuring high-availability, replication, and performance tuning. As noted on its product page (*https://oreil.ly/wLQPC*), AWS offers managed database services that help address these challenges and cover a broad range of database types (relational, key-value/NoSQL, in-memory, document, wide column, graph, time series, ledger). When choosing a database type and data model, you must keep speed, volume, and access patterns in mind.

The managed database services on AWS integrate with many services to provide you additional functionality from security, operations, and development perspectives. In this chapter, you will explore Amazon Relational Database Service (RDS), NoSQL usage with Amazon DynamoDB, and the ways to migrate, secure, and operate these database types at scale. For example, you will learn how to integrate Secrets Manager with an RDS database to automatically rotate database user passwords. You will also learn how to leverage IAM authentication to reduce the application dependency on database passwords entirely, granting access to RDS through IAM permissions instead. You'll explore autoscaling with DynamoDB and learn about why this is important from a cost and performance perspective.

Some people think that Route 53 is a database (*https://oreil.ly/Da83G*) but we disagree :-)

Some database engines in the past have used certain terminology for replica configurations, default root user names, primary tables, etc. We took care to use inclusive terminology throughout this chapter (and the whole book) wherever possible. We support the movement to use inclusive terminology in these commercial and open source database engines.

Workstation Configuration

Follow the "General workstation setup steps for CLI recipes" on page xvii to validate your configuration and set up the required environment variables. Then, clone the chapter code repository:

```
git clone https://github.com/AWSCookbook/Databases
```

During some of the steps in this chapter, you will create passwords and temporarily save them as environment variables to use in subsequent steps. Make sure that you unset the environment variables by following the cleanup steps when you complete the recipe. We use this approach for simplicity of understanding. A more secure method (such as the method used in Recipe 1.8) should be used in production environments.

4.1 Creating an Amazon Aurora Serverless PostgreSQL Database

Problem

You have a web application that receives unpredictable requests that require storage in a relational database. You need a database solution that can scale with usage and be cost-effective. You would like to build a solution that has low operational overhead and must be compatible with your existing PostgreSQL-backed application.

Solution

Configure and create an Aurora Serverless database cluster with a complex password. Then, apply a customized scaling configuration and enable automatic pause after inactivity. The scaling activity in response to the policy is shown in Figure 4-1.

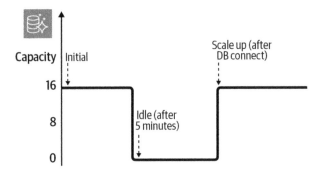

Figure 4-1. Aurora Serverless cluster scaling compute

Prerequisites

- VPC with isolated subnets created in two AZs and associated route tables.
- EC2 instance deployed. You will need the ability to connect to this for testing.

Preparation

Follow the steps in this recipe's folder in the chapter code repository (*https://github.com/AWSCookbook/Databases*).

Steps

1. Use AWS Secrets Manager to generate a complex password:

```
ADMIN_PASSWORD=$(aws secretsmanager get-random-password \
    --exclude-punctuation \
    --password-length 41 --require-each-included-type \
    --output text \
    --query RandomPassword)
```

 We are excluding punctuation characters from the password that we are creating because PostgreSQL does not support them. See the "Naming constraints in Amazon RDS" table (*https://oreil.ly/z0LvJ*).

2. Create a database subnet group specifying the VPC subnets to use for the cluster. Database subnet groups simplify the placement of RDS elastic network interfaces (ENIs):

```
aws rds create-db-subnet-group \
    --db-subnet-group-name awscookbook401subnetgroup \
    --db-subnet-group-description "AWSCookbook401 subnet group" \
    --subnet-ids $SUBNET_ID_1 $SUBNET_ID_2
```

You should see output similar to the following:

```
{
  "DBSubnetGroup": {
  "DBSubnetGroupName": "awscookbook402subnetgroup",
  "DBSubnetGroupDescription": "AWSCookbook401 subnet group",
  "VpcId": "vpc-<<VPCID>>",
  "SubnetGroupStatus": "Complete",
  "Subnets": [
    {
    "SubnetIdentifier": "subnet-<<SUBNETID>>",
    "SubnetAvailabilityZone": {
      "Name": "us-east-1b"
    },
    "SubnetOutpost": {},
    "SubnetStatus": "Active"
    },
  ...
```

3. Create a VPC security group for the database:

```
DB_SECURITY_GROUP_ID=$(aws ec2 create-security-group \
    --group-name AWSCookbook401sg \
    --description "Aurora Serverless Security Group" \
    --vpc-id $VPC_ID --output text --query GroupId)
```

4. Create a database cluster, specifying an engine-mode of serverless:

```
aws rds create-db-cluster \
    --db-cluster-identifier awscookbook401dbcluster \
    --engine aurora-postgresql \
    --engine-mode serverless \
    --engine-version 10.14 \
    --master-username dbadmin \
    --master-user-password $ADMIN_PASSWORD \
    --db-subnet-group-name awscookbook401subnetgroup \
    --vpc-security-group-ids $DB_SECURITY_GROUP_ID
```

You should see output similar to the following:

```
{
  "DBCluster": {
  "AllocatedStorage": 1,
  "AvailabilityZones": [
    "us-east-1f",
    "us-east-1b",
    "us-east-1a"
  ],
  "BackupRetentionPeriod": 1,
  "DBClusterIdentifier": "awscookbook401dbcluster",
  "DBClusterParameterGroup": "default.aurora-postgresql10",
  "DBSubnetGroup": "awscookbook401subnetgroup",
  "Status": "creating",
  ...
```

5. Wait for the Status to read available; this will take a few moments:

```
aws rds describe-db-clusters \
    --db-cluster-identifier awscookbook401dbcluster \
    --output text --query DBClusters[0].Status
```

6. Modify the database to automatically scale with new autoscaling capacity targets (8 min, 16 max) and enable `AutoPause` after five minutes of inactivity:

```
aws rds modify-db-cluster \
    --db-cluster-identifier awscookbook401dbcluster --scaling-configuration \

MinCapacity=8,MaxCapacity=16,SecondsUntilAutoPause=300,TimeoutAction='ForceApplyC
apacityChange',AutoPause=true
```

You should see output similar to what you saw for step 4.

In practice, you may want to use a different `AutoPause` value. To determine what is appropriate for your use, evaluate your performance needs and Aurora pricing (*https://oreil.ly/ o6mAP*).

Wait at least five minutes and observe that the database's capacity has scaled down to 0:

```
aws rds describe-db-clusters \
    --db-cluster-identifier awscookbook401dbcluster \
    --output text --query DBClusters[0].Capacity
```

The `AutoPause` feature automatically sets the capacity of the cluster to 0 after inactivity. When your database activity resumes (e.g., with a query or connection), the capacity value is automatically set to your configured minimum scaling capacity value.

7. Grant your EC2 instance's security group access to the default PostgreSQL port:

```
aws ec2 authorize-security-group-ingress \
    --protocol tcp --port 5432 \
    --source-group $INSTANCE_SG \
    --group-id $DB_SECURITY_GROUP_ID
```

You should see output similar to the following:

```
{
  "Return": true,
  "SecurityGroupRules": [
  {
    "SecurityGroupRuleId": "sgr-<<ID>>",
    "GroupId": "sg-<<ID>>",
    "GroupOwnerId": "111111111111",
    "IsEgress": false,
    "IpProtocol": "tcp",
    "FromPort": 5432,
    "ToPort": 5432,
    "ReferencedGroupInfo": {
    "GroupId": "sg-<<ID>>"
    }
    }
```

```
        ]
    }
```

Validation checks. List the endpoint for the RDS cluster:

```
aws rds describe-db-clusters \
    --db-cluster-identifier awscookbook401dbcluster \
    --output text --query DBClusters[0].Endpoint
```

You should see something similar to this:

```
awscookbook401dbcluster.cluster-<<unique>>.us-east-1.rds.amazonaws.com
```

Retrieve the password for your RDS cluster:

```
echo $ADMIN_PASSWORD
```

Connect to the EC2 instance by using SSM Session Manager (see Recipe 1.6):

```
aws ssm start-session --target $INSTANCE_ID
```

Install the PostgreSQL package so you can use the `psql` command to connect to the database:

```
sudo yum -y install postgresql
```

Connect to the database. This may take a moment as the database capacity is scaling up from 0. You'll need to copy and paste the password (outputted previously):

```
psql -h $HOST_NAME -U dbadmin -W -d postgres
```

Here is an example of connecting to a database using the `psql` command:

```
sh-4.2$ psql -h awscookbook401dbcluster.cluster-<<unique>>.us-
east-1.rds.amazonaws.com -U dbadmin -W -d postgres
Password for user dbadmin:(paste in the password)
```

Quit psql:

```
\q
```

Exit the Session Manager session:

```
exit
```

Check the capacity of the cluster again to observe that the database has scaled up to the minimum value that you configured:

```
aws rds describe-db-clusters \
    --db-cluster-identifier awscookbook401dbcluster \
    --output text --query DBClusters[0].Capacity
```

Cleanup

Follow the steps in this recipe's folder in the chapter code repository (*https://github.com/AWSCookbook/Databases*).

The default behavior of deleting an RDS cluster is to take a final snapshot as a safety mechanism. We chose to skip this behavior by adding the --skip-final-snapshot option to ensure you do not incur any costs for storing the snapshot in your AWS account. In a real-world scenario, you would likely want to retain the snapshot for a period of time in case you needed to re-create the existing database from the snapshot.

Discussion

The cluster will automatically scale capacity to meet the needs of your usage. Setting MaxCapacity=16 limits the upper bound of your capacity to prevent runaway usage and unexpected costs. The cluster will set its capacity to 0 when no connection or activity is detected. This is triggered when the SecondsUntilAutoPause value is reached.

When you enable AutoPause=true for your cluster, you pay for only the underlying storage during idle times. The default (and minimum) "inactivity period" is five minutes. Connecting to a paused cluster will cause the capacity to scale up to MinCapacity.

Not all database engines and versions are available with the serverless engine. At the time of writing, the Aurora FAQ states (*https://oreil.ly/P5A2B*) that Aurora Serverless is currently available for Aurora with MySQL 5.6 compatibility and for Aurora with PostgreSQL 10.7+ compatibility.

The user guide (*https://oreil.ly/MJpCb*) states that Aurora Serverless scaling is measured in capacity units (CUs) that correspond to compute and memory reserved for your cluster. This capability is a good fit for many workloads and use cases from development to batch-based workloads, and production workloads where traffic is unpredictable and costs associated with potential over-provisioning are a concern. By not needing to calculate baseline usage patterns, you can start developing quickly, and the cluster will automatically respond to the demand that your application requires.

If you currently use a "provisioned" capacity type cluster on Amazon RDS and would like to start using Aurora Serverless, you can snapshot your current database and restore it from within the AWS Console or from the command line to perform a migration. If your current database is not on RDS, you can use your database engine's dump and restore features or use the AWS Database Migration Service (AWS DMS) to migrate to RDS.

At the time of this writing, Amazon Aurora Serverless v2 is in preview (*https://oreil.ly/TVurx*).

The user guide (*https://oreil.ly/GMEVT*) mentions that Aurora Serverless further builds on the existing Aurora platform, which replicates your database's underlying storage six ways across three Availability Zones. While this replication is a benefit for resiliency, you should still use automated backups for your database to guard against operational errors. Aurora Serverless has automated backups enabled by default, and the backup retention can be increased up to 35 days if needed.

Per the documentation (*https://oreil.ly/Wq91f*), if your database cluster has been idle for more than seven days, the cluster will be backed up with a snapshot. If this occurs, the database cluster is restored when there is a request to connect to it.

Challenge

Change the max capacity to 64 and idle time to 10 minutes for the database cluster.

See Also

Recipe 4.2, "Using IAM Authentication with an RDS Database"

Recipe 4.7, "Migrating Databases to Amazon RDS Using AWS DMS"

4.2 Using IAM Authentication with an RDS Database

Problem

You have a server that connects to a database with a password and would like to instead use rotating temporary credentials.

Solution

First you will enable IAM authentication for your database. You will then configure the IAM permissions for the EC2 instance to use. Finally, create a new user on the database, retrieve the IAM authentication token, and verify connectivity (see Figure 4-2).

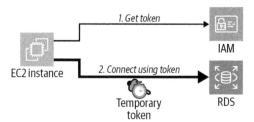

Figure 4-2. IAM authentication from an EC2 instance to an RDS database

Prerequisites

- VPC with isolated subnets created in two AZs and associated route tables.
- An RDS MySQL instance.
- EC2 instance deployed. You will need the ability to connect to this for configuring MySQL and testing.

Preparation

Follow the steps in this recipe's folder in the chapter code repository (*https://github.com/AWSCookbook/Databases*).

Steps

1. Enable IAM database authentication on the RDS database instance:

```
aws rds modify-db-instance \
    --db-instance-identifier $RDS_DATABASE_ID \
    --enable-iam-database-authentication \
    --apply-immediately
```

You should see output similar to the following:

```
{
  "DBInstance": {
    "DBInstanceIdentifier": "awscookbookrecipe402",
    "DBInstanceClass": "db.m5.large",
    "Engine": "mysql",
    "DBInstanceStatus": "available",
    "MasterUsername": "admin",
    "DBName": "AWSCookbookRecipe402",
    "Endpoint": {
      "Address": "awscookbookrecipe402.<<ID>>.us-east-1.rds.amazonaws.com",
      "Port": 3306,
      "HostedZoneId": "<<ID>>"
    },
    ...
```

IAM database authentication is available for only the database engines listed in this AWS article (*https://oreil.ly/jUIQ0*).

2. Retrieve the RDS database instance resource ID:

```
DB_RESOURCE_ID=$(aws rds describe-db-instances \
    --query \
    'DBInstances[?DBName==`AWSCookbookRecipe402`].DbiResourceId' \
    --output text)
```

3. Create a file called *policy.json* with the following content (a *policy-template.json* file is provided in the repository):

```
{
  "Version": "2012-10-17",
  "Statement": [
    {
      "Effect": "Allow",
      "Action": [
        "rds-db:connect"
      ],
      "Resource": [
        "arn:aws:rds-db:AWS_REGION:AWS_ACCOUNT_ID:dbuser:DBResourceId/db_user"
      ]
    }
  ]
}
```

In the preceding example, db_user must match the name of the user in the database that we would like to allow to connect.

4. Replace the values in the template file by using the sed command with environment variables you have set:

```
sed -e "s/AWS_ACCOUNT_ID/${AWS_ACCOUNT_ID}/g" \
    -e "s|AWS_REGION|${AWS_REGION}|g" \
    -e "s|DBResourceId|${DB_RESOURCE_ID}|g" \
    policy-template.json > policy.json
```

5. Create an IAM policy using the file you just created:

```
aws iam create-policy --policy-name AWSCookbook402EC2RDSPolicy \
    --policy-document file://policy.json
```

You should see output similar to the following:

```
{
  "Policy": {
  "PolicyName": "AWSCookbook402EC2RDSPolicy",
  "PolicyId": "<<ID>>",
  "Arn": "arn:aws:iam::111111111111:policy/AWSCookbook402EC2RDSPolicy",
  "Path": "/",
  "DefaultVersionId": "v1",
  "AttachmentCount": 0,
  "PermissionsBoundaryUsageCount": 0,
  "IsAttachable": true,
  "CreateDate": "2021-09-21T21:18:54+00:00",
  "UpdateDate": "2021-09-21T21:18:54+00:00"
  }
}
```

6. Attach the IAM policy AWSCookbook402EC2RDSPolicy to the IAM role that the EC2 is using:

```
aws iam attach-role-policy --role-name $INSTANCE_ROLE_NAME \
    --policy-arn arn:aws:iam::$AWS_ACCOUNT_ID:policy/AWSCookbook402EC2RDSPolicy
```

7. Retrieve the RDS admin password from Secrets Manager:

```
RDS_ADMIN_PASSWORD=$(aws secretsmanager get-secret-value \
    --secret-id $RDS_SECRET_ARN \
    --query SecretString | jq -r | jq .password | tr -d '"')
```

8. Output text so that you can use it later when you connect to the EC2 instance.

List the endpoint for the RDS cluster:

```
echo $RDS_ENDPOINT
```

You should see output similar to the following:

```
awscookbookrecipe402.<<unique>>.us-east-1.rds.amazonaws.com
```

List the password for the RDS cluster:

```
echo $RDS_ADMIN_PASSWORD
```

9. Connect to the EC2 instance using SSM Session Manager (see Recipe 1.6):

```
aws ssm start-session --target $INSTANCE_ID
```

10. Install MySQL:

```
sudo yum -y install mysql
```

11. Connect to the database. You'll need to copy and paste the password and hostname (outputted in steps 7 and 8):

```
mysql -u admin -p$DB_ADMIN_PASSWORD -h $RDS_ENDPOINT
```

You should see output similar to the following:

```
Welcome to the MariaDB monitor. Commands end with ; or \g.
Your MySQL connection id is 18
Server version: 8.0.23 Source distribution
Copyright (c) 2000, 2018, Oracle, MariaDB Corporation Ab and others.
Type 'help;' or '\h' for help. Type '\c' to clear the current input statement.
MySQL [(none)]>
```

In the `mysql` command in step 11, there is no space between the `-p` flag and the first character of the password.

12. Create a new database user to associate with the IAM authentication:
    ```
    CREATE USER db_user@'%' IDENTIFIED WITH AWSAuthenticationPlugin as 'RDS';
    GRANT SELECT ON *.* TO 'db_user'@'%';
    ```

    For both commands in step 12, you should see output similar to the following:
    ```
    Query OK, 0 rows affected (0.01 sec)
    ```

13. Now, exit the `mysql` prompt:
    ```
    quit
    ```

Validation checks.   While still on the EC2 instance, download the RDS Root CA (certificate authority) file provided by Amazon (*https://oreil.ly/2T2v5*) from the *rds-downloads* S3 bucket:

```
sudo wget https://s3.amazonaws.com/rds-downloads/rds-ca-2019-root.pem
```

Set the Region by grabbing the value from the instance's metadata:

```
export AWS_DEFAULT_REGION=$(curl --silent http://169.254.169.254/latest/dynamic/
instance-identity/document \
| awk -F'"' ' /region/ {print $4}')
```

Generate the RDS authentication token and save it as a variable. You'll need to copy and paste the hostname (outputted in step 8):

```
TOKEN="$(aws rds generate-db-auth-token --hostname $RDS_ENDPOINT --port 3306 --
username db_user)"
```

Connect to the database using the RDS authentication token with the new `db_user`. You'll need to copy and paste the hostname (outputted in step 8):

```
mysql --host=$RDS_ENDPOINT --port=3306 \
    --ssl-ca=rds-ca-2019-root.pem \
--user=db_user --password=$TOKEN
```

Run a SELECT query at the `mysql` prompt to verify that this user has the SELECT *.* grant that you applied:

```
SELECT user FROM mysql.user;
```

You should see output similar to the following:

```
MySQL [(none)]> SELECT user FROM mysql.user;
+------------------+
| user             |
+------------------+
| admin            |
| db_user          |
| mysql.infoschema |
```

```
| mysql.session  |
| mysql.sys      |
| rdsadmin       |
+------------------+
6 rows in set (0.00 sec)
```

Exit the `mysql` prompt:

```
quit
```

Exit the Session Manager session:

```
exit
```

Cleanup

Follow the steps in this recipe's folder in the chapter code repository (*https://github.com/AWSCookbook/Databases*).

Discussion

Instead of a password in your MySQL connection string, you retrieved and used a token associated with the EC2 instance's IAM role. The documentation for IAM (*https://oreil.ly/ahOrb*) states that this token lasts for 15 minutes. If you install an application on this EC2 instance, the code can regularly refresh this token using the AWS SDK. There is no need to rotate passwords for your database user because the old token will be invalidated after 15 minutes.

You can create multiple database users associated with specific grants to allow your application to maintain different levels of access to your database. The grants happen within the database, not within the IAM permissions. IAM controls the `db-connect` action for the specific user. This IAM action allows the authentication token to be retrieved. That username is mapped from IAM to the GRANT(s) by using the same username within the database as in the *policy.json* file:

```
{
  "Version": "2012-10-17",
  "Statement": [
    {
      "Effect": "Allow",
      "Action": [
        "rds-db:connect"
      ],
      "Resource": [
        "arn:aws:rds-db:AWS_REGION::dbuser:DBResourceId/db_user"
      ]
    }
  ]
}
```

In this recipe, you also enabled encryption in transit by specifying the SSL certificate bundle that you downloaded to the EC2 instance in your database connection command. This encrypts the connection between your application and your database. This is a good security practice and is often required for many compliance standards. The connection string you used to connect with the IAM authentication token indicated an SSL certificate as one of the connection parameters. The certificate authority bundle is available to download from AWS (*https://oreil.ly/TJBbg*) and use within your application.

Challenge

Try connecting to the database from a Lambda function using IAM authentication. We have provided a *lambda_function.py* file in the repository to get you started.

4.3 Leveraging RDS Proxy for Database Connections from Lambda

Problem

You have a serverless function that is accessing a relational database and you need to implement connection pooling to minimize the number of database connections and improve performance.

Solution

Create an RDS Proxy, associate it with your RDS MySQL database, and configure your Lambda to connect to the proxy instead of accessing the database directly (see Figure 4-3).

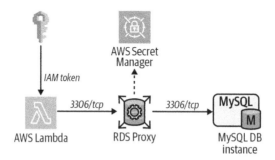

Figure 4-3. Lambda connection path to database via RDS Proxy

Prerequisites

• VPC with isolated subnets created in two AZs and associated route tables

- An RDS MySQL instance
- A Lambda function that you would like to connect to your RDS database

Preparation

Follow the steps in this recipe's folder in the chapter code repository (*https://github.com/AWSCookbook/Databases*).

Steps

1. Create a file called *assume-role-policy.json* with the following content (file provided in the repository):

    ```
    {
      "Version": "2012-10-17",
      "Statement": [
        {
          "Effect": "Allow",
          "Principal": {
            "Service": "rds.amazonaws.com"
          },
          "Action": "sts:AssumeRole"
        }
      ]
    }
    ```

2. Create an IAM role for the RDS Proxy using the *assume-role-policy.json* file:

    ```
    aws iam create-role --assume-role-policy-document \
        file://assume-role-policy.json --role-name AWSCookbook403RDSProxy
    ```

    You should see output similar to the following:

    ```
    {
      "Role": {
      "Path": "/",
      "RoleName": "AWSCookbook403RDSProxy",
      "RoleId": "<<ID>>",
      "Arn": "arn:aws:iam::111111111111:role/AWSCookbook403RDSProxy",
      "CreateDate": "2021-09-21T22:33:57+00:00",
      "AssumeRolePolicyDocument": {
        "Version": "2012-10-17",
        "Statement": [
        {
          "Effect": "Allow",
          "Principal": {
            "Service": "rds.amazonaws.com"
          },
          "Action": "sts:AssumeRole"
        }
        ]
      }
      }
    }
    ```

3. Create a security group to be used by the RDS Proxy:

```
RDS_PROXY_SG_ID=$(aws ec2 create-security-group \
    --group-name AWSCookbook403RDSProxySG \
    --description "Lambda Security Group" --vpc-id $VPC_ID \
    --output text --query GroupId)
```

4. Create the RDS Proxy. This will take a few moments:

```
RDS_PROXY_ENDPOINT_ARN=$(aws rds create-db-proxy \
    --db-proxy-name $DB_NAME \
    --engine-family MYSQL \
    --auth '{
            "AuthScheme": "SECRETS",
            "SecretArn": "'"$RDS_SECRET_ARN"'",
            "IAMAuth": "REQUIRED"
        }' \
    --role-arn arn:aws:iam::$AWS_ACCOUNT_ID:role/AWSCookbook403RDSProxy \
    --vpc-subnet-ids $ISOLATED_SUBNETS \
    --vpc-security-group-ids $RDS_PROXY_SG_ID \
    --require-tls --output text \
    --query DBProxy.DBProxyArn)
```

Wait for the RDS Proxy to become available:

```
aws rds describe-db-proxies \
    --db-proxy-name $DB_NAME \
    --query DBProxies[0].Status \
    --output text
```

5. Retrieve the RDS_PROXY_ENDPOINT:

```
RDS_PROXY_ENDPOINT=$(aws rds describe-db-proxies \
    --db-proxy-name $DB_NAME \
    --query DBProxies[0].Endpoint \
    --output text)
```

6. Next you need an IAM policy that allows the Lambda function to generate IAM authentication tokens. Create a file called *template-policy.json* with the following content (file provided in the repository):

```
{
  "Version": "2012-10-17",
  "Statement": [
    {
      "Effect": "Allow",
      "Action": [
        "rds-db:connect"
      ],
      "Resource": [
        "arn:aws:rds-db:AWS_REGION:AWS_ACCOUNT_ID:dbuser:RDSProxyID/admin"
      ]
    }
  ]
}
```

7. Separate out the Proxy ID from the RDS Proxy endpoint ARN. The Proxy ID is required for configuring IAM policies in the following steps:

```
RDS_PROXY_ID=$(echo $RDS_PROXY_ENDPOINT_ARN | awk -F: '{ print $7} ')
```

8. Replace the values in the template file by using the `sed` command with environment variables you have set:

```
sed -e "s/AWS_ACCOUNT_ID/${AWS_ACCOUNT_ID}/g" \
    -e "s|AWS_REGION|${AWS_REGION}|g" \
    -e "s|RDSProxyID|${RDS_PROXY_ID}|g" \
policy-template.json > policy.json
```

9. Create an IAM policy using the file you just created:

```
aws iam create-policy --policy-name AWSCookbook403RdsIamPolicy \
    --policy-document file://policy.json
```

You should see output similar to the following:

```
{
  "Policy": {
  "PolicyName": "AWSCookbook403RdsIamPolicy",
  "PolicyId": "<<Id>>",
  "Arn": "arn:aws:iam::111111111111:policy/AWSCookbook403RdsIamPolicy",
  "Path": "/",
  "DefaultVersionId": "v1",
  "AttachmentCount": 0,
  "PermissionsBoundaryUsageCount": 0,
  "IsAttachable": true,
  "CreateDate": "2021-09-21T22:50:24+00:00",
  "UpdateDate": "2021-09-21T22:50:24+00:00"
  }
}
```

10. Attach the policy to the DBAppFunction Lambda function's role:

```
aws iam attach-role-policy --role-name $DB_APP_FUNCTION_ROLE_NAME \
    --policy-arn arn:aws:iam::$AWS_ACCOUNT_ID:policy/AWSCookbook403RdsIamPolicy
```

Use this command to check when the proxy enters the available status and then proceed:

```
aws rds describe-db-proxies --db-proxy-name $DB_NAME \
    --query DBProxies[0].Status \
    --output text
```

11. Attach the `SecretsManagerReadWrite` policy to the RDS Proxy's role:

```
aws iam attach-role-policy --role-name AWSCookbook403RDSProxy \
    --policy-arn arn:aws:iam::aws:policy/SecretsManagerReadWrite
```

In a production scenario, you would want to scope this permission down to the minimal secret resources that your application needs to access, rather than grant `SecretsManagerReadWrite`, which allows read/write for all secrets.

12. Add an ingress rule to the RDS instance's security group that allows access on TCP port 3306 (the default MySQL engine TCP port) from the RDS Proxy security group:

```
aws ec2 authorize-security-group-ingress \
    --protocol tcp --port 3306 \
```

```
    --source-group $RDS_PROXY_SG_ID \
    --group-id $RDS_SECURITY_GROUP
```

You should see output similar to the following:

```
{
  "Return": true,
  "SecurityGroupRules": [
  {
    "SecurityGroupRuleId": "sgr-<<ID>>",
    "GroupId": "sg-<<ID>>",
    "GroupOwnerId": "111111111111",
    "IsEgress": false,
    "IpProtocol": "tcp",
    "FromPort": 3306,
    "ToPort": 3306,
    "ReferencedGroupInfo": {
    "GroupId": "sg-<<ID>>"
    }
  }
  ]
}
```

 Security groups can reference other security groups. Because of dynamic IP addresses within VPCs, this is considered the best way to grant access without opening up your security group too wide. For more information, see Recipe 2.5.

13. Register targets with the RDS Proxy:

```
aws rds register-db-proxy-targets \
    --db-proxy-name $DB_NAME \
    --db-instance-identifiers $RDS_DATABASE_ID
```

You should see output similar to the following:

```
{
  "DBProxyTargets": [
  {
    "Endpoint": "awscookbook403db.<<ID>>.us-east-1.rds.amazonaws.com",
    "RdsResourceId": "awscookbook403db",
    "Port": 3306,
    "Type": "RDS_INSTANCE",
    "TargetHealth": {
    "State": "REGISTERING"
    }
  }
  ]
}
```

Check the status of the target registration with this command. Wait until the State reaches AVAILABLE:

```
aws rds describe-db-proxy-targets \
    --db-proxy-name awscookbookrecipe403 \
    --query Targets[0].TargetHealth.State \
    --output text
```

14. Add an ingress rule to the RDS Proxy security group that allows access on TCP port 3306 from the Lambda App function's security group:

```
aws ec2 authorize-security-group-ingress \
    --protocol tcp --port 3306 \
    --source-group $DB_APP_FUNCTION_SG_ID \
    --group-id $RDS_PROXY_SG_ID
```

You should see output similar to the following:

```
{
  "Return": true,
  "SecurityGroupRules": [
  {
    "SecurityGroupRuleId": "sgr-<<ID>>",
    "GroupId": "sg-<<ID>>",
    "GroupOwnerId": "111111111111",
    "IsEgress": false,
    "IpProtocol": "tcp",
    "FromPort": 3306,
    "ToPort": 3306,
    "ReferencedGroupInfo": {
    "GroupId": "sg-<<ID>>"
    }
  }
  ]
}
```

15. Modify the Lambda function to now use the RDS Proxy endpoint as the DB_HOST, instead of connecting directly to the database:

```
aws lambda update-function-configuration \
    --function-name $DB_APP_FUNCTION_NAME \
    --environment Variables={DB_HOST=$RDS_PROXY_ENDPOINT}
```

You should see output similar to the following:

```
{
  "FunctionName": "cdk-aws-cookbook-403-LambdaApp<<ID>>",
  "FunctionArn": "arn:aws:lambda:us-east-1:111111111111:function:cdk-aws-
cookbook-403-LambdaApp<<ID>>",
  "Runtime": "python3.8",
  "Role": "arn:aws:iam::111111111111:role/cdk-aws-cookbook-403-
LambdaAppServiceRole<<ID>>",
  "Handler": "lambda_function.lambda_handler",
  "CodeSize": 665,
  "Description": "",
  "Timeout": 600,
  "MemorySize": 1024,
  ...
```

Validation checks. Run the Lambda function with this command to validate that the function can connect to RDS using your RDS Proxy:

```
aws lambda invoke \
    --function-name $DB_APP_FUNCTION_NAME \
    response.json && cat response.json
```

You should see output similar to the following:

```
{
  "StatusCode": 200,
  "ExecutedVersion": "$LATEST"
}
"Successfully connected to RDS via RDS Proxy!"
```

Cleanup

Follow the steps in this recipe's folder in the chapter code repository (*https://github.com/AWSCookbook/Databases*).

Discussion

Connection pooling is important to consider when you use Lambda with RDS. Since the function could be executed with a lot of concurrency and frequency depending on your application, the number of raw connections to your database can grow and impact performance. By using RDS Proxy to manage the connections to the database, fewer connections are needed to the actual database. This setup increases performance and efficiency.

Without RDS Proxy, a Lambda function might establish a new connection to the database each time the function is invoked. This behavior depends on the execution environment, runtimes (*https://oreil.ly/tkrh5*) (Python, NodeJS, Go, etc.), and the way you instantiate connections to the database from the function code. In cases with large amounts of function concurrency, this could result in large amounts of TCP connections to your database, reducing database performance and increasing latency. Per the documentation (*https://oreil.ly/7zUhZ*), RDS Proxy helps manage the connections from Lambda by managing them as a "pool," so that as concurrency increases, RDS Proxy increases the actual connections to the database only as needed, offloading the TCP overhead to RDS Proxy.

SSL encryption in transit is supported by RDS Proxy when you include the certificate bundle provided by AWS in your database connection string. RDS Proxy supports MySQL and PostgreSQL RDS databases. For a complete listing of all supported database engines and versions, see this support document (*https://oreil.ly/7zUhZ*).

 You can also architect to be efficient with short-lived database connections by leveraging the RDS Data API within your application, which leverages a REST API exposed by Amazon RDS. For an example on the RDS Data API, see Recipe 4.8.

Challenge

Enable enhanced logging for the RDS Proxy. This is useful for debugging.

4.4 Encrypting the Storage of an Existing Amazon RDS for MySQL Database

Problem

You need to encrypt the storage of an existing database.

Solution

Create a read replica of your existing database, take a snapshot of the read replica, copy the snapshot to an encrypted snapshot, and restore the encrypted snapshot to a new encrypted database, as shown in Figure 4-4.

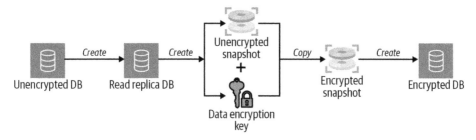

Figure 4-4. Process of encrypting an RDS database using a snapshot

Prerequisites

- VPC with isolated subnets created in two AZs and associated route tables
- An RDS MySQL instance with an RDS subnet group

Preparation

Follow the steps in this recipe's folder in the chapter code repository (*https://github.com/AWSCookbook/Databases*).

Steps

1. Verify that the storage for the database is not encrypted:
   ```
   aws rds describe-db-instances \
       --db-instance-identifier $RDS_DATABASE_ID \
       --query DBInstances[0].StorageEncrypted
   ```
   You should see `false` outputted.

2. Create a KMS key to use to encrypt your database snapshot later. Store the key ID in an environment variable:

```
KEY_ID=$(aws kms create-key \
    --tags TagKey=Name,TagValue=AWSCookbook404RDS \
    --description "AWSCookbook RDS Key" \
    --query KeyMetadata.KeyId \
    --output text)
```

3. Create an alias to easily reference the key that you created:
```
aws kms create-alias \
    --alias-name alias/awscookbook404 \
    --target-key-id $KEY_ID
```

4. Create a read replica of your existing unencrypted database:
```
aws rds create-db-instance-read-replica \
    --db-instance-identifier awscookbook404db-rep \
    --source-db-instance-identifier $RDS_DATABASE_ID \
    --max-allocated-storage 10
```

You should see output similar to the following:
```
{
  "DBInstance": {
  "DBInstanceIdentifier": "awscookbook404db-rep",
  "DBInstanceClass": "db.m5.large",
  "Engine": "mysql",
  "DBInstanceStatus": "creating",
  "MasterUsername": "admin",
  "DBName": "AWSCookbookRecipe404",
  "AllocatedStorage": 8,
  "PreferredBackupWindow": "05:51-06:21",
  "BackupRetentionPeriod": 0,
  "DBSecurityGroups": [],
...
```

By creating a read replica, you allow the snapshot to be created from it and therefore not affect the performance of the primary database.

Wait for the DBInstanceStatus to become "available":
```
aws rds describe-db-instances \
    --db-instance-identifier awscookbook404db-rep \
    --output text --query DBInstances[0].DBInstanceStatus
```

5. Take an unencrypted snapshot of your read replica:
```
aws rds create-db-snapshot \
    --db-instance-identifier awscookbook404db-rep \
    --db-snapshot-identifier awscookbook404-snapshot
```

You should see output similar to the following:
```
{
  "DBSnapshot": {
  "DBSnapshotIdentifier": "awscookbook404-snapshot",
  "DBInstanceIdentifier": "awscookbook404db-rep",
  "Engine": "mysql",
```

```
"AllocatedStorage": 8,
"Status": "creating",
"Port": 3306,
"AvailabilityZone": "us-east-1b",
"VpcId": "vpc-<<ID>>",
"InstanceCreateTime": "2021-09-21T22:46:07.785000+00:00",
```

Wait for the **Status** of the snapshot to become available:

```
aws rds describe-db-snapshots \
    --db-snapshot-identifier awscookbook404-snapshot \
    --output text --query DBSnapshots[0].Status
```

6. Copy the unencrypted snapshot to a new snapshot while encrypting by specifying your KMS key:

```
aws rds copy-db-snapshot \
--copy-tags \
--source-db-snapshot-identifier awscookbook404-snapshot \
--target-db-snapshot-identifier awscookbook404-snapshot-enc \
--kms-key-id alias/awscookbook404
```

You should see output similar to the following:

```
{
"DBSnapshot": {
"DBSnapshotIdentifier": "awscookbook404-snapshot-enc",
"DBInstanceIdentifier": "awscookbook404db-rep",
"Engine": "mysql",
"AllocatedStorage": 8,
"Status": "creating",
"Port": 3306,
"AvailabilityZone": "us-east-1b",
"VpcId": "vpc-<<ID>>",
"InstanceCreateTime": "2021-09-21T22:46:07.785000+00:00",
"MasterUsername": "admin",
...
```

 Specifying a KMS key with the copy-snapshot command encrypts the copied snapshot. Restoring an encrypted snapshot to a new database results in an encrypted database.

Wait for the **Status** of the encrypted snapshot to become available:

```
aws rds describe-db-snapshots \
    --db-snapshot-identifier awscookbook404-snapshot-enc \
    --output text --query DBSnapshots[0].Status
```

7. Restore the encrypted snapshot to a new RDS instance:

```
aws rds restore-db-instance-from-db-snapshot \
    --db-subnet-group-name $RDS_SUBNET_GROUP \
    --db-instance-identifier awscookbook404db-enc \
    --db-snapshot-identifier awscookbook404-snapshot-enc
```

You should see output similar to the following:

```
{
  "DBInstance": {
    "DBInstanceIdentifier": "awscookbook404db-enc",
    "DBInstanceClass": "db.m5.large",
    "Engine": "mysql",
    "DBInstanceStatus": "creating",
    "MasterUsername": "admin",
    "DBName": "AWSCookbookRecipe404",
    "AllocatedStorage": 8,
...
```

Validation checks.   Wait for `DBInstanceStatus` to become available:

```
aws rds describe-db-instances \
    --db-instance-identifier awscookbook404db-enc \
    --output text --query DBInstances[0].DBInstanceStatus
```

Verify that the storage is now encrypted:

```
aws rds describe-db-instances \
    --db-instance-identifier awscookbook404db-enc \
    --query DBInstances[0].StorageEncrypted
```

You should see `true` outputted.

Cleanup

Follow the steps in this recipe's folder in the chapter code repository (*https://github.com/AWSCookbook/Databases*).

Discussion

When you complete the steps, you need to reconfigure your application to point to a new database endpoint hostname. To perform this with minimal downtime, you can configure a Route 53 DNS record (*https://oreil.ly/SFZuW*) that points to your database endpoint. Your application would be configured to use the DNS record. Then you would shift your database traffic over to the new encrypted database by updating the DNS record with the new database endpoint DNS.

Encryption at rest is a security approach left up to end users in the AWS shared responsibility model (*https://oreil.ly/n6Cz3*), and often it is required to achieve or maintain compliance with regulatory standards. The encrypted snapshot you took could also be automatically copied to another Region, as well as exported to S3 for archival/backup purposes.

Challenge

Create an RDS database from scratch that initially has encrypted storage and migrate your data from your existing database to the new database using AWS DMS, as shown in Recipe 4.7.

4.5 Automating Password Rotation for RDS Databases

Problem

You would like to implement automatic password rotation for a database user.

Solution

Create a password and place it in AWS Secrets Manager. Configure a rotation interval for the secret containing the password. Finally, create a Lambda function using AWS-provided code, and configure the function to perform the password rotation. This configuration allows the password rotation automation to perform as shown in Figure 4-5.

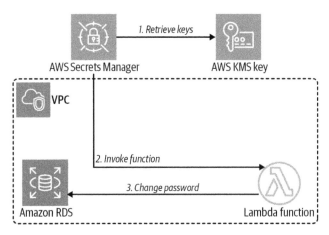

Figure 4-5. Secrets Manager Lambda function integration

Prerequisites

- VPC with isolated subnets created in two AZs and associated route tables.
- MySQL RDS instance and EC2 instance deployed. You will need the ability to connect to these for testing.

Preparation

Follow the steps in this recipe's folder in the chapter code repository (*https://github.com/AWSCookbook/Databases*).

Steps

1. Use AWS Secrets Manager to generate a password that meets RDS requirements:

```
RDS_ADMIN_PASSWORD=$(aws secretsmanager get-random-password \
    --exclude-punctuation \
    --password-length 41 --require-each-included-type \
    --output text --query RandomPassword)
```

 You can call the Secrets Manager GetRandomPassword (*https://oreil.ly/7DAG9*) API method to generate random strings of characters for various uses beyond password generation.

2. Change the admin password for your RDS database to the one you just created:

```
aws rds modify-db-instance \
    --db-instance-identifier $RDS_DATABASE_ID \
    --master-user-password $RDS_ADMIN_PASSWORD \
    --apply-immediately
```

You should see output similar to the following:

```
{
  "DBInstance": {
  "DBInstanceIdentifier": "awscookbook405db",
  "DBInstanceClass": "db.m5.large",
  "Engine": "mysql",
  "DBInstanceStatus": "available",
  "MasterUsername": "admin",
  "DBName": "AWSCookbookRecipe405",
  ...
```

3. Create a file with the following content called *rdscreds-template.json* (file provided in the repository):

```
{
  "username": "admin",
  "password": "PASSWORD",
  "engine": "mysql",
  "host": "HOST",
  "port": 3306,
  "dbname": "DBNAME",
  "dbInstanceIdentifier": "DBIDENTIFIER"
}
```

4. Use sed to modify the values in *rdscreds-template.json* to create *rdscreds.json*:

```
sed -e "s/AWS_ACCOUNT_ID/${AWS_ACCOUNT_ID}/g" \
    -e "s|PASSWORD|${RDS_ADMIN_PASSWORD}|g" \
    -e "s|HOST|${RdsEndpoint}|g" \
    -e "s|DBNAME|${DbName}|g" \
    -e "s|DBIDENTIFIER|${RdsDatabaseId}|g" \
    rdscreds-template.json > rdscreds.json
```

5. Download code from the AWS Samples GitHub repository (*https://oreil.ly/H5kgh*) for the Rotation Lambda function:

```
wget https://raw.githubusercontent.com/aws-samples/aws-secrets-manager-rotation-
lambdas/master/SecretsManagerRDSMySQLRotationSingleUser/lambda_function.py
```

AWS provides information and templates for different database rotation scenarios in this article (*https://oreil.ly/IdYkf*).

6. Compress the file containing the code:

```
zip lambda_function.zip lambda_function.py
```

You should see output similar to the following:

```
adding: lambda_function.py (deflated 76%)
```

7. Create a new security group for the Lambda function to use:

```
LAMBDA_SG_ID=$(aws ec2 create-security-group \
    --group-name AWSCookbook405LambdaSG \
    --description "Lambda Security Group" --vpc-id $VPC_ID \
    --output text --query GroupId)
```

8. Add an ingress rule to the RDS instances security group that allows access on TCP port 3306 from the Lambda's security group:

```
aws ec2 authorize-security-group-ingress \
    --protocol tcp --port 3306 \
    --source-group $LAMBDA_SG_ID \
    --group-id $RDS_SECURITY_GROUP
```

You should see output similar to the following:

```
{
  "Return": true,
  "SecurityGroupRules": [
  {
    "SecurityGroupRuleId": "sgr-<<ID>>",
    "GroupId": "sg-<<ID>>",
    "GroupOwnerId": "111111111111",
    "IsEgress": false,
    "IpProtocol": "tcp",
    "FromPort": 3306,
    "ToPort": 3306,
    "ReferencedGroupInfo": {
    "GroupId": "sg-<<ID>>"
    }
  }
  ]
}
```

9. Create a file named *assume-role-policy.json* with the following content (file provided in the repository):

```
{
  "Version": "2012-10-17",
  "Statement": [
  {
    "Effect": "Allow",
    "Principal": {
    "Service": "lambda.amazonaws.com"
    },
```

```
     "Action": "sts:AssumeRole"
    }
    ]
}
```

10. Create an IAM role with the statement in the provided *assume-role-policy.json* file using this command:

```
aws iam create-role --role-name AWSCookbook405Lambda \
    --assume-role-policy-document file://assume-role-policy.json
```

You should see output similar to the following:

```
{
  "Role": {
  "Path": "/",
  "RoleName": "AWSCookbook405Lambda",
  "RoleId": "<<ID>>",
  "Arn": "arn:aws:iam::111111111111:role/AWSCookbook405Lambda",
  "CreateDate": "2021-09-21T23:01:57+00:00",
  "AssumeRolePolicyDocument": {
    "Version": "2012-10-17",
    "Statement": [
...
```

11. Attach the IAM managed policy for `AWSLambdaVPCAccess` to the IAM role:

```
aws iam attach-role-policy --role-name AWSCookbook405Lambda \
    --policy-arn arn:aws:iam::aws:policy/service-role/
AWSLambdaVPCAccessExecutionRole
```

12. Attach the IAM managed policy for `SecretsManagerReadWrite` to the IAM role:

```
aws iam attach-role-policy --role-name AWSCookbook405Lambda \
    --policy-arn arn:aws:iam::aws:policy/SecretsManagerReadWrite
```

The IAM role that you associated with the Lambda function to rotate the password used the `SecretsManagerReadWrite` managed policy. In a production scenario, you would want to scope this down to limit which secrets the Lambda function can interact with.

13. Create the Lambda function to perform the secret rotation using the code:

```
LAMBDA_ROTATE_ARN=$(aws lambda create-function \
    --function-name AWSCookbook405Lambda \
    --runtime python3.8 \
    --package-type "Zip" \
    --zip-file fileb://lambda_function.zip \
    --handler lambda_function.lambda_handler --publish \
    --environment Variables={SECRETS_MANAGER_ENDPOINT=https://secretsmanager.
$AWS_REGION.amazonaws.com} \
    --layers $PyMysqlLambdaLayerArn \
    --role \
arn:aws:iam::$AWS_ACCOUNT_ID:role/AWSCookbook405Lambda \
    --output text --query FunctionArn \
    --vpc-config SubnetIds=${ISOLATED_SUBNETS},SecurityGroupIds=$LAMBDA_SG_ID)
```

Use this command to determine when the Lambda function has entered the Active state:

```
aws lambda get-function --function-name $LAMBDA_ROTATE_ARN \
    --output text --query Configuration.State
```

14. Add a permission to the Lambda function so that Secrets Manager can invoke it:

```
aws lambda add-permission --function-name $LAMBDA_ROTATE_ARN \
    --action lambda:InvokeFunction --statement-id secretsmanager \
    --principal secretsmanager.amazonaws.com
```

You should see output similar to the following:

```
{
    "Statement": "{\"Sid\":\"secretsmanager\",\"Effect\":\"Allow\",\"Principal\":
{\"Service\":\"secretsmanager.amazonaws.com\"},\"Action\":\"lambda:InvokeFunction
\",\"Resource\":\"arn:aws:lambda:us-
east-1:111111111111:function:AWSCookbook405Lambda\"}"
}
```

15. Set a unique suffix to use for the secret name to ensure you can reuse this pattern for additional automatic password rotations if desired:

```
AWSCookbook405SecretName=AWSCookbook405Secret-$(aws secretsmanager \
    get-random-password \
    --exclude-punctuation \
    --password-length 6 --require-each-included-type \
    --output text \
    --query RandomPassword)
```

16. Create a secret in Secrets Manager to store your admin password:

```
aws secretsmanager create-secret --name $AWSCookbook405SecretName \
    --description "My database secret created with the CLI" \
    --secret-string file://rdscreds.json
```

You should see output similar to the following:

```
{
    "ARN": "arn:aws:secretsmanager:us-
east-1:1111111111111:secret:AWSCookbook405Secret-T4tErs-AlJcLn",
    "Name": "AWSCookbook405Secret-<<Random>>",
    "VersionId": "<<ID>>"
}
```

17. Set up automatic rotation every 30 days and specify the Lambda function to perform rotation for the secret you just created:

```
aws secretsmanager rotate-secret \
    --secret-id $AWSCookbook405SecretName \
    --rotation-rules AutomaticallyAfterDays=30 \
    --rotation-lambda-arn $LAMBDA_ROTATE_ARN
```

You should see output similar to the following:

```
{
    "ARN": "arn:aws:secretsmanager:us-
east-1:1111111111111:secret:AWSCookbook405Secret-<<unique>>",
    "Name": "AWSCookbook405Secret-<<unique>>",
    "VersionId": "<<ID>>"
}
```

The `rotate-secret` command triggers an initial rotation of the password. You will trigger an extra rotation of the password in the next step to demonstrate how to perform rotations on demand.

18. Perform another rotation of the secret:

```
aws secretsmanager rotate-secret --secret-id $AWSCookbook405SecretName
```

You should see output similar to the output from step 17. Notice that the Version Id will be different from the last command indicating that the secret has been rotated.

Validation checks. Retrieve the RDS admin password from Secrets Manager:

```
RDS_ADMIN_PASSWORD=$(aws secretsmanager get-secret-value --secret-id
$AWSCookbook405SecretName --query SecretString | jq -r | jq .password | tr -d '"')
```

List the endpoint for the RDS cluster:

```
echo $RDS_ENDPOINT
```

Retrieve the password for your RDS cluster:

```
echo $RDS_ADMIN_PASSWORD
```

Connect to the EC2 instance by using SSM Session Manager (see Recipe 1.6):

```
aws ssm start-session --target $INSTANCE_ID
```

Install the MySQL client:

```
sudo yum -y install mysql
```

Connect to the database to verify that the latest rotated password is working. You'll need to copy and paste the password (outputted previously):

```
mysql -u admin -p$password -h $hostname
```

Run a SELECT statement on the `mysql.user` table to validate administrator permissions:

```
SELECT user FROM mysql.user;
```

You should see output similar to the following:

```
+------------------+
| user             |
+------------------+
| admin            |
| mysql.infoschema |
| mysql.session    |
| mysql.sys        |
| rdsadmin         |
+------------------+
5 rows in set (0.00 sec)
```

Exit from the `mysql` prompt:

```
quit
```

Exit the Session Manager session:

```
exit
```

Cleanup

Follow the steps in this recipe's folder in the chapter code repository (*https://github.com/AWSCookbook/Databases*).

Discussion

The AWS-provided Lambda function stores the rotated password in Secrets Manager. You can then configure your application to retrieve secrets from Secrets Manager directly; or the Lambda function you configured to update the Secrets Manager values could also store the password in a secure location of your choosing. You would need to grant the Lambda additional permissions to interact with the secure location you choose and add some code to store the new value there. This method could also be applied to rotate the passwords for nonadmin database user accounts by following the same steps after you have created the user(s) in your database.

The Lambda function you deployed is Python-based and connects to a MySQL engine-compatible database. The Lambda runtime environment does not have this library included by default, so you specified a Lambda layer with the `aws lambda create-function` command. This layer is required so that the PyMySQL library was available to the function in the Lambda runtime environment, and it was deployed for you as part of the preparation step when you ran `cdk deploy`.

Challenge

Create another Lambda function and a separate IAM role. Grant this new function access to the same secret.

See Also

Recipe 5.2, "Packaging Libraries with Lambda Layers"

4.6 Autoscaling DynamoDB Table Provisioned Capacity

Problem

You have a DynamoDB database table with a low provisioned throughput. You realize that your application load is variable and you may need to scale up or scale down your provisioned throughput based on the variability of the incoming application load.

Solution

Configure read and write scaling by setting a scaling target and a scaling policy for the read and write capacity of the DynamoDB table by using AWS application autoscaling, as shown in Figure 4-6.

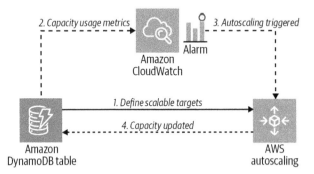

Figure 4-6. DynamoDB autoscaling configuration

Prerequisite

- A DynamoDB table

Preparation

Follow the steps in this recipe's folder in the chapter code repository (*https://github.com/AWSCookbook/Databases*).

Steps

1. Navigate to this recipe's directory in the chapter repository:

   ```
   cd 406-Auto-Scaling-DynamoDB
   ```

2. Register a `ReadCapacityUnits` scaling target for the DynamoDB table:

   ```
   aws application-autoscaling register-scalable-target \
       --service-namespace dynamodb \
       --resource-id "table/AWSCookbook406" \
       --scalable-dimension "dynamodb:table:ReadCapacityUnits" \
       --min-capacity 5 \
       --max-capacity 10
   ```

3. Register a `WriteCapacityUnits` scaling target for the DynamoDB table:

   ```
   aws application-autoscaling register-scalable-target \
       --service-namespace dynamodb \
       --resource-id "table/AWSCookbook406" \
   ```

```
--scalable-dimension "dynamodb:table:WriteCapacityUnits" \
--min-capacity 5 \
--max-capacity 10
```

4. Create a scaling policy JSON file for read capacity scaling (*read-policy.json* provided in the repository):

```
{
  "PredefinedMetricSpecification": {
    "PredefinedMetricType": "DynamoDBReadCapacityUtilization"
  },
  "ScaleOutCooldown": 60,
  "ScaleInCooldown": 60,
  "TargetValue": 50.0
}
```

5. Create a scaling policy JSON file for write capacity scaling (*write-policy.json* file provided in the repository):

```
{
  "PredefinedMetricSpecification": {
    "PredefinedMetricType": "DynamoDBWriteCapacityUtilization"
  },
  "ScaleOutCooldown": 60,
  "ScaleInCooldown": 60,
  "TargetValue": 50.0
}
```

DynamoDB-provisioned capacity (*https://oreil.ly/gWTDb*) uses capacity units to define the read and write capacity of your tables. The target value that you set defines when to scale based on the current usage. Scaling cooldown parameters define, in seconds, how long to wait to scale again after a scaling operation has taken place. For more information, see the API reference for autoscaling `TargetTrackingScalingPolicyConfiguration` (*https:// oreil.ly/cWtJI*).

6. Apply the read scaling policy to the table by using the *read-policy.json* file:

```
aws application-autoscaling put-scaling-policy \
--service-namespace dynamodb \
--resource-id "table/AWSCookbook406" \
--scalable-dimension "dynamodb:table:ReadCapacityUnits" \
--policy-name "AWSCookbookReadScaling" \
--policy-type "TargetTrackingScaling" \
--target-tracking-scaling-policy-configuration \
file://read-policy.json
```

7. Apply the write scaling policy to the table using the *write-policy.json* file:

```
aws application-autoscaling put-scaling-policy \
--service-namespace dynamodb \
--resource-id "table/AWSCookbook406" \
--scalable-dimension "dynamodb:table:WriteCapacityUnits" \
```

```
--policy-name "AWSCookbookWriteScaling" \
--policy-type "TargetTrackingScaling" \
--target-tracking-scaling-policy-configuration \
file://write-policy.json
```

Validation checks.   You can observe the autoscaling configuration for your table by selecting it in the DynamoDB console and looking under the "Additional settings" tab.

Cleanup

Follow the steps in this recipe's folder in the chapter code repository (*https://github.com/AWSCookbook/Databases*).

Discussion

 These steps will autoscale read and write capacities independently for your DynamoDB table, which helps you achieve the lowest operating cost model for your application's specific requirements.

DynamoDB allows for two capacity modes: *provisioned* and *on-demand*. When using provisioned capacity mode, you are able to select the number of data reads and writes per second. The pricing guide (*https://oreil.ly/QtLJP*) notes that you are charged according to the capacity units you specify. Conversely, with on-demand capacity mode, you pay per request for the data reads and writes your application performs on your tables. In general, using on-demand mode can result in higher costs over provisioned mode for especially transactionally heavy applications.

You need to understand your application and usage patterns when selecting a provisioned capacity for your tables. If you set the capacity too low, you will experience slow database performance and your application could enter error and wait states, since the DynamoDB API will return `ThrottlingException` and `Provisioned ThroughputExceededException` responses to your application when these limits are met. If you set the capacity too high, you are paying for unneeded capacity. Enabling autoscaling allows you to define minimum and maximum target values by setting a scaling target, while also allowing you to define when the autoscaling trigger should go into effect for scaling up, and when it should begin to scale down your capacity. This allows you to optimize for both cost and performance while taking advantage of the DynamoDB service. To see a list of the scalable targets that you configured for your table, you can use the following command:

```
aws application-autoscaling describe-scalable-targets \
    --service-namespace dynamodb \
    --resource-id "table/AWSCookbook406"
```

For more information on DynamoDB capacities and how they are measured, see this support document (*https://oreil.ly/uAFIs*).

Challenge

Create a Lambda function that monitors the performance of your DynamoDB table, and then modify the autoscaling target minimums and maximums accordingly.

4.7 Migrating Databases to Amazon RDS Using AWS DMS

Problem

You need to move data from a source database to a target database.

Solution

Configure the VPC security groups and IAM permissions to allow AWS Database Migration Service (DMS) connectivity to the databases. Then, configure the DMS endpoints for the source and target databases. Next, configure a DMS replication task. Finally, start the replication task. An architecture diagram of the solution is shown in Figure 4-7.

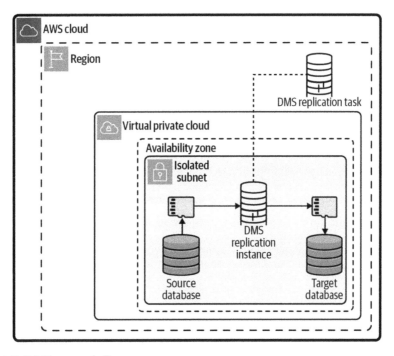

Figure 4-7. DMS network diagram

Preparation

Follow the steps in this recipe's folder in the chapter code repository (*https://github.com/AWSCookbook/Databases*).

Steps

1. Create a security group for the replication instance:

   ```
   DMS_SG_ID=$(aws ec2 create-security-group \
       --group-name AWSCookbook407DMSSG \
       --description "DMS Security Group" --vpc-id $VPC_ID \
       --output text --query GroupId)
   ```

2. Grant the DMS security group access to the source and target databases on TCP port 3306:

   ```
   aws ec2 authorize-security-group-ingress \
       --protocol tcp --port 3306 \
       --source-group $DMS_SG_ID \
       --group-id $SOURCE_RDS_SECURITY_GROUP
   aws ec2 authorize-security-group-ingress \
       --protocol tcp --port 3306 \
       --source-group $DMS_SG_ID \
       --group-id $TARGET_RDS_SECURITY_GROUP
   ```

3. Create a role for DMS by using the *assume-role-policy.json* provided:

   ```
   aws iam create-role --role-name dms-vpc-role \
       --assume-role-policy-document file://assume-role-policy.json
   ```

    The DMS service requires an IAM role with a specific name and a specific policy. The command you ran previously satisfies this requirement. You may also already have this role in your account if you have used DMS previously. This command would result in an error if that is the case, and you can proceed with the next steps without concern.

4. Attach the managed DMS policy to the role:

   ```
   aws iam attach-role-policy --role-name dms-vpc-role --policy-arn \
   arn:aws:iam::aws:policy/service-role/AmazonDMSVPCManagementRole
   ```

5. Create a replication subnet group for the replication instance:

   ```
   REP_SUBNET_GROUP=$(aws dms create-replication-subnet-group \
       --replication-subnet-group-identifier awscookbook407 \
       --replication-subnet-group-description "AWSCookbook407" \
       --subnet-ids $ISOLATED_SUBNETS \
       --query ReplicationSubnetGroup.ReplicationSubnetGroupIdentifier \
       --output text)
   ```

6. Create a replication instance and save the ARN in a variable:

   ```
   REP_INSTANCE_ARN=$(aws dms create-replication-instance \
       --replication-instance-identifier awscookbook407 \
       --no-publicly-accessible \
   ```

```
--replication-instance-class dms.t2.medium \
--vpc-security-group-ids $DMS_SG_ID \
--replication-subnet-group-identifier $REP_SUBNET_GROUP \
--allocated-storage 8 \
--query ReplicationInstance.ReplicationInstanceArn \
--output text)
```

Wait until the `ReplicationInstanceStatus` reaches available; check the status by using this command:

```
aws dms describe-replication-instances \
    --filter=Name=replication-instance-id,Values=awscookbook407 \
    --query ReplicationInstances[0].ReplicationInstanceStatus
```

 You used the `dms.t2.medium` replication instance size for this example. You should choose an instance size appropriate to handle the amount of data you will be migrating. DMS transfers tables in parallel, so you will need a larger instance size for larger amounts of data. For more information, see this user guide document (*https://oreil.ly/vzBOB*) about best practices for DMS.

7. Retrieve the source and target DB admin passwords from Secrets Manager and save to environment variables:

```
RDS_SOURCE_PASSWORD=$(aws secretsmanager get-secret-value --secret-id
$RDS_SOURCE_SECRET_NAME --query
SecretString --output text | jq .password | tr -d '"')

RDS_TARGET_PASSWORD=$(aws secretsmanager get-secret-value --secret-id
$RDS_TARGET_SECRET_NAME --query
SecretString --output text | jq .password | tr -d '"')
```

8. Create a source endpoint for DMS and save the ARN to a variable:

```
SOURCE_ENDPOINT_ARN=$(aws dms create-endpoint \
    --endpoint-identifier awscookbook407source \
    --endpoint-type source --engine-name mysql \
    --username admin --password $RDS_SOURCE_PASSWORD \
    --server-name $SOURCE_RDS_ENDPOINT --port 3306 \
    --query Endpoint.EndpointArn --output text)
```

9. Create a target endpoint for DMS and save the ARN to a variable:

```
TARGET_ENDPOINT_ARN=$(aws dms create-endpoint \
    --endpoint-identifier awscookbook407target \
    --endpoint-type target --engine-name mysql \
    --username admin --password $RDS_TARGET_PASSWORD \
    --server-name $TARGET_RDS_ENDPOINT --port 3306 \
    --query Endpoint.EndpointArn --output text)
```

10. Create your replication task:

```
REPLICATION_TASK_ARN=$(aws dms create-replication-task \
    --replication-task-identifier awscookbook-task \
    --source-endpoint-arn $SOURCE_ENDPOINT_ARN \
    --target-endpoint-arn $TARGET_ENDPOINT_ARN \
    --replication-instance-arn $REP_INSTANCE_ARN \
    --migration-type full-load \
    --table-mappings file://table-mapping-all.json \
    --query ReplicationTask.ReplicationTaskArn --output text)
```

Wait for the status to reach ready. To check the status of the replication task, use the following:

```
aws dms describe-replication-tasks \
    --filters "Name=replication-task-arn,Values=$REPLICATION_TASK_ARN" \
    --query "ReplicationTasks[0].Status"
```

11. Start the replication task:

```
aws dms start-replication-task \
    --replication-task-arn $REPLICATION_TASK_ARN \
    --start-replication-task-type start-replication
```

Validation checks. Monitor the progress of the replication task:

```
aws dms describe-replication-tasks
```

Use the AWS Console or the `aws dms describe-replication-tasks` operation to validate that your tables have been migrated:

```
aws dms describe-replication-tasks \
    --query ReplicationTasks[0].ReplicationTaskStats
```

You can also view the status of the replication task in the DMS console.

Cleanup

Follow the steps in this recipe's folder in the chapter code repository (*https://github.com/AWSCookbook/Databases*).

Discussion

 You could also run `full-load-and-cdc` to continuously replicate changes on the source to the destination to minimize your application downtime when you cut over to the new database.

DMS comes with functionality to test source and destination endpoints from the replication instance. This is a handy feature to use when working with DMS to validate that you have the configuration correct before you start to run replication tasks. Testing connectivity from the replication instance to both of the endpoints you configured can be done through the DMS console or the command line with the following commands:

```
aws dms test-connection \
    --replication-instance-arn $rep_instance_arn \
    --endpoint-arn $source_endpoint_arn

aws dms test-connection \
    --replication-instance-arn $rep_instance_arn \
    --endpoint-arn $target_endpoint_arn
```

The `test-connection` operation takes a few moments to complete. You can check the status and the results of the operation by using this command:

```
aws dms describe-connections --filter \
"Name=endpoint-arn,Values=$source_endpoint_arn,$target_endpoint_arn"
```

The DMS service supports many types of source (*https://oreil.ly/TowD5*) and target (*https://oreil.ly/8vggA*) databases within your VPC, another AWS account, or databases hosted in a non-AWS environment. The service can also transform data for you if your source and destination are different types of databases by using additional configuration in the *table-mappings.json* file. For example, the data type of a column in an Oracle database may have a different format than the equivalent type in a PostgreSQL database. The AWS Schema Conversion Tool (*https://oreil.ly/Tnt1a*) (SCT) can assist with identifying these necessary transforms, and also generate configuration files to use with DMS.

Challenge

Enable full load and ongoing replication (*https://oreil.ly/h8bPq*) to continuously replicate from one database to another.

4.8 Enabling REST Access to Aurora Serverless Using RDS Data API

Problem

You have a PostgreSQL database and would like to connect to it without having your application manage persistent database connections.

Solution

First, enable the Data API for your database and configure the IAM permissions for your EC2 instance. Then, test from both the CLI and RDS console. This allows your application to connect to your Aurora Serverless database, as shown in Figure 4-8.

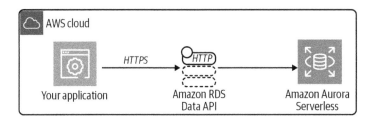

Figure 4-8. An application using the RDS Data API

Prerequisites

- VPC with isolated subnets created in two AZs and associated route tables.
- PostgreSQL RDS instance and EC2 instance deployed. You will need the ability to connect to these for testing.

Preparation

Follow the steps in this recipe's folder in the chapter code repository (*https://github.com/AWSCookbook/Databases*).

Steps

1. Enable the Data API on your Aurora Serverless cluster:

```
aws rds modify-db-cluster \
    --db-cluster-identifier $CLUSTER_IDENTIFIER \
    --enable-http-endpoint \
    --apply-immediately
```

2. Ensure that `HttpEndpointEnabled` is set to `true`:

```
aws rds describe-db-clusters \
    --db-cluster-identifier $CLUSTER_IDENTIFIER \
    --query DBClusters[0].HttpEndpointEnabled
```

3. Test a command from your CLI:

```
aws rds-data execute-statement \
    --secret-arn "$SECRET_ARN" \
    --resource-arn "$CLUSTER_ARN" \
    --database "$DATABASE_NAME" \
    --sql "select * from pg_user" \
    --output json
```

(Optional) You can also test access via the AWS Console using the Amazon RDS Query Editor. First run these two commands from your terminal so you can copy and paste the values:

```
echo $SECRET_ARN
echo $DATABASE_NAME
```

4. Log in to the AWS Console with admin permissions and go to the RDS console. On the lefthand sidebar menu, click Query Editor. Fill out the values and select "Connect to database," as shown in Figure 4-9.

Figure 4-9. Connect to database settings

5. Run the same query and view the results below the Query Editor (see Figure 4-10):

```
SELECT * from pg_user;
```

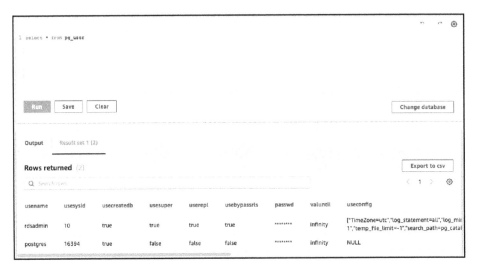

Figure 4-10. RDS Query Editor

6. Configure your EC2 instance to use the Data API with your database cluster. Create a file called *policy-template.json* with the following content (file provided in the repository):

```
{
  "Version": "2012-10-17",
  "Statement": [
  {
    "Action": [
    "rds-data:BatchExecuteStatement",
    "rds-data:BeginTransaction",
    "rds-data:CommitTransaction",
    "rds-data:ExecuteStatement",
    "rds-data:RollbackTransaction"
    ],
    "Resource": "*",
    "Effect": "Allow"
  },
  {
    "Action": [
    "secretsmanager:GetSecretValue",
    "secretsmanager:DescribeSecret"
    ],
    "Resource": "SecretArn",
    "Effect": "Allow"
  }
  ]
}
```

7. Replace the values in the template file by using the **sed** command with environment variables you have set:

```
sed -e "s/SecretArn/${SECRET_ARN}/g" \
    policy-template.json > policy.json
```

8. Create an IAM policy by using the file you just created:

```
aws iam create-policy --policy-name AWSCookbook408RDSDataPolicy \
    --policy-document file://policy.json
```

9. Attach the IAM policy for `AWSCookbook408RDSDataPolicy` to your EC2 instance's IAM role:

```
aws iam attach-role-policy --role-name $INSTANCE_ROLE_NAME \
    --policy-arn arn:aws:iam::$AWS_ACCOUNT_ID:policy/AWSCookbook408RDSDataPolicy
```

Validation checks.   Create and populate some SSM parameters to store values so that you can retrieve them from your EC2 instance:

```
aws ssm put-parameter \
    --name "Cookbook408DatabaseName" \
    --type "String" \
    --value $DATABASE_NAME

aws ssm put-parameter \
    --name "Cookbook408ClusterArn" \
    --type "String" \
    --value $CLUSTER_ARN

aws ssm put-parameter \
    --name "Cookbook408SecretArn" \
    --type "String" \
    --value $SECRET_ARN
```

Connect to the EC2 instance by using SSM Session Manager (see Recipe 1.6):

```
aws ssm start-session --target $INSTANCE_ID
```

Set the Region:

```
export AWS_DEFAULT_REGION=us-east-1
```

Retrieve the SSM parameter values and set them to environment values:

```
DatabaseName=$(aws ssm get-parameters \
    --names "Cookbook408DatabaseName" \
        --query "Parameters[*].Value" --output text)

SecretArn=$(aws ssm get-parameters \
    --names "Cookbook408SecretArn" \
        --query "Parameters[*].Value" --output text)

ClusterArn=$(aws ssm get-parameters \
    --names "Cookbook408ClusterArn" \
        --query "Parameters[*].Value" --output text)
```

Run a query against the database:

```
aws rds-data execute-statement \
    --secret-arn "$SecretArn" \
    --resource-arn "$ClusterArn" \
```

```
      --database "$DatabaseName" \
      --sql "select * from pg_user" \
      --output json
```

Exit the Session Manager session:

```
exit
```

Cleanup

Follow the steps in this recipe's folder in the chapter code repository (*https://github.com/AWSCookbook/Databases*).

Discussion

The Data API exposes an HTTPS endpoint for usage with Aurora and uses IAM authentication to allow your application to execute SQL statements on your database over HTTPS instead of using classic TCP database connectivity.

 Per the Aurora user guide (*https://oreil.ly/wvADq*), all calls to the Data API are synchronous, and the default timeout for a query is 45 seconds. If your queries take longer than 45 seconds, you can use the `continueAfterTimeout` parameter to facilitate long-running queries.

As is the case with other AWS service APIs that use IAM authentication, all activities performed with the Data API are captured in CloudTrail to ensure an audit trail is present, which can help satisfy your security and audit requirements. You can control and delegate access to the Data API endpoint by using IAM policies associated with roles for your application. For example, if you wanted to grant your application the ability to only read from your database using the Data API, you could write a policy that omits the `rds-data:CommitTransaction` and `rds-data:RollbackTransaction` permissions.

The Query Editor within the RDS console provides a web-based means of access for executing SQL queries against your database. This is a convenient mechanism for developers and DBAs to quickly accomplish bespoke tasks. The same privileges that you assigned your EC2 instance in this recipe would need to be granted to your developer and DBA via IAM roles.

Challenge

Create and deploy a Lambda function that has permissions to access the RDS Data API that you provisioned.

CHAPTER 5

Serverless

5.0 Introduction

The technology industry term *serverless* can sometimes lead to confusion in that servers are involved with the cloud services associated with this model of execution. The advantage is that end users do not need to worry about managing the underlying infrastructure and platform. The cloud provider (in this case, AWS) is responsible for all of the management, operating system updates, availability, capacity, and more.

In terms of "serverless" services available on AWS (*https://oreil.ly/5CIjp*), many options are available to take advantage of the benefits. Here are some examples:

- AWS Lambda and Amazon Fargate for compute
- Amazon EventBridge, Amazon SNS, Amazon SQS, and Amazon API Gateway for application integration
- Amazon S3, Amazon DynamoDB, and Amazon Aurora Serverless for datastores

The main benefits of serverless on AWS are as follows:

Cost savings
    You pay for only what you use.

Scalability
    Scale up to what you need; scale down to save costs.

Less management
    There are no servers to deploy or systems to manage.

Flexibility
    Many programming languages are supported in AWS Lambda.

The recipes in this chapter will enable you to explore several of the AWS services that fall under the "serverless" umbrella. You will find opportunities to extend the solutions with challenges and get experience with some new services that are leading the serverless industry trend.

Workstation Configuration

Follow the "General workstation setup steps for CLI recipes" on page xvii to validate your configuration and set up the required environment variables. Then, clone the chapter code repository:

```
git clone https://github.com/AWSCookbook/Serverless
```

Chapter Prerequisites

IAM role for Lambda function execution

Create a file named *assume-role-policy.json* with the following content (file provided in root of the chapter repository):

```
{
  "Version": "2012-10-17",
  "Statement": [
  {
    "Effect": "Allow",
    "Principal": {
    "Service": "lambda.amazonaws.com"
    },
    "Action": "sts:AssumeRole"
  }
  ]
}
```

> A similar role is created automatically when you create a Lambda function in the AWS Management Console and select "Create a new role from AWS policy templates" for the execution role.

Create an IAM role with the statement in the provided *assume-role-policy.json* file using this command:

```
aws iam create-role --role-name AWSCookbookLambdaRole \
    --assume-role-policy-document file://assume-role-policy.json
```

Attach the AWSLambdaBasicExecutionRole IAM managed policy to the IAM role:

```
aws iam attach-role-policy --role-name AWSCookbookLambdaRole \
    --policy-arn arn:aws:iam::aws:policy/service-role/AWSLambdaBasicExecutionRole
```

5.1 Configuring an ALB to Invoke a Lambda Function

Problem

You have a requirement that your entire web application must be exposed to the internet with a load balancer. Your application architecture includes serverless functions. You need a function to be able to respond to HTTP requests for specific URL paths.

Solution

Grant the Elastic Load Balancing service permission to invoke Lambda functions; then create a Lambda function. Create an ALB target group; then register the Lambda function with the target group. Associate the target group with the listener on your ALB. Finally, add a listener rule that directs traffic for the */function* path to the Lambda function (see Figure 5-1).

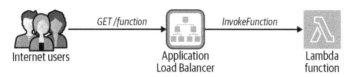

Figure 5-1. Lambda function invoked by ALB

Prerequisites

- VPC with public subnets in two AZs and associated route tables
- An Application Load Balancer that includes the following:
  — An associated security group that allows port 80 from the world

  — A listener on port 80
- IAM role that allows the Lambda function to execute (provided in chapter prerequisites)

Preparation

Follow the steps in this recipe's folder in the chapter code repository (*https://github.com/AWSCookbook/Serverless*).

Steps

1. Compress the function code provided in this recipe's directory in the repository. This code will be used for the Lambda function. You can modify this code if you wish, but we have provided code for you to use. For example, zip the code with the following command:

```
zip lambda_function.zip lambda_function.py
```

2. Create a Lambda function that will respond to HTTP requests:

```
LAMBDA_ARN=$(aws lambda create-function \
    --function-name AWSCookbook501Lambda \
    --runtime python3.8 \
    --package-type "Zip" \
    --zip-file fileb://lambda_function.zip \
    --handler lambda_function.lambda_handler --publish \
    --role \
    arn:aws:iam::$AWS_ACCOUNT_ID:role/AWSCookbookLambdaRole \
    --output text --query FunctionArn)
```

3. Create an ALB target group with the target type set to `lambda`:

```
TARGET_GROUP_ARN=$(aws elbv2 create-target-group \
    --name awscookbook501tg \
    --target-type lambda --output text \
    --query TargetGroups[0].TargetGroupArn)
```

4. Use the `add-permission` command to give the Elastic Load Balancing service permission to invoke your Lambda function:

```
aws lambda add-permission \
    --function-name $LAMBDA_ARN \
    --statement-id load-balancer \
    --principal elasticloadbalancing.amazonaws.com \
    --action lambda:InvokeFunction \
    --source-arn $TARGET_GROUP_ARN
```

5. Use the `register-targets` command to register the Lambda function as a target:

```
aws elbv2 register-targets \
    --target-group-arn $TARGET_GROUP_ARN \
    --targets Id=$LAMBDA_ARN
```

6. Modify the listener for your ALB on port 80; then create a rule that forwards traffic destined for the */function* path to your target group:

```
RULE_ARN=$(aws elbv2 create-rule \
    --listener-arn $LISTENER_ARN --priority 10 \
    --conditions Field=path-pattern,Values='/function' \
    --actions Type=forward,TargetGroupArn=$TARGET_GROUP_ARN \
    --output text --query Rules[0].RuleArn)
```

Validation checks.   Test the invocation to verify that the Lambda function is invoked when requesting */function*:

```
curl -v $LOAD_BALANCER_DNS/function
```

Cleanup

Follow the steps in this recipe's folder in the chapter code repository (*https://github.com/AWSCookbook/Serverless*).

Discussion

Developers and software architects can leverage Lambda functions to provide a programmatic response to some kind of event within a larger system. This type of compute is most often used when the functions are responsible for a small unit of work. AWS added the ability for Application Load Balancers to invoke Lambda functions (*https://oreil.ly/R15DP*) in 2018.

When an end user requests a specific URL path (configured by the developer) on an ALB, the ALB can pass the request to a Lambda function to handle the response. The ALB then receives the output from the function and hands the result back to the end user as an HTTP response. ALBs can have multiple paths and targets configured for a single load balancer, sending portions of traffic to specific targets (Lambda functions, containers, EC2 instances, etc.) ALBs also support routing to Lambda functions using header values (*https://oreil.ly/ljYBe*). This simple architecture is extremely cost-effective and highly scalable.

This flexibility allows for a single ALB to handle all the traffic for your application and provides for a nice building block when architecting a system that needs to be exposed via HTTP/HTTPS.

Challenge 1

Add a Fargate task that responds to another path on your ALB.

Challenge 2

Try using an Amazon API Gateway (*https://aws.amazon.com/api-gateway*) to play in front of your Lambda function.

5.2 Packaging Libraries with Lambda Layers

Problem

You have Python code using external libraries that you need to include with your serverless function deployments.

Solution

Create a folder and use `pip` to install a Python package to the folder. Then, `zip` the folder and use the *.zip* file to create a Lambda layer that your function will leverage (see Figure 5-2).

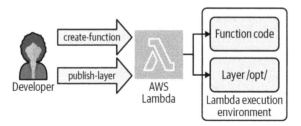

Figure 5-2. Lambda function layer creation and representation

Prerequisite

- IAM role that allows Lambda functions to execute (provided in chapter prerequisites)

Steps

1. In the root of this chapter's repository, `cd` to the *502-Packaging-Libraries-with-Lambda-Layers* directory and follow the subsequent steps:

   ```
   cd 502-Packaging-Libraries-with-Lambda-Layers/
   ```

2. Zip up *lambda_function.py* provided in the repository:

   ```
   zip lambda_function.zip lambda_function.py
   ```

   You should see output similar to the following:

   ```
   updating: lambda_function.py (deflated 49%)
   ```

3. Create a Lambda function that we will add a layer to:

   ```
   LAMBDA_ARN=$(aws lambda create-function \
       --function-name AWSCookbook502Lambda \
       --runtime python3.8 \
       --package-type "Zip" \
       --zip-file fileb://lambda_function.zip \
       --handler lambda_function.lambda_handler --publish \
       --role \
       arn:aws:iam::$AWS_ACCOUNT_ID:role/AWSCookbookLambdaRole \
       --output text --query FunctionArn)
   ```

4. Create a directory for the layer contents:

   ```
   mkdir python
   ```

5. Use `pip` to install the latest `requests` module to the directory:

   ```
   pip install requests --target="./python"
   ```

You should see output similar to the following:

```
Collecting requests
  Using cached requests-2.26.0-py2.py3-none-any.whl (62 kB)
Collecting certifi>=2017.4.17
  Using cached certifi-2021.5.30-py2.py3-none-any.whl (145 kB)
Collecting idna<4,>=2.5
  Using cached idna-3.2-py3-none-any.whl (59 kB)
Collecting urllib3<1.27,>=1.21.1
  Using cached urllib3-1.26.7-py2.py3-none-any.whl (138 kB)
Collecting charset-normalizer~=2.0.0
  Using cached charset_normalizer-2.0.6-py3-none-any.whl (37 kB)
Installing collected packages: urllib3, idna, charset-normalizer, certifi,
requests
Successfully installed certifi-2021.5.30 charset-normalizer-2.0.6 idna-3.2
requests-2.26.0 urllib3-1.26.7
```

6. Zip the contents of the directory:

```
zip -r requests-layer.zip ./python
```

You should see output similar to the following:

```
adding: python/ (stored 0%)
adding: python/bin/ (stored 0%)
adding: python/bin/normalizer (deflated 28%)
adding: python/requests-2.26.0.dist-info/ (stored 0%)
adding: python/requests-2.26.0.dist-info/RECORD (deflated 55%)
adding: python/requests-2.26.0.dist-info/LICENSE (deflated 65%)
adding: python/requests-2.26.0.dist-info/WHEEL (deflated 14%)
adding: python/requests-2.26.0.dist-info/top_level.txt (stored 0%)
adding: python/requests-2.26.0.dist-info/REQUESTED (stored 0%)
adding: python/requests-2.26.0.dist-info/INSTALLER (stored 0%)
adding: python/requests-2.26.0.dist-info/METADATA (deflated 58%)
```

Lambda layers require a specific folder structure. You create this folder structure when you use pip to install the requests module to the Python folder within your directory:

```
$ tree -L 1 python/
python/
├── bin
├── certifi
├── certifi-2020.12.5.dist-info
├── chardet
├── chardet-4.0.0.dist-info
├── idna
├── idna-2.10.dist-info
├── requests
├── requests-2.25.1.dist-info
├── urllib3
└── urllib3-1.26.4.dist-info

11 directories, 0 files
```

7. Publish the layer and set an environment variable to use in the next steps:

```
LAYER_VERSION_ARN=$(aws lambda publish-layer-version \
    --layer-name AWSCookbook502RequestsLayer \
    --description "Requests layer" \
    --license-info "MIT" \
    --zip-file fileb://requests-layer.zip \
    --compatible-runtimes python3.8 \
    --output text --query LayerVersionArn)
```

8. Update the Lambda to use the layer that you created:

```
aws lambda update-function-configuration \
    --function-name AWSCookbook502Lambda \
    --layers $LAYER_VERSION_ARN
```

You should see output similar to the following:

```
{
  "FunctionName": "AWSCookbook502Lambda",
  "FunctionArn": "arn:aws:lambda:us-
east-1:111111111111:function:AWSCookbook502Lambda",
  "Runtime": "python3.8",
  "Role": "arn:aws:iam::111111111111:role/AWSCookbookLambdaRole",
  "Handler": "lambda_function.lambda_handler",
  "CodeSize": 691,
  "Description": "",
  "Timeout": 3,
  "MemorySize": 128,
  ...
```

Validation checks. Test the Lambda:

```
aws lambda invoke \
    --function-name AWSCookbook502Lambda \
    response.json && cat response.json
```

Cleanup

Follow the steps in this recipe's folder in the chapter code repository (*https://
github.com/AWSCookbook/Serverless*).

Discussion

Lambda layers can be used to extend the packages available within the default
Lambda runtimes and also to provide your own custom runtimes for your functions.
The default runtimes are associated with Amazon Linux. Custom runtimes can be
developed on top of Amazon Linux to support your own programming language
requirements. See this tutorial (*https://oreil.ly/XTWHX*) to publish a custom runtime.

In this recipe, you packaged the Python `requests` module as a layer and deployed a
Python function that uses that module. Layers can be used by multiple functions,
shared with other AWS accounts, and they can also be version-controlled so that you

can deploy and test new versions of your layers without impacting existing versions that are being used for your functions.

Challenge

Create another Lambda function that uses the same layer.

5.3 Invoking Lambda Functions on a Schedule

Problem

You need to run a serverless function once per minute.

Solution

Add a permission to your Lambda function to allow the EventBridge service to invoke the function. Then configure an EventBridge rule using a schedule expression for one minute that targets your function (see Figure 5-3).

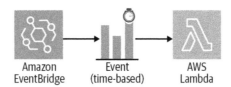

Figure 5-3. EventBridge triggering a time-based invocation of a Lambda function

Prerequisites

- Lambda function that you want to trigger
- IAM role that allows Lambda functions to execute (provided in chapter prerequisites)

Preparation

Follow the steps in this recipe's folder in the chapter code repository (*https://github.com/AWSCookbook/Serverless*).

Steps

1. Create an events rule with a scheduled expression with a rate of one minute:

```
RULE_ARN=$(aws events put-rule --name "EveryMinuteEvent" \
    --schedule-expression "rate(1 minute)")
```

You can use rate expressions and Cron formats (*https://cron tab.guru*) for schedule expressions when defining a time-based event rule. The Cron expression syntax for the rule you created would look like the following:

```
RULE_ARN=$(aws events put-rule --name
"EveryMinuteEvent" \
--schedule-expression "cron(* * * ? *)")
```

For more information about schedule expressions, see this support document (*https://oreil.ly/K7e8Z*).

2. Add a permission to the Lambda function so that the EventBridge service can invoke it:

```
aws lambda add-permission --function-name $LAMBDA_ARN \
    --action lambda:InvokeFunction --statement-id events \
    --principal events.amazonaws.com
```

You should see output similar to the following:

```
{
  "Statement": "{\"Sid\":\"events\",\"Effect\":\"Allow\",\"Principal\":{\"Service
\":\"events.amazonaws.com\"},\"Action\":\"lambda:InvokeFunction\",\"Resource\":
\"arn:aws:lambda:us-east-1:111111111111:function:AWSCookbook503Lambda\"}"
}
```

3. Add your Lambda function as a target for the rule that you created:

```
aws events put-targets --rule EveryMinuteEvent \
    --targets "Id"="1","Arn"="$LAMBDA_ARN"
```

You should see output similar to the following:

```
{
  "FailedEntryCount": 0,
  "FailedEntries": []
}
```

There are many available target options. For the latest list, check the documentation (*https://oreil.ly/Rggow*).

Validation checks. Tail the CloudWatch Logs log group to observe the function invoked every 60 seconds:

```
aws logs tail "/aws/lambda/AWSCookbook503Lambda" --follow --since 10s
```

You may have to wait a few moments for the log group to be created. If the log group doesn't exist, you will get the following error:

```
An error occurred (ResourceNotFoundException) when calling
the FilterLogEvents operation: The specified log group does
not exist.
```

You should see output similar to the following:

```
$ $ aws logs tail "/aws/lambda/AWSCookbook503Lambda" --follow --since 10s
2021-06-12T21:17:30.605000+00:00 2021/06/12/
[$LATEST]4d1335bf8b0846938cb585871db38374 START RequestId:
685481eb-9279-4007-854c-f99289bf9609 Version: $LATEST
2021-06-12T21:17:30.607000+00:00 2021/06/12/
[$LATEST]4d1335bf8b0846938cb585871db38374 AWS Cookbook Lambda
function run at 2021-06-12 21:17:30.607500
2021-06-12T21:17:30.608000+00:00 2021/06/12/
[$LATEST]4d1335bf8b0846938cb585871db38374 END RequestId:
685481eb-9279-4007-854c-f99289bf9609
2021-06-12T21:17:30.608000+00:00 2021/06/12/
[$LATEST]4d1335bf8b0846938cb585871db38374 REPORT RequestId:
685481eb-9279-4007-854c-f99289bf9609   Duration: 0.94 ms    Billed Duration: 1
ms    Memory Size: 128 MB
Max Memory Used: 51 MB
...
```

You can exit the tail session by pressing Ctrl-C.

Notice that subsequent runs occur at one-minute increments from the time that you added the Lambda function as a target for your event rule.

Cleanup

Follow the steps in this recipe's folder in the chapter code repository (*https://github.com/AWSCookbook/Serverless*).

Discussion

There are many reasons you would want to run functions on a schedule:

- Checking stock prices
- Checking the weather
- Starting scheduled processes
- Scheduling EC2 starting and stop

Being able to run serverless functions on a schedule without provisioning resources allows costs and management to be kept at a minimum. There are no servers to update, and you don't need to pay for them when they are idle.

Challenge

Pause and then enable the event rule. Here is a hint:

```
aws events disable-rule --name "EveryMinuteEvent"
aws events enable-rule --name "EveryMinuteEvent"
```

EventBridge was formerly known as Amazon CloudWatch Events (*https://oreil.ly/K4ElM*). EventBridge is now the preferred way to schedule events and uses the same API as CloudWatch Events.

When you need an AWS service to interact with another AWS service, you need to explicitly grant the permissions. In this case, EventBridge needs to be granted the permissions to invoke a Lambda function by using the `aws lambda add-permission` command.

5.4 Configuring a Lambda Function to Access an EFS File System

Problem

You have an existing network share that is accessible by servers, but you want to be able to process files on it with serverless functions.

Solution

You will create a Lambda function and mount your EFS file system to it (see Figure 5-4).

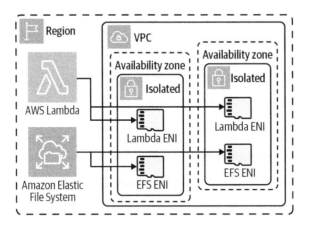

Figure 5-4. Lambda function accessing ENIs within the subnet of a VPC

Prerequisites

- VPC with isolated subnets in two AZs and associated route tables
- EFS file system with content that you want to access

- IAM role that allows the Lambda function to execute (provided in chapter prerequisites)

Preparation

Follow the steps in this recipe's folder in the chapter code repository (*https://github.com/AWSCookbook/Serverless*).

Steps

1. Create a new security group for the Lambda function to use:

   ```
   LAMBDA_SG_ID=$(aws ec2 create-security-group \
       --group-name AWSCookbook504LambdaSG \
       --description "Lambda Security Group" --vpc-id $VPC_ID \
       --output text --query GroupId)
   ```

2. Add an ingress rule to the EFS file system's security group that allows access on TCP port 2049 from the Lambda function's security group:

   ```
   aws ec2 authorize-security-group-ingress \
       --protocol tcp --port 2049 \
       --source-group $LAMBDA_SG_ID \
       --group-id $EFS_SECURITY_GROUP
   ```

   You should see output similar to the following:

   ```
   {
     "Return": true,
     "SecurityGroupRules": [
     {
       "SecurityGroupRuleId": "sgr-0f837d0b090ba38de",
       "GroupId": "sg-0867c2c4ca6f4ab83",
       "GroupOwnerId": "611652777867",
       "IsEgress": false,
       "IpProtocol": "tcp",
       "FromPort": 2049,
       "ToPort": 2049,
       "ReferencedGroupInfo": {
       "GroupId": "sg-0c71fc94eb6cd1ae3"
       }
       }
     ]
   }
   ```

3. Create an IAM role using the statement in the provided *assume-role-policy.json* file using this command:

   ```
   aws iam create-role --role-name AWSCookbook504Role \
       --assume-role-policy-document file://assume-role-policy.json
   ```

4. You need to give your Lambda function the ability to execute within a VPC, so attach the IAM managed policy for AWSLambdaVPCAccessExecutionRole to the IAM role:

```
aws iam attach-role-policy --role-name AWSCookbook504Role \
    --policy-arn arn:aws:iam::aws:policy/service-role/
AWSLambdaVPCAccessExecutionRole
```

5. Zip up the *lambda_function.py* provided in the repository:

```
zip lambda_function.zip lambda_function.py
```

6. Create a Lambda function specifying the `ACCESS_POINT_ARN` of the EFS file system:

```
LAMBDA_ARN=$(aws lambda create-function \
    --function-name AWSCookbook504Lambda \
    --runtime python3.8 \
    --package-type "Zip" \
    --zip-file fileb://lambda_function.zip \
    --handler lambda_function.lambda_handler --publish \
    --role \
    arn:aws:iam::$AWS_ACCOUNT_ID:role/AWSCookbook504Role \
    --file-system-configs Arn="$ACCESS_POINT_ARN",LocalMountPath="/mnt/efs" \
    --output text --query FunctionArn \
    --vpc-config SubnetIds=${ISOLATED_SUBNETS},SecurityGroupIds=${LAMBDA_SG_ID})
```

7. Use this command to determine when the Lambda function has entered the active state (this may take a few moments):

```
aws lambda get-function --function-name $LAMBDA_ARN \
    --output text --query Configuration.State
```

Validation checks. Execute the Lambda function to display the file's contents:

```
aws lambda invoke \
    --function-name $LAMBDA_ARN \
    response.json && cat response.json
```

Cleanup

Follow the steps in this recipe's folder in the chapter code repository (*https://github.com/AWSCookbook/Serverless*).

Discussion

As a developer or software architect, you start to see the benefits of serverless technologies when you connect serverless compute to serverless persistent storage (filesystems and databases both). The compute and storage operational overhead is drastically reduced when using these types of services within applications. You can provision and scale your storage on demand while relying on AWS to manage the underlying infrastructure for you. While many applications will use an object-style storage service such as Amazon S3, others are best suited to a somewhat more traditional file-style storage service. Combining Lambda and EFS, as shown in this recipe, solves this problem with ease.

By integrating Amazon EFS with AWS Lambda, you can build solutions like the following:

- Persistent storage for applications
- Maintenance activities
- Event-driven notifications
- Event-driven file processing

The fully managed nature and the pay-per-use aspects of these services allow for the design, building, deployment, and operation of cost-effective and modern application architectures.

Challenge 1

Create another Lambda function that has access to the same EFS file system.

Challenge 2

Create a Lambda function that runs on a scheduled interval to detect if any files have been changed in the last 30 days.

See Also

Recipe 5.9, "Accessing VPC Resources with Lambda"

5.5 Running Trusted Code in Lambda Using AWS Signer

Problem

You need to ensure that a serverless function deployed in your environment is running code from trusted sources. You need to verify the integrity of the code and have confidence that the code has not been modified after it has been signed.

Solution

Create a signing profile and then start a signing job for your code by using AWS Signer. Finally, deploy a Lambda function that references your signing configuration and uses the signed code (see Figure 5-5).

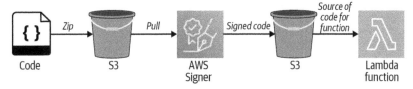

Figure 5-5. Signing process for Lambda function code

Prerequisites

- S3 bucket with versioning enabled and source code copied to it
- S3 bucket for AWS Signer to use a destination
- IAM role that allows the Lambda function to execute (provided in chapter prerequisites)

Preparation

Follow the steps in this recipe's folder in the chapter code repository (*https://github.com/AWSCookbook/Serverless*).

Steps

1. Get the version of the object in S3 that you will use. This is a zip of the code to be used in your Lambda function. You'll need this when you start the signing job:

```
OBJ_VER_ID=$(aws s3api list-object-versions \
    --bucket awscookbook505-src-$RANDOM_STRING \
    --prefix lambda_function.zip \
    --output text --query Versions[0].VersionId)
```

2. Create a signing profile:

```
SIGNING_PROFILE_ARN=$(aws signer put-signing-profile \
    --profile-name AWSCookbook505_$RANDOM_STRING \
    --platform AWSLambda-SHA384-ECDSA \
    --output text --query arn)
```

 You can find a list of the available signing platforms by running this command:

```
aws signer list-signing-platforms
```

3. Create a code-signing configuration for Lambda that refers to the signing profile:

```
CODE_SIGNING_CONFIG_ARN=$(aws lambda create-code-signing-config \
    --allowed-publishers SigningProfileVersionArns=$SIGNING_PROFILE_ARN \
    --output text --query CodeSigningConfig.CodeSigningConfigArn)
```

4. Start the signing job:

```
SIGNING_JOB_ID=$(aws signer start-signing-job \
    --source 's3={bucketName=awscookbook505-src-'"$
{RANDOM_STRING}"'",key=lambda_function.zip,version='"$OBJ_VER_ID"'}' \
    --destination 's3={bucketName=awscookbook505-dst-'"$
{RANDOM_STRING}"'",prefix=signed-}' \
    --profile-name AWSCookbook505_$RANDOM_STRING \
    --output text --query jobId)
```

Wait a few moments and then verify that the signing job was successful:

```
aws signer list-signing-jobs --status Succeeded
```

You should see output similar to the following:

```
{
  "jobs": [
  {
    "jobId": "efd392ae-2503-4c78-963f-8f40a58d770f",
    "source": {
    "s3": {
      "bucketName": "awscookbook505-src-<<unique>>",
      "key": "lambda_function.zip",
      "version": "o.MffnpzjBmaBR1yzvoti0AnluovMtMf"
    }
    },
    "signedObject": {
    "s3": {
      "bucketName": "awscookbook505-dst-<<unique>>",
      "key": "signed-efd392ae-2503-4c78-963f-8f40a58d770f.zip"
    }
    },
    "signingMaterial": {},
    "createdAt": "2021-06-13T11:52:51-04:00",
    "status": "Succeeded",
  ...
```

5. Retrieve the S3 object key of the resulting signed code:

```
OBJECT_KEY=$(aws s3api list-objects-v2 \
    --bucket awscookbook505-dst-$RANDOM_STRING \
    --prefix 'signed-' \
    --output text --query Contents[0].Key)
```

6. Create a Lambda function that uses the signed code:

```
LAMBDA_ARN=$(aws lambda create-function \
    --function-name AWSCookbook505Lambda \
    --runtime python3.8 \
    --package-type "Zip" \
    --code S3Bucket=awscookbook505-dst-$RANDOM_STRING,S3Key=$OBJECT_KEY \
    --code-signing-config-arn $CODE_SIGNING_CONFIG_ARN \
    --handler lambda_function.lambda_handler --publish \
    --role \
    arn:aws:iam::$AWS_ACCOUNT_ID:role/AWSCookbookLambdaRole \
    --output text --query FunctionArn)
```

7. Use this command to determine when the Lambda function has entered the active state:

```
aws lambda get-function --function-name $LAMBDA_ARN \
    --output text --query Configuration.State
```

Validation checks. View your Lambda function in that console. Notice that you can't edit the code. You will see the message, "Your function has signed code and can't be edited inline."

Cleanup

Follow the steps in this recipe's folder in the chapter code repository (*https://github.com/AWSCookbook/Serverless*).

Discussion

Security-focused administrators and application developers can use this approach to implement a DevSecOps strategy by enforcing rules that allow only trusted code to be deployed in a given environment. By using AWS Signer (*https://oreil.ly/sPLFP*), you can ensure that you are running only trusted code in your environments. This helps meet compliance requirements and increases the security posture of your application.

By using a digital signature generated by AWS Signer, your code is validated against a cryptographic fingerprint, and enforcement policies can be applied to restrict the deployment and execution of code. This capability paves the way to a strategic shift from "reactive" to "preventive" controls in your security and compliance governance.

Challenge 1

Make a modification to the source code, sign it, and update the Lambda function.

Challenge 2

You can change your `CodeSigningPolicies` from `Warn` to `Enforce`—this will block deployments if validation checks of the signature aren't successful. Deploy a function that leverages this capability to ensure you are running only signed code in your environment:

```
"CodeSigningPolicies": {
        "UntrustedArtifactOnDeployment": "Warn"
    },
```

5.6 Packaging Lambda Code in a Container Image

Problem

You want to use your existing container-based development processes and tooling to package your serverless code.

Solution

Create a Docker image and push it to an Amazon Elastic Container Registry (ECR) repository. Create a Lambda function with the `package-type` of `Image` and code that references an image URL in ECR (see Figure 5-6).

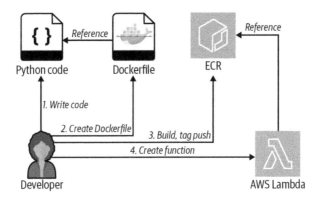

Figure 5-6. Deploying Lambda code packaged in a Docker image

Prerequisites

- ECR repository
- IAM role that allows the Lambda function to execute (provided in chapter prerequisites)
- Docker installed

Preparation

Follow the steps in this recipe's folder in the chapter code repository (*https://github.com/AWSCookbook/Serverless*).

Steps

1. Get ECR login information and pass to Docker:

   ```
   aws ecr get-login-password | docker login --username AWS \
       --password-stdin $AWS_ACCOUNT_ID.dkr.ecr.$AWS_REGION.amazonaws.com
   ```

   You should see output similar to the following:

   ```
   Login Succeeded
   ```

2. Create a file called *app.py* with the following code that you would like to execute in Lambda (file provided in the repository):

   ```
   import sys
   def handler(event, context):
       return 'Hello from the AWS Cookbook ' + sys.version + '!'
   ```

3. Create a file called *Dockerfile* with the following content that builds on an AWS-provided base image and references your Python code (file provided in the repository):

   ```
   FROM public.ecr.aws/lambda/python:3.8
   ```

```
COPY app.py   ./
CMD ["app.handler"]
```

4. In the folder where the *Dockerfile* and *app.py* files exist, build the container image. The process will take a few minutes to complete:

```
docker build -t aws-cookbook506-image .
```

You should see output similar to the following:

```
[+] Building 19.1s (4/6)
 => [internal] load build definition from Dockerfile
    0.0s
 => => transferring dockerfile: 36B
    0.0s
 => [internal] load .dockerignore
    0.0s
 => => transferring context: 2B
    0.0s
 => [internal] load metadata for public.ecr.aws/lambda/python:3.8
    2.2s
 => [internal] load build context
    0.0s
 ...
```

5. Add an additional tag to the image to allow it to be pushed to ECR:

```
docker tag \
    aws-cookbook506-image:latest \
    $AWS_ACCOUNT_ID.dkr.ecr.$AWS_REGION.amazonaws.com/aws-cookbook-506repo:latest
```

6. Push the image to the ECR repository. The process should take a few minutes to complete:

```
docker push \
    $AWS_ACCOUNT_ID.dkr.ecr.$AWS_REGION.amazonaws.com/aws-cookbook-506repo:latest
```

You should see output similar to the following:

```
The push refers to repository [111111111111.dkr.ecr.us-east-1.amazonaws.com/aws-
cookbook-506repo]
5efc5a3f50dd: Pushed
a1f8e0568112: Pushing [=====>                        ]    10.3MB/98.4MB
bcf453d1de13: Pushing [>                             ]   3.244MB/201.2MB
f6ae2f36d5d7: Pushing [=============================>]   4.998MB/8.204MB
5959c8f9752b: Pushed
3e5452c20c48: Pushed
9c4b6b04eac3: Pushing [>
```

7. Create a Lambda function with the Docker image by specifying a `--code` value that is the `ImageUri` of the Docker image :

```
LAMBDA_ARN=$(aws lambda create-function \
    --function-name AWSCookbook506Lambda \
    --package-type "Image" \
    --code ImageUri=$AWS_ACCOUNT_ID.dkr.ecr.$AWS_REGION.amazonaws.com/aws-
cookbook-506repo:latest \
    --role \
    arn:aws:iam::$AWS_ACCOUNT_ID:role/AWSCookbookLambdaRole \
    --output text --query FunctionArn)
```

The `--runtime` and `--handler` parameters are not necessary or supported when creating a function that uses a container image.

Use this command to determine when the Lambda function has entered the active state:

```
aws lambda get-function --function-name $LAMBDA_ARN \
    --output text --query Configuration.State
```

Validation checks. In the AWS Console, navigate to the Lambda→Functions menu. Notice that the "Package type" for your function is `Image`.

Invoke the function and view the response:

```
aws lambda invoke \
    --function-name $LAMBDA_ARN response.json && cat response.json
```

You should see output similar to the following:

```
{
  "StatusCode": 200,
  "ExecutedVersion": "$LATEST"
}
"Hello from the AWS Cookbook 3.8.8 (default, Mar 8 2021, 20:13:42) \n[GCC 7.3.1
20180712 (Red Hat 7.3.1-12)]!"
```

Cleanup

Follow the steps in this recipe's folder in the chapter code repository (*https://github.com/AWSCookbook/Serverless*).

Discussion

If your application code is packaged in container images, AWS Lambda provides this ability to package your function code inside container images. This allows for alignment with existing build, test, package, and deploy pipelines that you may already be using. You can package application code up to 10 GB in size for your functions. You can use the base images that AWS provides or create your own images, as long as you include a runtime interface client (*https://oreil.ly/N4wd7*) that is required by the Lambda runtime environment.

You can store your container images on Amazon ECR, and your function must be in the same account as the ECR repository where you have stored your container image.

Challenge

Update the application code, create a new image, push it to ECR, and update the Lambda function.

5.7 Automating CSV Import into DynamoDB from S3 with Lambda

Problem

You need to load data from S3 into DynamoDB when files are uploaded to S3.

Solution

Use a Lambda function to load the S3 data into DynamoDB and configure an S3 notification specifying the Lambda function to trigger on S3:PutObject events (see Figure 5-7).

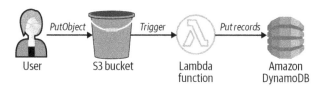

Figure 5-7. Using a Lambda function to load data into a DynamoDB table

Steps

1. Navigate to this recipe's directory in the chapter repository:

```
cd 507-Importing-CSV-to-DynamoDB-from-S3
```

2. Create a DynamoDB table:

```
aws dynamodb create-table \
    --table-name 'AWSCookbook507' \
    --attribute-definitions 'AttributeName=UserID,AttributeType=S' \
    --key-schema 'AttributeName=UserID,KeyType=HASH' \
    --sse-specification 'Enabled=true,SSEType=KMS' \
    --provisioned-throughput \
    'ReadCapacityUnits=5,WriteCapacityUnits=5'
```

3. Set a unique suffix to use for the S3 bucket name:

```
RANDOM_STRING=$(aws secretsmanager get-random-password \
    --exclude-punctuation --exclude-uppercase \
    --password-length 6 --require-each-included-type \
    --output text \
    --query RandomPassword)
```

4. Create an S3 bucket:

```
aws s3api create-bucket --bucket awscookbook507-$RANDOM_STRING
```

5. Create a role for a Lambda function allowing S3 and DynamoDB usage (file provided in the repository):

```
aws iam create-role --role-name AWSCookbook507Lambda \
    --assume-role-policy-document file://assume-role-policy.json
```

6. Attach the IAM managed policy for `AmazonS3ReadOnlyAccess` to the IAM role:

```
aws iam attach-role-policy --role-name AWSCookbook507Lambda \
    --policy-arn arn:aws:iam::aws:policy/AmazonS3ReadOnlyAccess
```

7. Attach the IAM managed policy for `AmazonDynamoDBFullAccess` to the IAM role:

```
aws iam attach-role-policy --role-name AWSCookbook507Lambda \
    --policy-arn arn:aws:iam::aws:policy/AmazonDynamoDBFullAccess
```

> It is best to scope the Lambda function permission to the spe-
> cific DynamoDB table resource rather than `AmazonDynamoDB`
> `FullAccess` (we used it for simplicity here). See Recipe 1.2 for
> details on how to create a more narrowly scoped permission.

8. Attach the `AWSLambdaBasicExecutionRole` IAM managed policy to the IAM role:

```
aws iam attach-role-policy --role-name AWSCookbook507Lambda \
    --policy-arn arn:aws:iam::aws:policy/service-role/AWSLambdaBasicExecutionRole
```

9. Zip the function code:

```
zip lambda_function.zip lambda_function.py
```

10. Create a Lambda function by using the provided code and specifying the code:

```
LAMBDA_ARN=$(aws lambda create-function \
    --function-name AWSCookbook507Lambda \
    --runtime python3.8 \
    --package-type "Zip" \
    --zip-file fileb://lambda_function.zip \
    --handler lambda_function.lambda_handler --publish \
    --environment Variables={bucket=awscookbook507-$RANDOM_STRING} \
    --role \
    arn:aws:iam::$AWS_ACCOUNT_ID:role/AWSCookbook507Lambda \
    --output text --query FunctionArn)
```

11. Grant the S3 service invoke permissions for the Lambda function:

```
aws lambda add-permission --function-name $LAMBDA_ARN \
    --action lambda:InvokeFunction --statement-id s3invoke \
    --principal s3.amazonaws.com
```

12. Create a *notification-template.json* file to use as the event definition for automatically triggering the Lambda function when your file (*sample_data.csv*) is uploaded. A file you can use is provided in the repository:

```
{
  "LambdaFunctionConfigurations": [
    {
      "Id": "awscookbook507event",
      "LambdaFunctionArn": "LAMBDA_ARN",
      "Events": [
        "s3:ObjectCreated:*"
      ],
      "Filter": {
        "Key": {
          "FilterRules": [
            {
```

```
                    "Name": "prefix",
                    "Value": "sample_data.csv"
                  }
                ]
              }
            }
          }
        ]
      }
```

13. You can use the sed command to replace the values in the provided *notification-template.json* file with the environment variables you have created:

    ```
    sed -e "s/LAMBDA_ARN/${LAMBDA_ARN}/g" \
        notification-template.json > notification.json
    ```

14. Configure the S3 bucket notification settings to trigger the Lambda function (one-liner config). NotificationConfiguration→LambdaConfigurations→Lambda ARN:

    ```
    aws s3api put-bucket-notification-configuration \
        --bucket awscookbook507-$RANDOM_STRING \
        --notification-configuration file://notification.json
    ```

15. Upload a file to S3 to trigger the import:

    ```
    aws s3 cp ./sample_data.csv s3://awscookbook507-$RANDOM_STRING
    ```

Validation checks.   View the results from your DynamoDB console, or use this CLI command to scan the table:

```
aws dynamodb scan --table-name AWSCookbook507
```

> One of the great features of DynamoDB is that it provides AWS API endpoints for easy CRUD operations by your application via the AWS SDK.

Cleanup

Follow the steps in this recipe's folder in the chapter code repository (*https://github.com/AWSCookbook/Serverless*).

Discussion

You can use AWS Lambda and Amazon DynamoDB together to build applications with massively scalable database persistence while minimizing the operational overhead required. Software architects and developers who are looking to build applications without worrying about server infrastructure may find it useful to use these two services together.

At the time of this writing, Lambda functions time out after 900 seconds (*https://oreil.ly/MnJNV*). This could cause an issue with large CSV files or if the DynamoDB table does not have sufficient write capacity.

Event-driven applications are also an important concept in building modern cloud-native applications on AWS. When you created the *notification.json* file, you specified your Lambda function and the S3 bucket, as well as a key pattern to watch for uploads to trigger the Lambda function when an object is put into the bucket. Using event-driven architecture helps minimize the cost and complexity associated with running your applications because the function logic is run only when needed.

Challenge 1

Add some new data to the *sample_data.csv* file, delete the file from your bucket, and re-upload the file to trigger the new import. Note that the existing data will remain, and the new data will be added.

Challenge 2

Change the S3 notification and the Lambda function to allow for other filenames to be used with the solution.

Challenge 3

Create a fine-grained IAM policy for your Lambda function that scopes down the function's granted access to the DynamoDB table.

5.8 Reducing Lambda Startup Times with Provisioned Concurrency

Problem

You need to ensure that a predetermined number (five) of invocations to your serverless function are as fast as possible. You need to eliminate any latency associated with cold starts.

Solution

Create a Lambda function and set the function concurrency to 5 (see Figure 5-8).

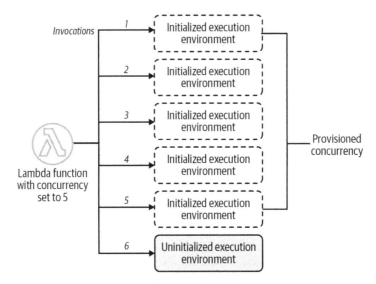

Figure 5-8. Provisioned concurrency for a Lambda function

Prerequisite

- IAM role that allows the Lambda function to execute (provided in chapter prerequisites)

Steps

1. Create a file called *lambda_function.py* with the following content (file provided in the repository):

```
from datetime import datetime
import time

def lambda_handler(event, context):
    time.sleep(5)
    print('AWS Cookbook Function run at {}'.format(str(datetime.now())))
```

2. Zip the function code:

```
zip lambda_function.zip lambda_function.py
```

3. Create a Lambda function:

```
aws lambda create-function \
    --function-name AWSCookbook508Lambda \
    --runtime python3.8 \
    --package-type "Zip" \
    --zip-file fileb://lambda_function.zip \
    --handler lambda_function.lambda_handler --publish \
    --timeout 20 \
    --role \
    arn:aws:iam::$AWS_ACCOUNT_ID:role/AWSCookbookLambdaRole
```

4. Use this command to determine when the Lambda function has entered the active state:

```
aws lambda get-function --function-name AWSCookbook509Lambda \
    --output text --query Configuration.State
```

Lambda function aliases (*https://oreil.ly/8vXHA*) allow you to reference a specific version of a function. Each Lambda function can have one or more aliases. The initial alias is named LATEST.

5. Configure the provisioned concurrency for the Lambda function:

```
aws lambda put-provisioned-concurrency-config \
    --function-name AWSCookbook508Lambda \
    --qualifier LATEST \
    --provisioned-concurrent-executions 5
```

Validation checks. Invoke the function six times in a row to see the limit hit:

```
aws lambda invoke --function-name AWSCookbook508Lambda response.json &
aws lambda invoke --function-name AWSCookbook508Lambda response.json
```

The Lambda function you deployed needs to be run in parallel to demonstrate the capability of the provisioned concurrency feature. You may want to write a simple script which runs this command multiple times in parallel to prove that the provisioned concurrency enabled.

Cleanup

Follow the steps in this recipe's folder in the chapter code repository (*https://github.com/AWSCookbook/Serverless*).

Discussion

Your code's execution environment provisioning is handled for you by the Lambda service. This is a benefit of it being a fully managed service on AWS. Since the execution environment is provisioned on demand, a small amount of time is required to provision this environment for you. This is referred to as a *cold start*. Lambda keeps your execution environment provisioned (or "warm") for a period of time so that if your function is invoked again, it will launch quickly. When you need your functions to respond quickly and achieve more concurrency, you can avoid the cold start and use provisioned concurrency to keep multiple copies of the execution environments "warm."

Some developers and software architects need to build solutions with time-sensitive requirements measured in milliseconds in microservice-based applications. When you use Lambda-provisioned concurrency, you minimize the amount of time your function needs to start up when it is invoked.

Challenge 1

Configure an API Gateway in front of your Lambda function and use a tool like bees with machine guns (*https://oreil.ly/EmxSn*) or ApacheBench (*https://oreil.ly/3i7WV*) to simulate user load.

Challenge 2

Configure application autoscaling to modify the provisioned concurrency for your Lambda function based on time and/or a performance metric (e.g., response time).

5.9 Accessing VPC Resources with Lambda

Problem

You need a serverless function to be able to access an ElastiCache cluster that has an endpoint in a VPC.

Solution

Create a Lambda function that has a Redis client connection and package and specifies VPC subnets and security groups. Then create ElastiCache subnet groups and an ElastiCache cluster. Invoke the Lambda and pass the cluster endpoint to the function to test (see Figure 5-9).

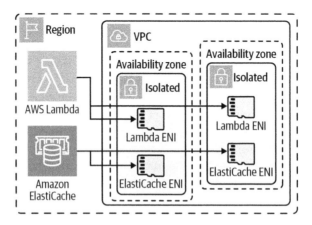

Figure 5-9. Lambda accessing an ElastiCache cluster in a VPC

Prerequisite

- IAM role that allows the Lambda function to execute (provided in chapter prerequisites)

Preparation

Follow the steps in this recipe's folder in the chapter code repository (*https://github.com/AWSCookbook/Serverless*).

Steps

1. You need to give your Lambda function the ability to execute within a VPC, so attach the IAM managed policy for AWSLambdaVPCAccess to the IAM role (created in the chapter prerequisites):

```
aws iam attach-role-policy --role-name AWSCookbookLambdaRole \
    --policy-arn arn:aws:iam::aws:policy/service-role/
AWSLambdaVPCAccessExecutionRole
```

2. Install the Redis Python package to the current directory from the Python Package Index (PyPI):

```
pip install redis -t .
```

3. Zip the function code:

```
zip -r lambda_function.zip lambda_function.py redis*
```

4. Create a security group for the Lambda:

```
LAMBDA_SG_ID=$(aws ec2 create-security-group \
    --group-name Cookbook509LambdaSG \
    --description "Lambda Security Group" --vpc-id $VPC_ID \
    --output text --query GroupId)
```

5. Create a Lambda function that will respond to HTTP requests:

```
LAMBDA_ARN=$(aws lambda create-function \
    --function-name AWSCookbook509Lambda \
    --runtime python3.8 \
    --package-type "Zip" \
    --zip-file fileb://lambda_function.zip \
    --handler lambda_function.lambda_handler --publish \
    --role arn:aws:iam::$AWS_ACCOUNT_ID:role/AWSCookbookLambdaRole \
    --output text --query FunctionArn \
    --vpc-config SubnetIds=${TRIMMED_ISOLATED_SUBNETS},SecurityGroupIds=$
{LAMBDA_SG_ID})
```

6. Create an ElastiCache subnet group:

```
aws elasticache create-cache-subnet-group \
    --cache-subnet-group-name "AWSCookbook509CacheSG" \
    --cache-subnet-group-description "AWSCookbook509CacheSG" \
    --subnet-ids $ISOLATED_SUBNETS
```

7. Create an ElastiCache Redis cluster with one node:

```
aws elasticache create-cache-cluster \
    --cache-cluster-id "AWSCookbook509CacheCluster" \
    --cache-subnet-group-name AWSCookbook509CacheSG \
    --engine redis \
    --cache-node-type cache.t3.micro \
    --num-cache-nodes 1
```

Wait for the cache cluster to be available.

8. Invoke the function and view the response replacing *HOSTNAME* with the host name of your cluster:

```
aws lambda invoke \
    --cli-binary-format raw-in-base64-out \
    --function-name $LAMBDA_ARN \
    --payload '{ "hostname": "HOSTNAME" }' \
    response.json && cat response.json
```

Cleanup

Follow the steps in this recipe's folder in the chapter code repository (*https://github.com/AWSCookbook/Serverless*).

Discussion

By default, Lambda functions do not have access to any VPC that you may have provisioned in your AWS environment. However, Lambda does support VPC connectivity by provisioning network interfaces in your VPC. ElastiCache requires compute nodes that have network interfaces in your VPC, so you need to configure Lambda within your VPC to allow it to access the ElastiCache nodes that you provision.

The compute memory that your function uses is not persistent if the function is invoked when the execution environment is spun down and restarted. If your application requires access to memory persistence (for example, in HTTP sessions), you can use the Amazon ElastiCache service to implement redis or memcached for session storage and key/value storage. These common solutions implement in-memory cache for fast read/write and allow you to scale horizontally with your application while maintaining memory persistence that your application requires.

Challenge 1

Configure your Lambda function to read and write additional values to Amazon ElastiCache for Redis.

CHAPTER 6

Containers

6.0 Introduction

A *container*, put simply, packages application code, binaries, configuration files, and libraries together into a single package, called a *container image*. By packaging everything together in this way, you can develop, test, and run applications with control and consistency. You can quickly start packaging up and testing containers that you build locally, while ensuring that the exact same runtime environment is present regardless of where it is running. This generally reduces the time it takes to build something and offer it to a wide audience, and ensures consistency whenever you deploy.

Containers are wholly "contained" environments that leverage the underlying compute and memory capabilities on the host where they are running (your laptop, a server in a closet, or the cloud). Multiple containers can be run on the same host at once without conflicts. You can also have multiple containers running with the intention of them communicating with one another. Imagine that you have a frontend web application running as a container that accesses a container running a backend for your website, and you might want to run multiple instances of them at once to handle more traffic. Running multiple containers at once and ensuring they are always available can present some challenges, which is why you enlist the help of a container *orchestrator*. Popular orchestrators come in many flavors, but some of the common ones you may have heard of are Kubernetes and Docker Swarm.

You have options for running containers on AWS, such as Amazon Elastic Container Service (Amazon ECS) and Amazon Elastic Kubernetes Service (Amazon EKS) as container orchestrators, and Amazon Elastic Cloud Compute (Amazon EC2) for deployments with custom requirements. Both of the AWS container orchestrator services mentioned (Amazon ECS and Amazon EKS) can run workloads on Amazon

EC2 or on the fully managed AWS Fargate compute engine. In other words, you can choose to control the underlying EC2 instance (or instances) responsible for running your containers on Amazon ECS and Amazon EKS, allowing some level of customization to your host, or you can use Fargate, which is fully managed by AWS—you don't have to worry about instance management. You can even use ECS and EKS within your own datacenter using ECS Anywhere and EKS Anywhere. AWS provides a comprehensive listing of all up-to-date container services on its website (*https://aws.amazon.com/containers*).

Some AWS services (AWS CodeDeploy, AWS CodePipeline, and Amazon Elastic Container Registry) can help streamline the development lifecycle and provide automation to your workflow. These integrate well with Amazon ECS and Amazon EKS. Some examples of AWS services that provide network capabilities are Amazon Virtual Private Cloud, AWS Elastic Load Balancing, AWS Cloud Map, and Amazon Route 53.You can address your logging and monitoring concerns with Amazon CloudWatch and the Amazon Managed Service for Prometheus (*https://aws.amazon.com/prometheus*). Fine-grained security capabilities can be provided by AWS Identity and Access Management (IAM) and AWS Key Management System (KMS). By following the recipes in this chapter, you will see how some of these services combine to meet your needs.

Workstation Configuration

Follow the "General workstation setup steps for CLI recipes" on page xvii to validate your configuration and set up the required environment variables. Then, clone the chapter code repository:

```
git clone https://github.com/AWSCookbook/Containers
```

Chapter Prerequisites

Docker installation and validation

Docker Desktop (*https://oreil.ly/Wfv89*) is recommended for Windows and Mac users; Docker Linux Engine (*https://oreil.ly/taxpH*) is recommended for Linux users. In the following recipes, you'll use Docker to create a consistent working environment on your particular platform. Be sure to install the latest stable version of Docker for your OS.

MacOS.

1. Follow instructions from Docker Desktop: *https://docs.docker.com/docker-for-mac/install.*

2. Run the Docker Desktop application after installation.

Windows.

1. Follow instructions from Docker Desktop: *https://docs.docker.com/desktop/windows/install.*

2. Run the Docker Desktop application after installation.

Linux.

1. Follow instructions from Docker Desktop: *https://docs.docker.com/engine/install.*

2. Start the Docker daemon on your distribution:

Validation the installation of Docker on your workstation with the following command:

```
docker --version
```

You should see output similar to the following:

```
Docker version 19.03.13, build 4484c46d9d
```

Run the `docker images` command to list images on your local machine:

```
REPOSITORY     TAG        IMAGE ID        CREATED         SIZE
```

6.1 Building, Tagging, and Pushing a Container Image to Amazon ECR

Problem

You need a repository to store built and tagged container images.

Solution

First, you will create a repository in Amazon ECR. Next, you will create a Dockerfile and use it to build a Docker image. Finally, you will apply two tags to the container image and push them both to the newly created ECR repository. This process is illustrated in Figure 6-1.

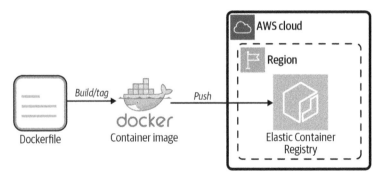

Figure 6-1. Solution workflow of build, tag, and push for container images

Steps

1. Log into the AWS Management Console and search for Elastic Container Registry. Click the "Create repository" button.

   Give your repository a name, keep all defaults (as shown in Figure 6-2), scroll to the bottom, and click "Create repository" again to finish.

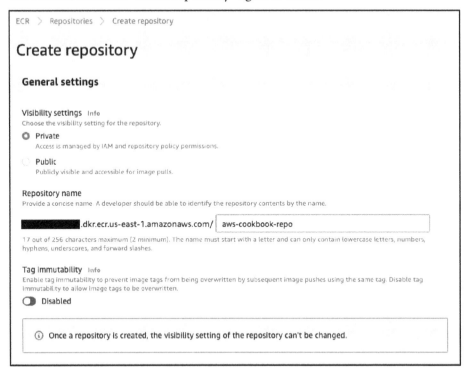

Figure 6-2. ECR repository creation

You now have a repository created on Amazon ECR that you can use to store container images. An example of the ECR console is shown in Figure 6-3.

Figure 6-3. Screenshot of created ECR repository

Alternatively, you can also create an ECR repository from the command line:

```
REPO=aws-cookbook-repo && \
        aws ecr create-repository --repository-name $REPO
```

You should see output similar to the following:

```
{
  "repository": {
    "repositoryArn": "arn:aws:ecr:us-east-1:111111111111:repository/aws-cookbook-repo",
    "registryId": "111111111111",
    "repositoryName": "aws-cookbook-repo",
    "repositoryUri": "611652777867.dkr.ecr.us-east-1.amazonaws.com/aws-cookbook-repo",
    "createdAt": "2021-10-02T19:57:56-04:00",
    "imageTagMutability": "MUTABLE",
    "imageScanningConfiguration": {
      "scanOnPush": false
    },
    "encryptionConfiguration": {
      "encryptionType": "AES256"
    }
  }
}
```

2. Create a simple Dockerfile:

```
echo FROM nginx:latest > Dockerfile
```

This command creates a Dockerfile (*https://oreil.ly/VCCb7*) that contains a single line instructing the Docker Engine to use the `nginx:latest` image as the base image. Since you use only the base image with no other lines in the Dockerfile, the resulting image is identical to the `nginx:latest` image. You could include some HTML files within this image by using the `COPY` and `ADD` Dockerfile directives.

3. Build and tag the image. This step may take a few moments as it downloads and combines the image layers:

```
docker build . -t \
    $AWS_ACCOUNT_ID.dkr.ecr.$AWS_REGION.amazonaws.com/aws-cookbook-repo:latest
```

4. Add an additional tag:

```
docker tag \
    $AWS_ACCOUNT_ID.dkr.ecr.$AWS_REGION.amazonaws.com/aws-cookbook-repo:latest \
    $AWS_ACCOUNT_ID.dkr.ecr.$AWS_REGION.amazonaws.com/aws-cookbook-repo:1.0
```

5. Get Docker login information:

```
aws ecr get-login-password | docker login --username AWS \
    --password-stdin $AWS_ACCOUNT_ID.dkr.ecr.us-east-1.amazonaws.com
```

Here is the output:

```
Login Succeeded
```

An authorization token needs to be provided each time an operation is executed against a private repository. Tokens last for 12 hours, so the command you ran would need to be manually refreshed at that interval on your command line. To help you with automating the task of obtaining authorization tokens, you can use the ECR Docker Credential Helper, available from the awslabs GitHub repository (*https://oreil.ly/xI0xD*).

6. Push each image tag to Amazon ECR:

```
docker push \
    $AWS_ACCOUNT_ID.dkr.ecr.$AWS_REGION.amazonaws.com/aws-cookbook-repo:latest
```

```
docker push \
    $AWS_ACCOUNT_ID.dkr.ecr.$AWS_REGION.amazonaws.com/aws-cookbook-repo:1.0
```

You will see "Layer already exists" for the image layer uploads on the second push. This is because the image already exists in the ECR repository due to the first push, but this step is still required to add the additional tag.

Validation checks. Now you can view both of the tagged images in Amazon ECR from the console, as shown in Figure 6-4.

Figure 6-4. Screenshot of the image with two tags

Alternatively, you can use the AWS CLI to list the images:

```
aws ecr list-images --repository-name aws-cookbook-repo
```

You should see output similar to the following:

```
{
    "imageIds": [
        {
            "imageDigest":
"sha256:99d0a53e3718cef59443558607d1e100b325d6a2b678cd2a48b05e5e22ffeb49",
            "imageTag": "1.0"
        },
        {
            "imageDigest":
"sha256:99d0a53e3718cef59443558607d1e100b325d6a2b678cd2a48b05e5e22ffeb49",
            "imageTag": "latest"
        }
    ]
}
```

Cleanup

Follow the steps in this recipe's folder in the chapter code repository (*https://github.com/AWSCookbook/Containers*).

Discussion

Having a repository for your container images is an important foundational component of the application development process. A private repository for your container images that you control is a best practice to increase the security of your application development process. You can grant access to other AWS accounts, IAM entities, and

AWS services with permissions for Amazon ECR. Now that you know how to create an ECR repository, you will be able to store your container images and use them with AWS services.

 Amazon ECR supports the popular Docker Image Manifest V2, Schema 2 (*https://oreil.ly/FeYVY*) and most recently Open Container Initiative (OCI) (*https://oreil.ly/tzgdd*) images. It can translate between these formats on pull. Legacy support is available for Manifest V2, Schema 1, and Amazon ECR can translate on the fly when interacting with legacy Docker client versions. The experience should be seamless for most Docker client versions in use today.

Container tagging allows you to version and keep track of your container images. You can apply multiple tags to an image, which can help you implement your versioning strategy and deployment process. For example, you may always refer to a "latest" tagged image in your dev environment, but your production environment can be locked to a specific version tag. The Docker CLI pushes tagged images to the repository and the tags can be used with pulls.

Challenge

Modify the Dockerfile, build a new image, tag it with a new version number, and put it to ECR.

6.2 Scanning Images for Security Vulnerabilities on Push to Amazon ECR

Problem

You want to automatically scan your container images for security vulnerabilities each time you push to a repository.

Solution

Enable automatic image scanning on a repository in Amazon ECR, push an image, and observe the scan results, as shown in Figure 6-5.

Prerequisite

- ECR repository

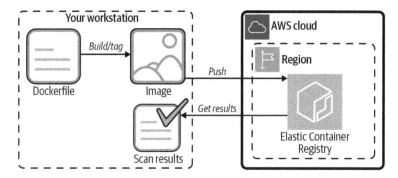

Figure 6-5. Container image scanning solution workflow

Preparation

Follow the steps in this recipe's folder in the chapter code repository (*https://github.com/AWSCookbook/Containers*).

Steps

1. Rather than building a new container image from a Dockerfile (as you did in Recipe 6.1), this time you are going to pull an old NGINX container image:

   ```
   docker pull nginx:1.14.1
   ```

2. On the command line, apply the scanning configuration to the repository you created:

   ```
   REPO=aws-cookbook-repo && \
       aws ecr put-image-scanning-configuration \
       --repository-name $REPO \
       --image-scanning-configuration scanOnPush=true
   ```

3. Get Docker login information:

   ```
   aws ecr get-login-password | docker login --username AWS \
       --password-stdin $AWS_ACCOUNT_ID.dkr.ecr.$AWS_REGION.amazonaws.com
   ```

4. Apply a tag to the image so that you can push it to the ECR repository:

   ```
   docker tag nginx:1.14.1 \
       $AWS_ACCOUNT_ID.dkr.ecr.$AWS_REGION.amazonaws.com/aws-cookbook-repo:old
   ```

5. Push the image:

   ```
   docker push \
       $AWS_ACCOUNT_ID.dkr.ecr.$AWS_REGION.amazonaws.com/aws-cookbook-repo:old
   ```

Validation checks. Shortly after the push is complete, you can examine the results of the security scan of the image in JSON format:

```
aws ecr describe-image-scan-findings \
    --repository-name aws-cookbook-repo --image-id imageTag=old
```

You should see output similar to the following:

```
{
  "imageScanFindings": {
    "findings": [
      {
        "name": "CVE-2019-3462",
        "description": "Incorrect sanitation of the 302 redirect field in HTTP
transport method of apt versions 1.4.8 and earlier can lead to content injection by
a MITM attacker, potentially leading to remote code execution on the target
machine.",
        "uri": "https://security-tracker.debian.org/tracker/CVE-2019-3462",
        "severity": "CRITICAL",
        "attributes": [
          {
            "key": "package_version",
            "value": "1.4.8"
          },
```

Cleanup

Follow the steps in this recipe's folder in the chapter code repository (*https://github.com/AWSCookbook/Containers*).

 Amazon ECR has a safety mechanism built in that does not let you delete a repository containing images. If the repository is not empty and the `delete-repository` command is failing, you can bypass this check by adding `--force` to the `delete-repository` command.

Discussion

The Common Vulnerabilities and Exposures (CVEs) (*https://cve.mitre.org*) database from the open source Clair project (*https://github.com/quay/clair*) is used by Amazon ECR for vulnerability scanning (*https://oreil.ly/ZSiob*). You are provided a Common Vulnerability Scoring System (CVSS) score to indicate the severity of any detected vulnerabilities. This helps you detect and remediate vulnerabilities in your container image. You can configure alerts for newly discovered vulnerabilities in images by using Amazon EventBridge and Amazon Simple Notification Service (Amazon SNS).

 The scanning feature does not continuously scan your images, so it is important to push your image versions routinely (or trigger a manual scan).

You can retrieve the results of the last scan for an image at any time with the command used in the last step of this recipe. Furthermore, you can use these commands as part of an automated CI/CD process that may validate whether or not an image has a certain CVSS score before deploying.

Challenge 1

Remediate the vulnerability by updating the image with the latest NGINX container image.

Challenge 2

Configure an SNS topic to send you an email when vulnerabilities are detected in your repository.

6.3 Deploying a Container Using Amazon Lightsail

Problem

You need to quickly deploy a container-based application and access it securely over the internet.

Solution

Deploy a plain NGINX container that listens on port 80 to Lightsail (*https://oreil.ly/SaZCa*). Lightsail provides a way to quickly deploy applications to AWS. The workflow is shown in Figure 6-6.

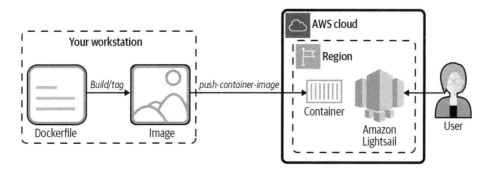

Figure 6-6. Amazon Lightsail serving a container image

Prerequisite

- In addition to Docker Desktop and the AWS CLI (version 2), you need to install the Lightsail Control plugin (lightsailctl) (*https://oreil.ly/Tn2B9*) for the AWS CLI.

Preparation

Follow the steps in this recipe's folder in the chapter code repository (*https://github.com/AWSCookbook/Containers*).

Steps

> Several power levels are available for Lightsail, each of which is priced according to the amount of compute power your container needs. We selected nano in this example. A list of power levels and associated costs is available in the Lightsail pricing guide (*https://oreil.ly/DSPNv*).

1. Once you have lightsailctl installed, create a new container service and give it a name, power parameter, and scale parameter:

   ```
   aws lightsail create-container-service \
       --service-name awscookbook --power nano --scale 1
   ```

   You should see output similar to the following:

   ```
   {
     "containerService": {
       "containerServiceName": "awscookbook",
       "arn": "arn:aws:lightsail:us-east-1:111111111111:ContainerService/124633d7-
   b625-48b2-b066-5826012904d5",
       "createdAt": "2020-11-15T10:10:55-05:00",
       "location": {
         "availabilityZone": "all",
         "regionName": "us-east-1"
       },
       "resourceType": "ContainerService",
       "tags": [],
       "power": "nano",
       "powerId": "nano-1",
       "state": "PENDING",
       "scale": 1,
       "isDisabled": false,
       "principalArn": "",
       "privateDomainName": "awscookbook.service.local",
       "url": "https://awscookbook.<<unique-id>>.us-east-1.cs.amazonlightsail.com/"
     }
   }
   ```

2. Pull a plain NGINX container image to use that listens on port 80/TCP.

   ```
   docker pull nginx
   ```

   Use the following command to ensure that the state of your container service has entered the READY state (this may take a few minutes):

   ```
   aws lightsail get-container-services --service-name awscookbook
   ```

3. When the container service is ready, push the container image to Lightsail:

   ```
   aws lightsail push-container-image --service-name awscookbook \
       --label awscookbook --image nginx
   ```

   You should see output similar to the following:

   ```
   7b5417cae114: Pushed
   Image "nginx" registered.
   Refer to this image as ":awscookbook.awscookbook.1" in deployments.
   ```

You can specify public image repositories or push your own image to your container service within Amazon Lightsail. Rather than using a private Amazon ECR location, your Lightsail images are kept within the Lightsail service. For more information, refer to the Lightsail documentation for image locations (*https://oreil.ly/Hi4Ny*).

4. Now you will associate the image you pushed with the container service you created for deployment. Create a file with the following contents and save it as *lightsail.json* (file provided in the code repository (*https://github.com/AWSCookbook/Containers*)):

```
{
  "serviceName": "awscookbook",
  "containers": {
    "awscookbook": {
      "image": ":awscookbook.awscookbook.1",
      "ports": {
        "80": "HTTP"
      }
    }
  },
  "publicEndpoint": {
    "containerName": "awscookbook",
    "containerPort": 80
  }
}
```

5. Create the deployment:

```
aws lightsail create-container-service-deployment \
    --service-name awscookbook --cli-input-json file://lightsail.json
```

View your container service again and wait for the ACTIVE state. This may take a few minutes:

```
aws lightsail get-container-services --service-name awscookbook
```

Note the endpoint URL at the end of the output.

Validation checks. Now, visit the endpoint URL in your browser, or use the curl on the command line (e.g., url: `https://awscookbook.un94eb3cd7hgk.us-east-1.cs.amazonlightsail.com`):

```
curl <<URL endpoint>>
```

You should see output similar to the following:

```
...
<h1>Welcome to nginx!</h1>
...
```

Cleanup

Follow the steps in this recipe's folder in the chapter code repository (*https://github.com/AWSCookbook/Containers*).

Discussion

Lightsail manages the TLS certificate, load balancer, compute, and storage. It can also manage MySQL and PostgreSQL databases as part of your deployment if your application requires it. Lightsail performs routine health checks on your application and will automatically replace a container you deploy that may have become unresponsive for some reason. Changing the power and scale parameters in the `lightsail create-container-service` command will allow you to create services for demanding workloads.

Using this recipe, you could deploy any common container-based application (e.g., Wordpress) and have it served on the internet in a short period of time. You could even point a custom domain alias (*https://oreil.ly/rB5Xf*) at your Lightsail deployment for an SEO-friendly URL.

Challenge

Scale your service so that it will be able to handle more traffic.

6.4 Deploying Containers Using AWS Copilot

Problem

You need a way to use your existing Dockerfile to quickly deploy and manage a load balanced web service using best practices in a private network.

Solution

Starting with a Dockerfile, you can use AWS Copilot (*https://oreil.ly/zH8YD*) to quickly deploy an application using an architecture shown in Figure 6-7.

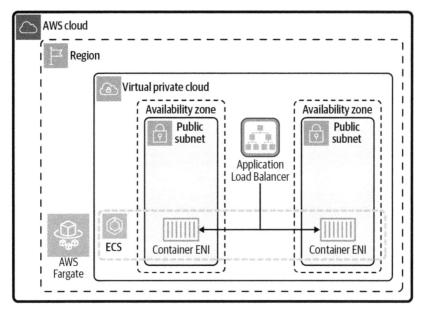

Figure 6-7. AWS Copilot load balanced web service infrastructure

Prerequisite

- AWS Copilot CLI (*https://oreil.ly/PvZlD*)

Preparation

Follow the steps in this recipe's folder in the chapter code repository (*https://github.com/AWSCookbook/Containers*).

Steps

1. Copilot requires an ECS service-linked role to allow Amazon ECS to perform actions on your behalf. This may already exist in your AWS account. To see if you have this role already, issue the following command:

   ```
   aws iam list-roles --path-prefix /aws-service-role/ecs.amazonaws.com/
   ```

   (If the role is displayed, you can skip the following role-creation step.)

   Create the ECS service-linked role if it does not exist:

   ```
   aws iam create-service-linked-role --aws-service-name ecs.amazonaws.com
   ```

IAM service-linked roles allow AWS services to securely interact with other AWS services on your behalf. See the AWS article (*https://oreil.ly/CwzCZ*) on using these roles.

2. cd to this recipe's directory in this chapter's code repository (*https://github.com/AWSCookbook/Containers*):

```
cd 604-Deploy-Container-With-Copilot-CLI
```

You could provide your own Dockerfile and content for this recipe. If you choose to use your own container with this recipe, ensure that the container listens on port 80/TCP. Or configure the alternate port with the copilot init command.

3. Now use AWS Copilot to deploy the sample NGINX Dockerfile to Amazon ECS:

```
copilot init --app web --name nginx --type 'Load Balanced Web Service' \
    --dockerfile './Dockerfile' --port 80 --deploy
```

If you don't specify any arguments to the copilot init command, it will walk you through a menu of options for your deployment.

The deployment will take a few moments. You can watch the progress of the deployment in your terminal.

Validation checks. After the deployment is complete, get information on the deployed service with this command:

```
copilot svc show
```

Cleanup

Follow the steps in this recipe's folder in the chapter code repository (*https://github.com/AWSCookbook/Containers*).

Discussion

Copilot exposes a command-line interface that simplifies deployments to Amazon ECS, AWS Fargate, and AWS App Runner. It helps streamline your development workflow and deployment lifecycle.

The `copilot init` command created a directory called *copilot* in your current working directory. You can view and customize the configuration by using the *manifest.yml* that is associated with your application.

 The test environment is the default environment created. You can add additional environments to suit your needs and keep your environments isolated from each other by using the `copilot env init` command.

Copilot configures all of the required resources for hosting containers on Amazon ECS according to many best practices. Some examples are deploying to multiple Availability Zones), using subnet tiers to segment traffic, and using AWS KMS to encrypt.

The AWS Copilot commands can also be embedded in your CI/CD pipeline to perform automated deployments. In fact, Copilot can orchestrate the creation and management of a CI/CD pipeline for you with the `copilot pipeline` command. For all of the current supported features and examples, visit the AWS Copilot home page (*https://aws.github.io/copilot-cli*).

Challenge

Reconfigure your Load Balanced Web Service to deploy to AWS App Runner (*https://oreil.ly/BvUTg*) instead of Amazon ECS.

6.5 Updating Containers with Blue/Green Deployments

Problem

You want to use a deployment strategy with your container-based application so you can update your application to the latest version without introducing downtime to customers, while also being able to easily roll back if the deployment was not successful.

Solution

Use AWS CodeDeploy to orchestrate your application deployments to Amazon ECS with the Blue/Green strategy, as shown in Figure 6-8.

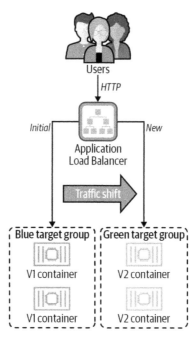

Figure 6-8. Blue/Green target group association

Preparation

Follow the steps in this recipe's folder in the chapter code repository (*https://github.com/AWSCookbook/Containers*).

Steps

1. With the CDK stack deployed, open a web browser and visit the `LOAD_BAL ANCER_DNS` address on TCP port 8080 that the CDK output displayed. You will see the "Blue" application running:

   ```
   E.g.:
   firefox $LOAD_BALANCER_DNS:8080
   or
   open http://$LOAD_BALANCER_DNS:8080
   ```

2. Create an IAM role with the statement in the provided *assume-role-policy.json* file using this command:

   ```
   aws iam create-role --role-name ecsCodeDeployRole \
       --assume-role-policy-document file://assume-role-policy.json
   ```

3. Attach the IAM managed policy for `CodeDeployRoleForECS` to the IAM role:

   ```
   aws iam attach-role-policy --role-name ecsCodeDeployRole \
       --policy-arn arn:aws:iam::aws:policy/AWSCodeDeployRoleForECS
   ```

4. Create a new ALB target group to use as the "Green" target group with CodeDeploy:

```
aws elbv2 create-target-group --name "GreenTG" --port 80 \
    --protocol HTTP --vpc-id $VPC_ID --target-type ip
```

5. Create the CodeDeploy application:

```
aws deploy create-application --application-name awscookbook-605 \
    --compute-platform ECS
```

CodeDeploy requires some configuration. We provided a template file for you (*codedeploy-template.json*) in this recipe's directory of the code repository (*https://github.com/AWSCookbook/Containers*).

6. Use the `sed` command to replace the values with the environment variables you exported with the *helper.py* script:

```
sed -e "s/AWS_ACCOUNT_ID/${AWS_ACCOUNT_ID}/g" \
    -e "s|PROD_LISTENER_ARN|${PROD_LISTENER_ARN}|g" \
    -e "s|TEST_LISTENER_ARN|${TEST_LISTENER_ARN}|g" \
    codedeploy-template.json > codedeploy.json
```

`sed` (short for *stream editor*) is a great tool to use for text find-and-replace operations as well as other types of text manipulation in your terminal sessions and scripts. In this case, `sed` is used to replace values in a template file with values output from `cdk deploy` set as environment variables.

7. Now, create a deployment group:

```
aws deploy create-deployment-group --cli-input-json file://codedeploy.json
```

AppSpec-template.yaml contains information about the application you are going to update. The CDK preprovisioned a task definition you can use.

8. Use the `sed` command to replace the value with the environment variable you exported with the *helper.py* script:

```
sed -e "s|FargateTaskGreenArn|${FARGATE_TASK_GREEN_ARN}|g" \
    appspec-template.yaml > appspec.yaml
```

9. Now copy the *AppSpec* file to the S3 bucket created by the CDK deployment so that CodeDeploy can use it to update the application:

```
aws s3 cp ./appspec.yaml s3://$BUCKET_NAME
```

10. One final configuration file needs to be created; this contains the instructions about the deployment. Use `sed` to modify the S3 bucket used in the *deployment-template.json* file:

```
sed -e "s|S3BucketName|${BUCKET_NAME}|g" \
    deployment-template.json > deployment.json
```

11. Now create a deployment with the deployment configuration:

```
aws deploy create-deployment --cli-input-json file://deployment.json
```

To get the status of the deployment, observe the status in the AWS Console (Developer Tools→CodeDeploy→Deployments, and click the deployment ID). You should see CodeDeploy in progress with the deployment, as shown in Figure 6-9.

Figure 6-9. Initial deployment status

Validation checks. Once the replacement task is serving 100% of the traffic, you can visit the same URL where you previously observed the Blue application running, replaced with the Green version of the application.

 You may need to refresh your browser or clear your cache to see the updated Green application.

Cleanup

Follow the steps in this recipe's folder in the chapter code repository (*https://github.com/AWSCookbook/Containers*).

Discussion

CodeDeploy offers several deployment strategies (*https://oreil.ly/18B4u*)—Canary, AllAtOnce, Blue/Green, etc.—and you can also create your own custom deployment strategies. You might customize the strategy to define a longer wait period for the cut-over window or to define other conditions to be met before traffic switchover occurs. In the default Blue/Green strategy, CodeDeploy keeps your previous version of the application running for five minutes while all traffic is routed to the new version. If you notice that the new version is not behaving properly, you can quickly route traffic back to the original version since it is still running in a separate AWS Application Load Balancer target group.

CodeDeploy uses ALB target groups to manage which application is considered "production." When you deployed the initial stack with the AWS CDK, the V1 Blue containers were registered with a target group associated with port 8080 on the ALB. After you initiate the deployment of the new version, CodeDeploy starts a brand new version of the ECS service, associates it with the Green target group you created, and then gracefully shifts all traffic to the Green target group. The final result is the Green V2 containers now being served on port 8080 of the ALB. The previous target group is now ready to execute the next Blue/Green deployment.

This is a common pattern to utilize with CI/CD. Your previous version can quickly be reactivated with a seamless rollback. If no rollback is needed, the initial version (V1) is terminated, and you can repeat the processes the next time you deploy, putting V3 in the Blue target group, shifting traffic to it when you are ready. Using this strategy helps you minimize the impact to users of new application versions while allowing more frequent deployments.

 Deployment conditions allow you to define deployment success criteria. You can use a combination of a custom deployment strategy and a deployment condition to build automation tests into your CodeDeploy process. This would allow you to ensure that all of your tests run and pass before traffic is sent to your new deployment.

Challenge

Trigger a rollback to the original V1 container deployment and observe the results.

6.6 Autoscaling Container Workloads on Amazon ECS

Problem

You need to deploy a containerized service that scales out during times of heavy traffic to meet demand.

Solution

Configure a CloudWatch alarm and scaling policy for an ECS service so that your service adds more containers when the CPU load increases, as shown in Figure 6-10.

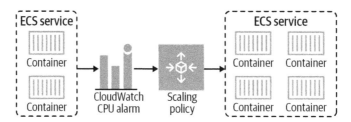

Figure 6-10. ECS service with a CloudWatch alarm and scaling policy

Preparation

Follow the steps in this recipe's folder in the chapter code repository (*https://github.com/AWSCookbook/Containers*).

Steps

1. Access the ECS service URL over the internet with the `curl` command (or your web browser) to verify the successful deployment:

   ```
   curl -v -m 3 $LOAD_BALANCER_DNS
   ```

2. Use verbose (**-v**) and three-second timeout (**-m 3**) to ensure you see the entire connection and have a timeout set. The following is an example command and output:

   ```
   curl -v -m 3 http://AWSCookbook.us-east-1.elb.amazonaws.com:80/
   *   Trying 1.2.3.4...
   * TCP_NODELAY set
   * Connected to AWSCookbook.us-east-1.elb.amazonaws.com (1.2.3.4) port 80<
   > GET / HTTP/1.1
   > Host: AWSCookbook.us-east-1.elb.amazonaws.com:80
   > User-Agent: curl/7.64.1
   > Accept: */*
   >
   < HTTP/1.1 200
   < Content-Type: application/json
   < Content-Length: 318
   ```

```
< Connection: keep-alive
<
{

"URL":"http://awscookbookloadtestloadbalancer-36821611.us-
east-1.elb.amazonaws.com:80/",
  "ContainerLocalAddress":"10.192.2.179:8080",
  "ProcessingTimeTotalMilliseconds":"0",
  "LoadBalancerPrivateIP":"10.192.2.241",
  "ContainerHostname":"ip-10-192-2-179.ec2.internal",
  "CurrentTime":"1605724705176"
}
Closing connection 0
```

 Run this same `curl` command several times in a row, and you
will notice the `ContainerHostname` and `ContainerLocalAd`
`dress` alternating between two addresses. This indicates that
Amazon ECS is load balancing between the two containers
you should expect to be running at all times, as defined by the
ECS service.

3. You will need to create a role for the autoscaling trigger to execute; this file is provided in this solution's directory in the code repository (*https://github.com/
AWSCookbook/Containers*):

```
aws iam create-role --role-name AWSCookbook606ECS \
    --assume-role-policy-document file://task-execution-assume-role.json
```

4. Attach the managed policy for autoscaling:

```
aws iam attach-role-policy --role-name AWSCookbook606ECS --policy-arn
arn:aws:iam::aws:policy/service-role/AmazonEC2ContainerServiceAutoscaleRole
```

5. Register an autoscaling target:

```
aws application-autoscaling register-scalable-target \
    --service-namespace ecs \
    --scalable-dimension ecs:service:DesiredCount \
    --resource-id service/$ECS_CLUSTER_NAME/AWSCookbook606 \
    --min-capacity 2 \
    --max-capacity 4
```

6. Set up an autoscaling policy for the autoscaling target using the sample configuration file specifying a 50% average CPU target:

```
aws application-autoscaling put-scaling-policy --service-namespace ecs \
    --scalable-dimension ecs:service:DesiredCount \
    --resource-id service/$ECS_CLUSTER_NAME/AWSCookbook606 \
    --policy-name cpu50-awscookbook-606 --policy-type TargetTrackingScaling \
    --target-tracking-scaling-policy-configuration file://scaling-policy.json
```

7. Now, to trigger a process within the container that simulates high CPU load, run
the same `curl` command, appending **cpu** to the end of the service URL:

```
curl -v -m 3 $LOAD_BALANCER_DNS/cpu
```

This command will time out after three seconds, indicating that the container is
running a CPU-intensive process as a result of visiting that URL (the ECS service
you deployed with the CDK runs a CPU load generator that we provided to simulate high CPU usage). The following is an example command and output:

```
curl -v -m 3 http://AWSCookbookLoadtestLoadBalancer-36821611.us-
east-1.elb.amazonaws.com:80/cpu
*    Trying 52.4.148.24...
* TCP_NODELAY set
* Connected to AWSCookbookLoadtestLoadBalancer-36821611.us-
east-1.elb.amazonaws.com (52.4.148.245) port 80 (#0)
> GET /cpu HTTP/1.1
> Host: AWSCookbookLoadtestLoadBalancer-36821611.us-east-1.elb.amazonaws.com:80
> User-Agent: curl/7.64.1
> Accept: */*
>
* Operation timed out after 3002 milliseconds with 0 bytes received
* Closing connection 0
curl: (28) Operation timed out after 3002 milliseconds with 0 bytes received
```

Validation checks.   Wait approximately five minutes. Then log into the AWS Console,
locate Elastic Container Service, go to the Clusters page, select the cluster deployed,
and select the ECS service. Verify that the Desired Count has increased to 4, the maximum scaling value that you configured. You can click the Tasks tab to view four container tasks now running for your service.

Click the Metrics tab to view the CPU usage for the service. You set the scaling target
at 50% to trigger the autoscaling actions, adding two additional containers to the service as a result of high CPU usage. An example metrics graph is shown in
Figure 6-11.

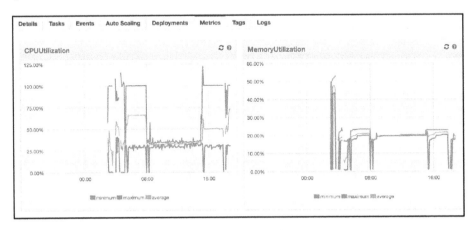

Figure 6-11. ECS service metrics on the AWS Console

Cleanup

Follow the steps in this recipe's folder in the chapter code repository (*https://github.com/AWSCookbook/Containers*).

Discussion

Autosccaling is an important mechanism to implement to save costs associated with running your applications on AWS services. It allows your applications to provision their own resources as needed during times when load may increase, and it removes their own resources during times when the application may be idle. Note that whenever you have an AWS service doing something like this on your behalf, you have to specifically grant permission for services to execute these functions via IAM.

The underlying data that provides the metrics for such operations is contained in the CloudWatch metrics service. There are many data points and metrics that you can use for configuring autoscaling; some of the most common ones are listed here:

- Network I/O
- CPU usage
- Memory used
- Number of transactions

In this recipe, you monitor the CPU usage metric on the ECS service. You set the metric at 50% and trigger the CPU load with a cURL call to the HTTP endpoint of the ECS service. Scaling metrics are dependent upon the type of applications you are running and the technologies you use to build them. As a best practice, you should observe your application metrics over a period of time to set a baseline before choosing metrics to implement autoscaling.

Challenge

Replace the provided sample CPU load application with your own containerized application and configure the target scaling policy to meet your needs.

6.7 Launching a Fargate Container Task in Response to an Event

Problem

You need to launch a container task to process incoming files.

Solution

Use Amazon EventBridge to trigger the launch of ECS container tasks on Fargate after a file is uploaded to S3, as shown in Figure 6-12.

Figure 6-12. Flow of container EventBridge pattern

Preparation

Follow the steps in this recipe's folder in the chapter code repository (*https://github.com/AWSCookbook/Containers*).

Steps

1. Configure CloudTrail to log events on the S3 bucket:

```
aws cloudtrail put-event-selectors --trail-name $CLOUD_TRAIL_ARN --event-
selectors "[{ \"ReadWriteType\":
\"WriteOnly\", \"IncludeManagementEvents\":false, \"DataResources\": [{ \"Type
\": \"AWS::S3::Object\",
\"Values\": [\"arn:aws:s3:::$BUCKET_NAME/input/\"] }],
\"ExcludeManagementEventSources\": [] }]"
```

Now create an assume-role policy JSON statement called *policy1.json* to use in the next step (this file is provided in the repository):

```
{
  "Version": "2012-10-17",
  "Statement": [
    {
      "Effect": "Allow",
      "Principal": {
        "Service": "events.amazonaws.com"
      },
      "Action": "sts:AssumeRole"
    }
  ]
}
```

2. Create the role and specify the *policy1.json* file:

```
aws iam create-role --role-name AWSCookbook607RuleRole \
    --assume-role-policy-document file://policy1.json
```

3. You will also need a policy document with the following content called *policy2.json* (this file is provided in the repository):

```
{
  "Version": "2012-10-17",
  "Statement": [
```

```
    {
      "Effect": "Allow",
      "Action": [
        "ecs:RunTask"
      ],
      "Resource": [
        "arn:aws:ecs:*:*:task-definition/*"
      ]
    },
    {
      "Effect": "Allow",
      "Action": "iam:PassRole",
      "Resource": [
        "*"
      ],
      "Condition": {
        "StringLike": {
          "iam:PassedToService": "ecs-tasks.amazonaws.com"
        }
      }
    }
  ]
}
```

4. Now attach the IAM policy JSON you just created to the IAM role:

```
aws iam put-role-policy --role-name AWSCookbook607RuleRole \
    --policy-name ECSRunTaskPermissionsForEvents \
    --policy-document file://policy2.json
```

5. Create an EventBridge rule that monitors the S3 bucket for file uploads:

```
aws events put-rule --name "AWSCookbookRule" --role-arn "arn:aws:iam::
$AWS_ACCOUNT_ID:role/AWSCookbook607RuleRole" --event-pattern "{\"source\":
[\"aws.s3\"],\"detail-type\":[\"AWS API Call via CloudTrail\"],\"detail\":
{\"eventSource\":[\"s3.amazonaws.com\"],\"eventName\":[\"CopyObject\",\"PutObject
\",\"CompleteMultipartUpload\"],\"requestParameters\":{\"bucketName\":
[\"$BUCKET_NAME\"]}}}"
```

6. Modify the value in *targets-template.json* and create a *targets.json* for use:

```
sed -e "s|AWS_ACCOUNT_ID|${AWS_ACCOUNT_ID}|g" \
    -e "s|AWS_REGION|${AWS_REGION}|g" \
    -e "s|ECSClusterARN|${ECS_CLUSTER_ARN}|g" \
    -e "s|TaskDefinitionARN|${TASK_DEFINITION_ARN}|g" \
    -e "s|VPCPrivateSubnets|${VPC_PRIVATE_SUBNETS}|g" \
    -e "s|VPCDefaultSecurityGroup|${VPC_DEFAULT_SECURITY_GROUP}|g" \
    targets-template.json > targets.json
```

7. Create a rule target that specifies the ECS cluster, ECS task definition, IAM role, and networking parameters. This specifies what the rule will trigger; in this case, launch a container on Fargate:

```
aws events put-targets --rule AWSCookbookRule \
    --targets file://targets.json
```

You should see output similar to the following:

```
{
  "FailedEntryCount": 0,
```

```
    "FailedEntries": []
  }
```

8. Check the S3 bucket to verify that it's empty before we populate it:

```
aws s3 ls s3://$BUCKET_NAME/
```

9. Copy the provided *maze.jpg* file to the S3 bucket. This will trigger the ECS task that launches a container with a Python library (*https://pypi.org/project/mazesolver*) to process the file:

```
aws s3 cp maze.jpg s3://$BUCKET_NAME/input/maze.jpg
```

This will trigger an ECS task to process the image file. Quickly, check the task with the `ecs list-tasks` command. The task will run for about two to three minutes:

```
aws ecs list-tasks --cluster $ECS_CLUSTER_ARN
```

You should see output similar to the following:

```
{
  "taskArns": [
    "arn:aws:ecs:us-east-1:111111111111:task/cdk-aws-cookbook-607-
AWSCookbookEcsCluster46494E6E-MX7kvtp1sYWZ/d86f16af55da56b5ca4874d6029"
  ]
}
```

Validation checks.   After a few minutes, observe the output directory created in the S3 bucket:

```
aws s3 ls s3://$BUCKET_NAME/output/
```

Download and view the output file:

```
aws s3 cp s3://$BUCKET_NAME/output/output.jpg ./output.jpg
```

Open *output.jpg* with a file viewer of your choice to view the file that was processed.

Cleanup

Follow the steps in this recipe's folder in the chapter code repository (*https://github.com/AWSCookbook/Containers*).

Discussion

Event-driven architecture is an important approach to application and process design in the cloud. This type of design allows for removing long-running application workloads in favor of serverless architectures, which can be more resilient and easily scale to peaks of higher usage when needed. When there are no events to handle in your application, you generally do not pay much for compute resources (if at all), so potential cost savings is also a point to consider when choosing an application architecture.

It is common to use Lambda functions with S3 for event-driven architectures, but for longer-running data-processing jobs and computational jobs like this one, Fargate is a better choice because the runtime is essentially infinite, while the maximum runtime for Lambda functions is limited.

Amazon ECS can run tasks and services. Services are made up of tasks, and generally, are long-running in that a service keeps a specific set of tasks running. Tasks can be short-lived; a container may start, process some data, and then gracefully exit after the task is complete. This is what you have achieved in this solution: a task was launched in response to an S3 event signaling a new object, and the container read the object, processed the file, and exited.

Challenge

While EventBridge is a powerful solution that can be used to orchestrate many types of event-driven solutions, you can achieve similar functionality with S3's triggers. Try to deploy and configure a Lambda function to be invoked directly from S3 events. Here is a hint. (*https://oreil.ly/rfTno*)

6.8 Capturing Logs from Containers Running on Amazon ECS

Problem

You have an application running in a container and want to inspect the application logs.

Solution

Send the logs from the container to Amazon CloudWatch. By specifying the `awslogs` driver within an ECS task definition and providing an IAM role that allows the container to write to CloudWatch logs, you are able to stream container logs to a location within Amazon CloudWatch. A high-level view of this configuration and process is shown in Figure 6-13.

Figure 6-13. Streaming container logs to CloudWatch

Preparation

Follow the steps in this recipe's folder in the chapter code repository (*https://github.com/AWSCookbook/Containers*).

Steps

1. Create a file called *task-execution-assume-role.json* with the following content. The file is provided in the root of this recipe's directory in the code repository.

    ```
    {
      "Version": "2012-10-17",
      "Statement": [
        {
          "Sid": "",
          "Effect": "Allow",
          "Principal": {
            "Service": "ecs-tasks.amazonaws.com"
          },
          "Action": "sts:AssumeRole"
        }
      ]
    }
    ```

2. Create an IAM role using the statement in the preceding file:

    ```
    aws iam create-role --role-name AWSCookbook608ECS \
        --assume-role-policy-document file://task-execution-assume-role.json
    ```

3. Attach the AWS managed IAM policy for ECS task execution to the IAM role that you just created:

    ```
    aws iam attach-role-policy --role-name AWSCookbook608ECS --policy-arn
    arn:aws:iam::aws:policy/service-
    role/AmazonECSTaskExecutionRolePolicy
    ```

4. Create a log group in CloudWatch:

    ```
    aws logs create-log-group --log-group-name AWSCookbook608ECS
    ```

5. Create a file called *taskdef.json* with the following content (a file is provided in this recipe's directory in the code repository):

    ```
    {
      "networkMode": "awsvpc",
      "containerDefinitions": [
        {
          "portMappings": [
            {
              "hostPort": 80,
              "containerPort": 80,
              "protocol": "tcp"
            }
          ],
          "essential": true,
          "entryPoint": [
            "sh",
            "-c"
          ],
    ```

```
    "logConfiguration": {
      "logDriver": "awslogs",
      "options": {
        "awslogs-group": "AWSCookbook608ECS",
        "awslogs-region": "us-east-1",
        "awslogs-stream-prefix": "LogStream"
      }
    },
    "name": "awscookbook608",
    "image": "httpd:2.4",
    "command": [
      "/bin/sh -c \"echo 'Hello AWS Cookbook Reader, this container is running
on ECS!' >
/usr/local/apache2/htdocs/index.html && httpd-foreground\""
    ]
  }
],
"family": "awscookbook608",
"requiresCompatibilities": [
  "FARGATE"
],
"cpu": "256",
"memory": "512"
}
```

6. Now that you have an IAM role and an ECS task definition configuration, you need to create the ECS task using the configuration and associate the IAM role:

```
aws ecs register-task-definition --execution-role-arn \
    "arn:aws:iam::$AWS_ACCOUNT_ID:role/AWSCookbook608ECS" \
    --cli-input-json file://taskdef.json
```

7. Run the ECS task on the ECS cluster that you created earlier in this recipe with the AWS CDK:

```
aws ecs run-task --cluster $ECS_CLUSTER_NAME \
    --launch-type FARGATE --network-configuration
"awsvpcConfiguration={subnets=[$VPC_PUBLIC_SUB
NETS],securityGroups=[$VPC_DEFAULT_SECURITY_GROUP],assign
PublicIp=ENABLED}" --task-definition awscookbook608
```

Validation checks.   Check the status of the task to make sure the task is running. First, find the Task's Amazon Resource Name (ARN):

```
TASK_ARNS=$(aws ecs list-tasks --cluster $ECS_CLUSTER_NAME \
    --output text --query taskArns)
```

Then use the task ARNs to check for the RUNNING state with the describe-tasks command output:

```
aws ecs describe-tasks --cluster $ECS_CLUSTER_NAME --tasks $TASK_ARNS
```

After the task has reached the RUNNING state (approximately 15 seconds), use the following commands to view logs:

```
aws logs describe-log-streams --log-group-name AWSCookbook608ECS
```

You should see output similar to the following:

```
{
  "logStreams": [
    {
      "logStreamName": "LogStream/webserver/97635dab942e48d1bab11dbe88c8e5c3",
      "creationTime": 1605584764184,
      "firstEventTimestamp": 1605584765067,
      "lastEventTimestamp": 1605584765067,
      "lastIngestionTime": 1605584894363,
      "uploadSequenceToken":
"49612420096740389364147985468451499506623702081936625922",
      "arn": "arn:aws:logs:us-east-1:111111111111:log-group:AWSCookbook608ECS:log-
stream:LogStream/webserver/97635dab942e48d1bab11dbe88c8e5c3",
      "storedBytes": 0
    }
  ]
}
```

Note the `logStreamName` from the output and then run the `get-log-events` command:

```
aws logs get-log-events --log-group-name AWSCookbook608ECS \
    --log-stream-name <<logStreamName>>
```

You should see output similar to the following:

```
{
  "events": [
    {
      "timestamp": 1605590555566,
      "message": "[Tue Nov 17 05:22:35.566054 2020] [mpm_event:notice] [pid 7:tid
140297116308608] AH00489: Apache/2.4.46 (Unix) configured -- resuming normal
operations",
      "ingestionTime": 1605590559713
    },
    {
      "timestamp": 1605590555566,
      "message": "[Tue Nov 17 05:22:35.566213 2020] [core:notice] [pid 7:tid
140297116308608] AH00094: Command line: 'httpd -D FOREGROUND'",
      "ingestionTime": 1605590559713
    }
  ],
  "nextForwardToken": "f/35805865872844590178623550035180924397996026459535048705",
  "nextBackwardToken": "b/35805865872844590178623550035180924397996026459535048704"
}
```

Cleanup

Follow the steps in this recipe's folder in the chapter code repository (*https:// github.com/AWSCookbook/Containers*).

Discussion

You made use of the `awslogs` driver and an IAM role, which allows the running task to write to a CloudWatch log group. This is a common pattern when working with containers on AWS, as you most likely need log output for troubleshooting and debugging your application. This configuration is handled by tools like Copilot since it is a common pattern, but when working with Amazon ECS directly, like defining and running a task, the configuration is critical for developers to know about.

The PID 1 process output (*https://oreil.ly/XY2UF*) to */dev/stdout* and */dev/stderr* is captured by the awslogs driver. In other words, the first process in the container is the only process logging to these streams. Be sure your application that you would like to see logs from is running with PID 1 inside of your container.

In order for most AWS services to communicate with one another, you must assign a role to them that allows the required level of permissions for the communication. This holds true when configuring logging to CloudWatch from a container ECS task; the container must have a role associated with it that allows the CloudWatchLogs operations via the `awslogs logConfiguration` driver (*https://oreil.ly/OrzrZ*):

```
{
  "Version": "2012-10-17",
  "Statement": [
    {
      "Effect": "Allow",
      "Action": [
        "logs:CreateLogGroup",
        "logs:CreateLogStream",
        "logs:PutLogEvents",
        "logs:DescribeLogStreams"
      ],
      "Resource": [
        "arn:aws:logs:*:*:*"
      ]
    }
  ]
}
```

CloudWatch logs allow for a central logging solution for many AWS services. When running multiple containers, it is important to be able to quickly locate logs for debugging purposes.

Challenge

You can tail (*https://oreil.ly/kFrGf*) the logs of a log stream to give you a more real-time view of the logs that your application is generating. This can help in your development and troubleshooting activities. Try using the `aws logs tail` command with your log stream while generating some output for you to observe.

CHAPTER 7

Big Data

7.0 Introduction

Data is sometimes referred to as "the new gold (*https://oreil.ly/6EDB0*)." Many companies are leveraging data in new and exciting ways every day as available data science tools continue to improve. You can now mine troves of historical data quickly for insights and patterns by using modern analytics tools. You might not yet know the queries and analysis you need to run against the data, but tomorrow you might be faced with a challenge that could be supported by historical data analysis using new and emerging techniques. With the advent of cheaper data storage, many organizations and individuals opt to keep data rather than discard it so that they can run historical analysis to gain business insights, discover trends, train AI/ML models, and be ready to implement future technologies that can use the data.

In addition to the amount of data you might collect over time, you are also collecting a wider variety of data types and structures at an increasingly faster velocity. Imagine that you might deploy IoT devices to collect sensor data, and as you continue to deploy these over time, you need a way to capture and store the data in a scalable way. This can be structured, semistructured, and unstructured data with schemas that might be difficult to predict as new data sources are ingested. You need tools to be able to transform and analyze your diverse data.

An informative and succinct AWS re:Invent 2020 presentation by Francis Jayakumar, "An Introduction to Data Lakes and Analytics on AWS (*https://oreil.ly/WcmSj*)," provides a high-level introduction to what is available on AWS for big data and analytics. We could have included so much in this chapter—enough to fill another book—but we will focus on foundational recipes for sending data to S3, discovering data on S3, and transforming data to give you examples of working with data on AWS.

Workstation Configuration

You will need a few things installed to be ready for the recipes in this chapter.

General setup

Follow the "General workstation setup steps for CLI recipes" on page xvii to validate your configuration and set up the required environment variables. Then, clone the chapter code repository:

```
git clone https://github.com/awscookbook/BigData
```

7.1 Using a Kinesis Stream for Ingestion of Streaming Data

Problem

You need a way to ingest streaming data for your applications.

Solution

Create a Kinesis stream and verify that it is working by using the AWS CLI to put a record on the stream, as shown in Figure 7-1.

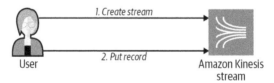

Figure 7-1. Using a Kinesis stream for ingestion of streaming data

Steps

1. Create a Kinesis stream:

```
aws kinesis create-stream --stream-name AWSCookbook701 --shard-count 1
```

> Shards (*https://oreil.ly/XKI0q*) are an important concept to understand with Kinesis streams as you scale your stream to handle larger velocities of incoming streaming data. Each shard can support up to five transactions per second for reads, up to a maximum total data read rate of 2 MB per second. For writes, each shard can support up to 1,000 records per second, up to a maximum total data write rate of 1 MB per second (including partition keys). You can re-shard your stream at any time if you need to handle more data.

2. Confirm that your stream is in ACTIVE state:

```
aws kinesis describe-stream-summary --stream-name AWSCookbook701
```

You should see output similar to the following:

```
{
    "StreamDescriptionSummary": {
        "StreamName": "AWSCookbook701",
        "StreamARN": "arn:aws:kinesis:us-east-1:111111111:stream/AWSCookbook701",
        "StreamStatus": "ACTIVE",
        "RetentionPeriodHours": 24,
        "StreamCreationTimestamp": "2021-10-12T17:12:06-04:00",
        "EnhancedMonitoring": [
            {
                "ShardLevelMetrics": []
            }
        ],
        "EncryptionType": "NONE",
        "OpenShardCount": 1,
        "ConsumerCount": 0
    }
}
```

Validation checks. Put a record on the Kinesis stream:

```
aws kinesis put-record --stream-name AWSCookbook701 \
    --partition-key 111 \
    --cli-binary-format raw-in-base64-out \
    --data={\"Data\":\"1\"}
```

You should see output similar to the following:

```
{
    "ShardId": "shardId-000000000000",
    "SequenceNumber": "49622914081337086513355510347442886426455090590105206786"
}
```

Get the record from the Kinesis stream. Get the shard iterator (*https://oreil.ly/dFx8m*) and run the get-records command:

```
SHARD_ITERATOR=$(aws kinesis get-shard-iterator \
    --shard-id shardId-000000000000 \
    --shard-iterator-type TRIM_HORIZON \
    --stream-name AWSCookbook701 \
    --query 'ShardIterator' \
    --output text)
aws kinesis get-records --shard-iterator $SHARD_ITERATOR \
    --query Records[0].Data --output text | base64 --decode
```

You should see output similar to the following:

```
{"Data":"1"}
```

The data is base64 encoded that you published to the stream. You queried the command output for the data element within the JSON object and piped the output to `base64 --decode` to validate that the record is what you published.

Cleanup

Follow the steps in this recipe's folder in the chapter code repository (*https://github.com/AWSCookbook/BigData*).

Discussion

Streaming data can come from a variety of sources. The sources putting records on streams are known as producers (*https://oreil.ly/ze6Wd*). Entities getting records from streams are known as consumers (*https://oreil.ly/dzRG2*). In the case of streaming data, you are dealing with real-time information, and you may need to act on it immediately or store it for usage later (see Recipe 7.2). Some common producer examples to think about are as follows:

- Real-time financial market data
- IoT and sensor data
- End-user clickstream activity from web and mobile applications

You can use the Kinesis Producer Library (KPL) and Kinesis Client Library (KCL) within your application for your specific needs. When consuming data from Kinesis streams, you can configure your application to read records from the stream and respond, invoke Lambda functions directly from the stream, or even use a Kinesis Data Analytics (*https://oreil.ly/lyR4E*) application (powered by Apache Flink) directly within the Kinesis service.

The Kinesis service will scale automatically to meet your needs, but you need to be aware of the quotas and limits (*https://oreil.ly/f7kq3*) to ensure that you do not exceed capacity with your shard configuration.

Challenge

Automatically trigger a Lambda function to process incoming Kinesis data.

7.2 Streaming Data to Amazon S3 Using Amazon Kinesis Data Firehose

Problem

You need to deliver incoming streaming data to object storage.

Solution

Create an S3 bucket, create a Kinesis stream, and configure Kinesis Data Firehose to deliver the stream data to the S3 bucket. The flow is shown in Figure 7-2.

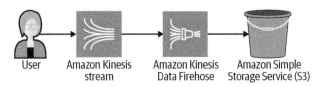

Figure 7-2. Streaming data to Amazon S3 using Amazon Kinesis Data Firehose

Prerequisites

- Kinesis stream
- S3 Bucket with a CSV file

Preparation

Follow the steps in this recipe's folder in the chapter code repository (*https://github.com/AWSCookbook/BigData*).

Steps

1. Open the Kinesis Data Firehose console (*https://oreil.ly/GG8yA*) and click the "Create delivery stream" button; choose Amazon Kinesis Data Streams for the source and Amazon S3 for the destination, as shown in Figure 7-3.

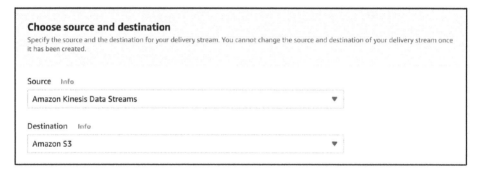

Figure 7-3. Choosing the source and destination in the Kinesis Data Firehose dialog

2. For Source settings, choose the Kinesis stream that you created in the preparation steps, as shown in Figure 7-4.

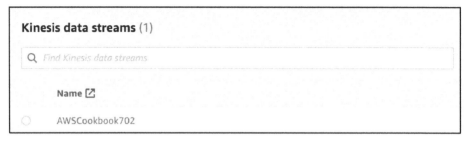

Figure 7-4. Choosing a Kinesis data stream

3. Keep the defaults (Disabled) for "Transform and convert records" options. For Destination settings, browse for and choose the S3 bucket that you created in the preparation steps as shown in Figure 7-5, and keep the defaults for the other options (disabled partitioning and no prefixes).

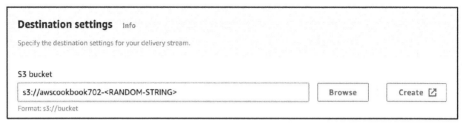

Figure 7-5. Kinesis Data Firehose destination configuration

4. Under the Advanced settings section, confirm that the "Create or update IAM role" is selected. This will create an IAM role that Kinesis can use to access the stream and S3 bucket, as shown in Figure 7-6.

Figure 7-6. Creating an IAM role for the Kinesis Data Firehose service

Validation checks. You can test delivery to the stream from within the Kinesis console. Click the Delivery streams link in the left navigation menu, choose the stream you created, expand the "Test with demo data" section, and click the "Start sending demo data" button. This will initiate sending sample data to your stream so you can verify that it is making it to your S3 bucket. A sample is shown in Figure 7-7.

Figure 7-7. Sending test data through a Kinesis Data Firehose

After a few minutes, you will see a folder structure and a file appear in your S3 bucket, similar to Figure 7-8.

Figure 7-8. S3 destination with Kinesis stream data delivered

If you download and inspect the file, you will see output similar to the following:

```
{"CHANGE":3.95,"PRICE":79.75,"TICKER_SYMBOL":"SLW","SECTOR":"ENERGY"}
{"CHANGE":7.27,"PRICE":96.37,"TICKER_SYMBOL":"ALY","SECTOR":"ENERGY"}
{"CHANGE":-5,"PRICE":81.74,"TICKER_SYMBOL":"QXZ","SECTOR":"HEALTHCARE"}
{"CHANGE":-0.6,"PRICE":98.4,"TICKER_SYMBOL":"NFLX","SECTOR":"TECHNOLOGY"}
{"CHANGE":-0.46,"PRICE":18.92,"TICKER_SYMBOL":"PLM","SECTOR":"FINANCIAL"}
{"CHANGE":4.09,"PRICE":100.46,"TICKER_SYMBOL":"ALY","SECTOR":"ENERGY"}
{"CHANGE":2.06,"PRICE":32.34,"TICKER_SYMBOL":"PPL","SECTOR":"HEALTHCARE"}
{"CHANGE":-2.99,"PRICE":38.98,"TICKER_SYMBOL":"KFU","SECTOR":"ENERGY"}
```

Cleanup

Follow the steps in this recipe's folder in the chapter code repository (*https://github.com/AWSCookbook/BigData*).

Discussion

As you begin to ingest data from various sources, your application may be consuming or reacting to streaming data in real time. In some cases, you may want to store the data from the stream to query or process it later. You can use Kinesis Data Firehose to deliver data to object storage (S3), Amazon Redshift, OpenSearch, and many third-party endpoints. You can also connect multiple delivery streams to a single producer stream to deliver data if you have to support multiple delivery locations from your streams.

 Kinesis Data Firehose scales automatically to handle the volume of data you need to deliver, meaning that you do not have to configure or provision additional resources if your data stream starts to receive large volumes of data. For more information on Kinesis Data Firehose features and capabilities, see the AWS documentation (*https://oreil.ly/9h2Bc*) for Kinesis Data Firehose.

If you need to transform data before it ends up in the destination via Firehose, you can configure transformations. A transformation will automatically invoke a Lambda function as your streaming data queues up (see this Firehose article (*https://oreil.ly/PW0LN*) for buffer size information). This is useful when you have to adjust the schema of a record before delivery, sanitize data for long-term storage on the fly (e.g., remove personally identifiable information), or join the data with other sources before delivery. The transformation Lambda function you invoke must follow the convention specified by the Kinesis Data Firehose API. To see some examples of Lambda functions, go to the AWS Serverless Application Repository (*https://oreil.ly/q7noh*) and search for "firehose."

Challenge

Configure a Firehose delivery with transformations to remove a field from the streaming data before delivery.

7.3 Automatically Discovering Metadata with AWS Glue Crawlers

Problem

You have CSV data files on object storage, and you would like to discover the schema and metadata about the files to use in further analysis and query operations.

Solution

Create an AWS Glue database, follow the crawler configuration wizard to configure a crawler to scan your S3 bucket data, run the crawler, and inspect the resulting table, as shown in Figure 7-9.

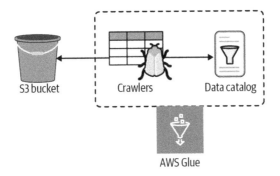

Figure 7-9. *Automatically discover metadata with AWS Glue crawlers*

Prerequisite

- An S3 bucket

Preparation

Follow the steps in this recipe's folder in the chapter code repository (*https://github.com/AWSCookbook/BigData*).

Steps

1. Log in to the AWS Console and navigate to the AWS Glue console, choose Databases from the left navigation menu and select "Add database," as shown in Figure 7-10.

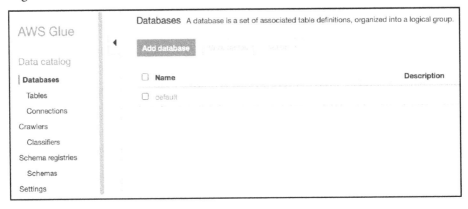

Figure 7-10. *Creating a database in the Glue data catalog*

2. Give your database a name (e.g., **awscookbook703**) and click Create. A sample dialog box is shown in Figure 7-11.

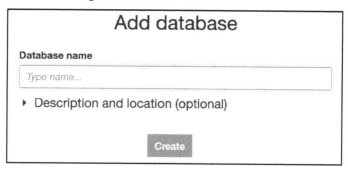

Figure 7-11. Database name dialog box

3. Select Tables from the left navigation menu and choose "Add tables" → "Add tables using a crawler," as shown in Figure 7-12.

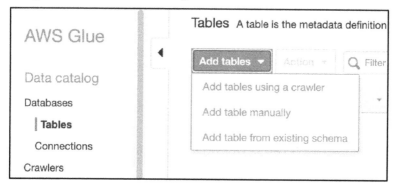

Figure 7-12. Adding a table to the Glue Data catalog

4. Follow the "Add crawler" wizard. For the crawler source type, choose "Data stores," crawl all folders, S3 as "Data store" (do not define a Connection), choose your S3 bucket and "data" folder in "Include path," and do not choose a sample size. Choose to create an IAM role, and suffix it with **AWSCookbook703**. For a frequency, choose "Run on demand," and select the database you created in step 2. Confirm the configuration on the "Review all steps" page and click Finish. An example review page is shown in Figure 7-13.

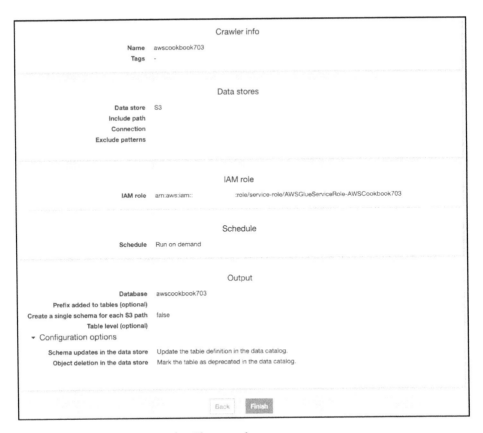

Figure 7-13. Review settings for Glue crawler

5. From the left navigation menu, select Crawlers. Choose the crawler that you created in step 4 and click "Run crawler," as shown in Figure 7-14.

The Glue crawler will take a few moments to run. Once it is complete, you can view the table properties of the discovered schema and metadata.

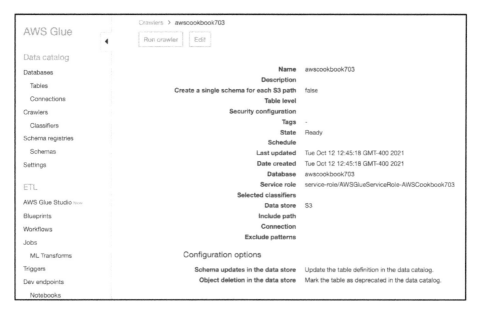

Figure 7-14. Glue crawler configuration summary

Validation checks. Verify the crawler configuration you created; you can use the AWS CLI or the Glue console. Note the LastCrawl status of SUCCEEDED:

```
aws glue get-crawler --name awscookbook703
```

You should see output similar to this:

```
{
  "Crawler": {
    "Name": "awscookbook703",
    "Role": "service-role/AWSGlueServiceRole-AWSCookbook703",
    "Targets": {
      "S3Targets": [
        {
          "Path": "s3://awscookbook704-<RANDOM_STRING>/data",
          "Exclusions": []
        }
      ],
      "JdbcTargets": [],
      "MongoDBTargets": [],
      "DynamoDBTargets": [],
      "CatalogTargets": []
    },
    "DatabaseName": "awscookbook703",
    "Classifiers": [],
    "RecrawlPolicy": {
      "RecrawlBehavior": "CRAWL_EVERYTHING"
    },
    "SchemaChangePolicy": {
```

```
      "UpdateBehavior": "UPDATE_IN_DATABASE",
      "DeleteBehavior": "DEPRECATE_IN_DATABASE"
    },
    "LineageConfiguration": {
      "CrawlerLineageSettings": "DISABLE"
    },
    "State": "READY",
    "CrawlElapsedTime": 0,
    "CreationTime": "2021-10-12T12:45:18-04:00",
    "LastUpdated": "2021-10-12T12:45:18-04:00",
    "LastCrawl": {
      "Status": "SUCCEEDED",
      "LogGroup": "/aws-glue/crawlers",
      "LogStream": "awscookbook703",
      "MessagePrefix": "16e867b7-e972-4ceb-b318-8e78370949d8",
      "StartTime": "2021-10-12T12:54:19-04:00"
    },
    "Version": 1
  }
}
```

 AWS Glue crawlers log information about their runs to Amazon CloudWatch logs. If you need to debug your crawlers' activity, you can inspect the logs in the */aws-glue/crawlers* log group.

In the Glue console, select the table that was created and click "View properties." You can also run an AWS CLI command to output the JSON:

```
aws glue get-table --database-name awscookbook703 --name data
```

The JSON properties should look similar to this:

```
{
  "StorageDescriptor": {
    "cols": {
      "FieldSchema": [
        {
          "name": "title",
          "type": "string",
          "comment": ""
        },
        {
          "name": "other titles",
          "type": "string",
          "comment": ""
        },
        {
          "name": "bl record id",
          "type": "bigint",
          "comment": ""
        }...<SNIP>...
      ]
```

```
    },
    "location": "s3://awscookbook703-<RANDOM_STRING>/data/",
    "inputFormat": "org.apache.hadoop.mapred.TextInputFormat",
    "outputFormat": "org.apache.hadoop.hive.ql.io.HiveIgnoreKeyTextOutputFormat",
    "compressed": "false",
    "numBuckets": "-1",
    "SerDeInfo": {
      "name": "",
      "serializationLib": "org.apache.hadoop.hive.serde2.lazy.LazySimpleSerDe",
      "parameters": {
        "field.delim": ","
      }
    },
    "bucketCols": [],
    "sortCols": [],
    "parameters": {
      "skip.header.line.count": "1",
      "sizeKey": "43017100",
      "objectCount": "1",
      "UPDATED_BY_CRAWLER": "awscookbook703",
      "CrawlerSchemaSerializerVersion": "1.0",
      "recordCount": "79367",
      "averageRecordSize": "542",
      "CrawlerSchemaDeserializerVersion": "1.0",
      "compressionType": "none",
      "classification": "csv",
      "columnsOrdered": "true",
      "areColumnsQuoted": "false",
      "delimiter": ",",
      "typeOfData": "file"
    },
    "SkewedInfo": {},
    "storedAsSubDirectories": "false"
  },
  "parameters": {
    "skip.header.line.count": "1",
    "sizeKey": "43017100",
    "objectCount": "1",
    "UPDATED_BY_CRAWLER": "awscookbook703",
    "CrawlerSchemaSerializerVersion": "1.0",
    "recordCount": "79367",
    "averageRecordSize": "542",
    "CrawlerSchemaDeserializerVersion": "1.0",
    "compressionType": "none",
    "classification": "csv",
    "columnsOrdered": "true",
    "areColumnsQuoted": "false",
    "delimiter": ",",
    "typeOfData": "file"
  }
}
```

Cleanup

Follow the steps in this recipe's folder in the chapter code repository (*https://github.com/AWSCookbook/BigData*).

Discussion

When you start to ingest and store large amounts of data from various sources to object storage like S3, you may want to temporarily query the data in place without loading into an intermediate database. Since you may not always know the schema or metadata of the data, you need to know some basics about it, such as where the data resides, what the files and partitioning look like, whether it's structured versus unstructured data, the size of data, and most importantly, the schema of the data. One specific feature of the AWS Glue service, Glue crawlers, allow you to discover metadata about the variety of data you have in storage. Crawlers (*https://oreil.ly/49nom*) connect to your data source (in this case, S3 bucket), scan the objects in the source, and populate a Glue Data Catalog database with tables associated with your data's schema.

 In addition to S3 bucket sources, you can use crawlers to scan Java Database Connectivity (JDBC) data stores and DynamoDB tables. In the case of a JDBC table, you will need to define a connection (*https://oreil.ly/Gasxy*) to allow Glue to use a network connection to your JDBC source.

Challenge

Configure your crawler to run on an interval so that your tables and metadata are automatically updated.

7.4 Querying Files on S3 Using Amazon Athena

Problem

You need to run a SQL query on CSV files stored on object storage without indexing them.

Solution

Configure an Amazon Athena results S3 bucket location, create a Data Catalog database and table in the Athena Editor, and run a SQL query on the data in the S3 bucket, as shown in Figure 7-15.

S3 bucket   Amazon
             Athena   Data catalog

Figure 7-15. Query files on S3 using Amazon Athena

Prerequisite

- S3 bucket with a CSV file containing data

Preparation

Follow the steps in this recipe's folder in the chapter code repository (*https://github.com/AWSCookbook/BigData*).

Steps

1. Log into the AWS Console and go to the Athena console; you should see something similar to Figure 7-16.

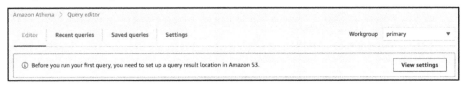

Figure 7-16. Athena console

2. In the Query Editor, click the Settings tab and configure a Query result location using the S3 bucket that you created and a prefix: `s3://bucket/folder/object/`. Click Manage, select the bucket, and click Choose. As an option, you can encrypt the results. See Figure 7-17 for an example.

Figure 7-17. Athena results destination configuration

3. Back in the Editor tab, run the following SQL statement to create a Data Catalog database:

```
CREATE DATABASE `awscookbook704db`
```

You should see output similar to Figure 7-18.

Figure 7-18. Database creation SQL statement

4. Run a new statement in the Query Editor to create a table within the database that references the S3 bucket location of the data and the schema of the data. Be sure to replace *BUCKET_NAME* with the name of the bucket that you created:

```
CREATE EXTERNAL TABLE IF NOT EXISTS default.`awscookbook704table`(
   `title` string,
   `other titles` string,
   `bl record id` bigint,
   `type of resource` string,
   `content type` string,
   `material type` string,
   `bnb number` string,
   `isbn` string,
   `name` string,
   `dates associated with name` string,
   `type of name` string,
   `role` string,
   `all names` string,
   `series title` string,
   `number within series` string,
   `country of publication` string,
   `place of publication` string,
   `publisher` string,
   `date of publication` string,
   `edition` string,
   `physical description` string,
   `dewey classification` string,
   `bl shelfmark` string,
   `topics` string,
   `genre` string,
   `languages` string,
   `notes` string)
ROW FORMAT SERDE 'org.apache.hadoop.hive.serde2.lazy.LazySimpleSerDe'
WITH SERDEPROPERTIES (
   'serialization.format' = ',',
```

```
    'field.delim' = ','
) LOCATION 's3://BUCKET_NAME/data/'
TBLPROPERTIES ('has_encrypted_data'='false');
```

 You can use an AWS Glue crawler to crawl your data on S3 and keep databases, tables, and metadata up-to-date automatically. See Recipe 7.3 for an example of configuring a Glue crawler with this example dataset.

Validation checks. Open the Query Editor and run a query to list the rows where the title is "Marvel universe":

```
SELECT * FROM awscookbook704table WHERE title='"Marvel universe"' LIMIT 100
```

You should see output similar to Figure 7-19.

Results (4)

Q *Search rows*

title	other titles	bl record id
"Marvel universe"	""	
"Marvel universe"	""	
"Marvel universe"	""	
"Marvel universe"	"Handbook of the Marvel universe ; Official handbook of the Marvel universe"	

Figure 7-19. Query results in the Athena console

Run a SQL query selecting the top 100 rows for the sample dataset:

```
SELECT * FROM awscookbook704table LIMIT 100;
```

Cleanup

Follow the steps in this recipe's folder in the chapter code repository (*https://github.com/AWSCookbook/BigData*).

Discussion

You may have had to use an extract, transform, load (ETL) process in the past to facilitate querying large amounts of data on demand. This process could have taken hours, if not days, if the volume of data was substantial. In the world of big data, the volume will only increase as time moves on, and you may not know what you need to query for when you initially start to ingest the data. This makes table schema design challenging. Chances are, as you ingest and collect data from various sources, you will be storing it in object storage. This is the *data lake* concept realized. Being able to query text-based data in place within your data lake is a powerful concept that you can use Amazon Athena for. You can use standard SQL to run queries against data directly on object storage (Amazon S3).

Athena requires knowing some basics about your data before you can run queries. This includes metadata, schema, and data locations. The concepts of tables, databases, and the Data Catalog (*https://oreil.ly/wLxfa*) are important to understand so that you can configure the Athena service to meet your needs. As you saw in Recipe 7.3, the Glue service can crawl your data to discover this information and keep it up-to-date so that you can always be ready to run queries against your data while it is stored in your data lake. You can use a Glue Data Catalog in the Athena service rather than defining your own schema to save you time.

 As you start to increase your usage of S3 as your central data repository (or in other words, a data lake), you may need to use several services together and also start to apply certain levels of permission to allow other team members to interact with and manage the data. AWS Lake Formation (*https://oreil.ly/wStEx*) is a managed service that brings services like S3, Glue, and Athena together with a robust permissions engine that can meet your needs.

 The Athena service will automatically scale for you, running queries in parallel for your large datasets, so you do not have to worry about provisioning any resources. For more information, see the Athena documentation (*https://oreil.ly/hWrqZ*).

Challenge

Configure Athena to use the Glue Data Catalog with a Glue crawler for a source dataset on S3 that you do not have a predefined schema for.

7.5 Transforming Data with AWS Glue DataBrew

Problem

You have data stored in a CSV and need to convert all characters in a column to uppercase before further processing can occur.

Solution

Start with a sample project in Glue DataBrew using a sample CSV dataset. Wait for the session to initiate and apply an uppercase format operation on the name column of the sample set. Inspect the results (see Figure 7-20).

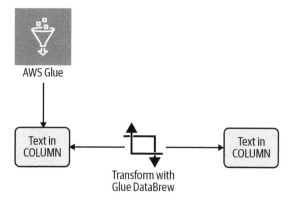

Figure 7-20. Transforming data with AWS Glue DataBrew

Steps

1. In the AWS Console, search for and navigate to the AWS Glue DataBrew console.

2. Click "Create sample project," select "Popular names for babies in 2020," create a new IAM role, enter a role suffix of your choosing, and then click "Create project," as shown in Figure 7-21. Your session will take a few moments to be prepared, and the status indicator should look similar to Figure 7-22.

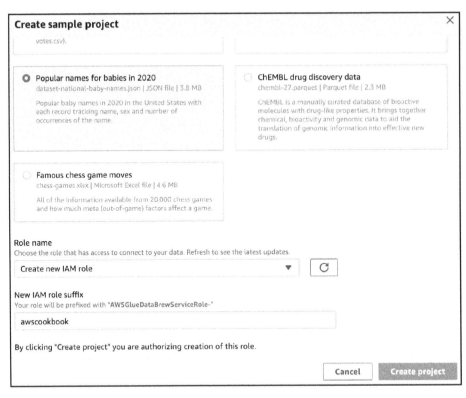

Figure 7-21. Creating a sample project in Glue DataBrew

Figure 7-22. Preparing a session in Glue DataBrew

3. When your session has been prepared, click FORMAT in the menu. Then from the drop-down menu, select "Change to uppercase," as shown in Figure 7-23.

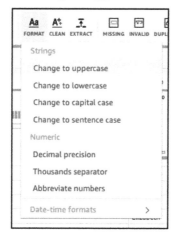

Figure 7-23. Beginning to format a string to uppercase

4. In the righthand menu, set the "Source column" to "name" and then click Apply, as shown in Figure 7-24.

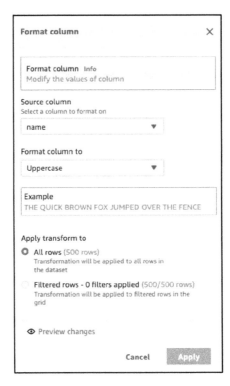

Figure 7-24. Formatting column to uppercase interface

Validation checks. View the updated name column, as shown in Figure 7-25.

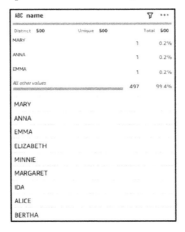

Figure 7-25. Results of the uppercase recipe step

From the ACTIONS menu in the top-right corner, select Download CSV, as shown in Figure 7-26.

Figure 7-26. Downloading CSV action

Cleanup

Follow the steps in this recipe's folder in the chapter code repository (*https://github.com/AWSCookbook/BigData*).

Discussion

When dealing with large amounts of heterogeneous data from various sources, you will find that you need to manipulate data in various ways to meet your use case. In the past, you would have to programmatically accomplish this using scripts, complicated ETL jobs, or third-party tools. You can use AWS DataBrew to streamline the tasks of formatting, cleaning, and extracting information from your data. You can perform complex joins and splits, and run custom functions within the DataBrew service using a visual interface.

DataBrew is an example of a low-code development platform (*https://oreil.ly/GKEer*) (LCDP) that enables you to quickly achieve outcomes that otherwise would require knowledge of more complicated development platforms. You use Glue DataBrew in your web browser to visually design recipe jobs (*https://oreil.ly/fNFFY*) to process your data, preview results, and automate your data-processing workflow. Once you have a recipe job saved, you can bring automation into your workflow by setting up an S3 trigger for your incoming data to have DataBrew process it and deliver it back to S3, the Glue Data Catalog, or a JDBC data source.

Challenge

Upload your own dataset. Create a job from the DataBrew console, configure it to deliver the results to S3 so you can use the job on demand or automatically with a trigger.

CHAPTER 8

AI/ML

8.0 Introduction

Machine learning (ML) and artificial intelligence (AI) are two of the hottest topics today. Scale provided by cloud computing and improved algorithms have enabled rapid advances in the abilities of computers to think like humans (aka "provide inferences"). Many mundane and boring tasks that required human intervention can now be automated because of AI.

AI and ML can get complex very quickly. Volumes of text have been written about each. Recipes in this chapter will allow you to explore some of the easy-to-implement AI services provided by AWS and get started building your own models. While you are working through the recipes, try to think about other problematic areas in society that could be well served by these technologies. From supply chain predictive maintenance to song suggestions, the opportunities are endless.

We could have written 100 pages on this topic, but these recipes are great to get started, and you can iterate from there. If you are looking to dive deeper, we suggest you check out *Data Science on AWS* by Chris Fregly and Antje Barth (O'Reilly, 2021).

Workstation Configuration

Follow the "General workstation setup steps for CLI recipes" on page xvii to validate your configuration and set up the required environment variables. Then, clone the chapter code repository:

```
git clone https://github.com/AWSCookbook/ArtificialIntelligence
```

8.1 Transcribing a Podcast

Problem

You need to create a text transcription of an MP3-based audio, such as a podcast.

Solution

Use Amazon Transcribe to generate an English language transcription and save the results to an S3 bucket (see Figure 8-1).

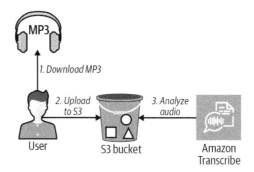

Figure 8-1. Using Amazon Transcribe with an MP3 file

Prerequisites

- S3 bucket
- jq CLI JSON processor

Preparation

Follow the steps in this recipe's folder in the chapter code repository (*https://github.com/AWSCookbook/ArtificialIntelligence*).

Steps

1. Download a podcast in MP3 format to upload to the S3 bucket:

   ```
   curl https://d1le29qyzha1u4.cloudfront.net/AWS_Podcast_Episode_453.mp3 \
       -o podcast.mp3
   ```

   You should see output similar to the following:

   ```
   % Total % Received % Xferd  Average Speed   Time    Time     Time  Current
                                Dload  Upload   Total   Spent    Left  Speed
   100 29.8M  100 29.8M    0      0   4613k      0  0:00:06  0:00:06 --:--:-- 5003k
   ```

You can find a list of the file formats supported by Amazon Transcribe in the documentation (*https://oreil.ly/eo3LQ*).

2. Copy the downloaded podcast to your S3 bucket:

```
aws s3 cp ./podcast.mp3 s3://awscookbook801-$RANDOM_STRING
```

You should see output similar to the following:

```
upload: ./podcast.mp3 to s3://awscookbook801-<<unique>>/podcast.mp3
```

3. Start a Transcribe transcription job using the AWS CLI:

```
aws transcribe start-transcription-job \
    --language-code 'en-US' \
    --media-format 'mp3' \
    --transcription-job-name 'awscookbook-801' \
    --media MediaFileUri=s3://awscookbook801-${RANDOM_STRING}/podcast.mp3 \
    --output-bucket-name "awscookbook801-${RANDOM_STRING}"
```

You should see output similar to the following:

```
{
    "TranscriptionJob": {
        "TranscriptionJobName": "awscookbook-801",
        "TranscriptionJobStatus": "IN_PROGRESS",
        "LanguageCode": "en-US",
        "MediaFormat": "mp3",
        "Media": {
            "MediaFileUri": "s3://awscookbook801-<<unique>>/podcast.mp3"
        },
        "StartTime": "2021-09-21T22:02:13.312000-04:00",
        "CreationTime": "2021-09-21T22:02:13.273000-04:00"
    }
}
```

Check the status of the transcription job using the AWS CLI. Wait until the Transcription Job Status is COMPLETED. This should take a few minutes:

```
aws transcribe get-transcription-job \
    --transcription-job-name awscookbook-801 \
    --output text \
    --query TranscriptionJob.TranscriptionJobStatus
```

Validation checks. Display the results of the Transcribe transcription job in your terminal:

```
aws s3 cp s3://awscookbook801-$RANDOM_STRING/awscookbook-801.json - \
    | jq '.results.transcripts[0].transcript' --raw-output
```

You should see output similar to the following:

```
This is episode 453 of the US podcast released on June 11, 2021 podcast confirmed.
Welcome to the official AWS podcast. Yeah. Mhm. Hello everyone and welcome back to
another episode of a W. S. Launch.
```

```
I'm Nicky, I'm your host. And today I am joined by Nathan Peck
...
```

Cleanup

Follow the steps in this recipe's folder in the chapter code repository (*https://github.com/AWSCookbook/ArtificialIntelligence*).

Discussion

Transcribing audio is a great way to allow voice recordings to be processed and analyzed in different ways at scale. Having the ability to easily transcribe audio files without gathering a large dataset and training your own AI model will save you time and open up many possibilities. Converting audio to text also allows you to easily perform natural language processing (NLP) to gain additional insights from the piece of media.

Here are some things to keep in mind when you are using Transcribe:

- Is the language supported (*https://oreil.ly/8NYOB*)?
- Do you need to identify speakers (*https://oreil.ly/E38Ch*) in a recording?
- Do you need to support streaming audio (*https://oreil.ly/uhrAr*)?

Challenge

Automate the process to trigger when new objects are uploaded to your S3 bucket by using EventBridge.

8.2 Converting Text to Speech

Problem

You need to generate audio files from text descriptions of products. This audio will be incorporated in advertisements so must be as human-like and high quality as possible.

Solution

You will use the neural engine of Amazon Polly to generate MP3s from the provided text (see Figure 8-2).

Figure 8-2. Text to speech with Amazon Polly

Steps

1. Create an initial sound file of text that you specify:

   ```
   aws polly synthesize-speech \
       --output-format mp3 \
       --voice-id Joanna \
       --text 'Acme products are of the very highest quality and lowest price.' \
       products.mp3
   ```

   You should see output similar to the following:

   ```
   {
     "ContentType": "audio/mpeg",
     "RequestCharacters": "63"
   }
   ```

2. Listen to the MP3. Here is an example on macOS CLI:

   ```
   afplay products.mp3
   ```

3. Change to the neural engine:

   ```
   aws polly synthesize-speech \
       --output-format mp3 \
       --voice-id Joanna \
       --engine neural \
       --text 'Acme products are of the very highest quality and lowest price.' \
       products-neural.mp3
   ```

   You will see similar output as you did in step 2.

4. Listen to the MP3. Here is an example on macOS CLI:

   ```
   afplay products-neural.mp3
   ```

5. Add some SSML tags (*https://oreil.ly/sdAQe*) to modify the speech speed:

   ```
   aws polly synthesize-speech \
       --output-format mp3 \
       --voice-id Joanna \
       --engine neural \
       --text-type ssml \
       --text '<speak>Acme products are of the very highest quality and <prosody
   rate="slow">lowest price</prosody></speak>' \
       products-neural-ssml.mp3
   ```

   You will see similar output as you did in steps 2 and 3.

6. Listen to the MP3. Here is an example on macOS CLI:

   ```
   afplay products-neural-ssml.mp3
   ```

A list of SSML tags supported by Polly is shown in this article (*https://oreil.ly/q148r*).

Discussion

Having the ability to easily generate lifelike audio from text allows for many creative uses. You no longer need voice actors to sit and rehearse recordings. You can now easily incorporate audio into your application. This can improve your customers' experience in many ways.

When creating audio with Polly, you should experiment with different voices and SSML tags (you might even want to create your own voice (*https://oreil.ly/vsIzj*)). Many of Polly's voices are available to create Amazon Alexa skills (*https://oreil.ly/A0xXZ*).

Challenge

Create a pronunciation lexicon (*https://oreil.ly/TQrQS*) for Polly to use.

8.3 Computer Vision Analysis of Form Data

Problem

You have a document and need to extract responses from it so that you can digitally process them.

Solution

You will install and use the Textractor (*https://oreil.ly/zPgXy*) tool provided by AWS to utilize the forms feature of Amazon Textract. This will pull the values from the form and associate them with their keys (e.g., Name). See Figure 8-3.

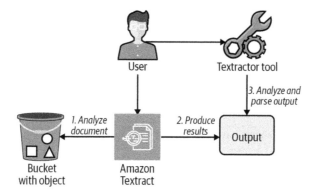

Figure 8-3. Analyzing a document with Amazon Textract and the textractor tool

Prerequisite

- S3 bucket

Preparation

Follow the steps in this recipe's folder in the chapter code repository (*https://github.com/AWSCookbook/ArtificialIntelligence*).

Steps

1. In the root of the Chapter 8 repository, cd to the *803-Computer-Vision-Analysis-of-Handwritten-Form-Data/* directory and follow the subsequent steps:

   ```
   cd 803-Computer-Vision-Analysis-of-Handwritten-Form-Data/
   ```

2. Copy the provided *registration_form.png* file (or your own) to the S3 bucket you created:

   ```
   aws s3 cp ./registration_form.png s3://awscookbook803-$RANDOM_STRING
   ```

   You should see output similar to the following:

   ```
   upload: ./registration_form.png to s3://awscookbook803-<<unique>>/
   registration_form.png
   ```

3. Analyze the document with Textract and redirect the output to a file:

   ```
   aws textract analyze-document \
       --document '{"S3Object":{"Bucket":"'"awscookbook803-${RANDOM_STRING}"'",
   "Name":"registration_form.png"}}' \
       --feature-types '["FORMS"]' > output.json
   ```

4. Get the Textractor tool from the *aws-samples* repository on GitHub:

   ```
   wget https://github.com/aws-samples/amazon-textract-textractor/blob/master/zip/
   textractor.zip?raw=true -O textractor.zip
   ```

Many great AWS samples and tools (*https://github.com/aws-samples*) are available on GitHub. It is a great place to check often for new ideas and approaches.

5. Unzip the archive:

```
unzip textractor.zip
```

6. Create a Python virtual environment (if you don't already have one created):

```
test -d .venv || python3 -m venv .venv
```

7. Activate the newly created Python virtual environment:

```
source .venv/bin/activate
```

8. Install the required Python modules for Textractor:

```
pip install -r requirements.txt
```

You should see output similar to the following:

```
Collecting tabulate
  Downloading tabulate-0.8.9-py3-none-any.whl (25 kB)
Installing collected packages: tabulate
Successfully installed tabulate-0.8.9
```

9. Install the boto3 module:

```
pip install boto3
```

10. Use the tool to analyze the registration form and parse the output:

```
python textractor.py \
    --documents s3://awscookbook803-${RANDOM_STRING}/registration_form.png \
    --text --forms
```

You should see output similar to the following:

```
**********************************************************
Total input documents: 1
**********************************************************

Textracting Document # 1: registration_form.png
==================================================
Calling Textract...
Received Textract response...
Generating output...
Total Pages in Document: 1
registration_form.png textracted successfully.

**********************************************************
Successfully textracted documents: 1
**********************************************************
```

Validation checks. Check out the form data extracted and confidence values:

```
cat registration_form-png-page-1-forms.csv | column -t -s,
```

You should see output similar to the following:

```
Key                      KeyConfidence  Value                               ValueConfidence
Average Score            97.0           285                                            97.0
Name:                    96.5           Elwood Blues                                   96.5
Date                     94.5           2/9/2021                                       94.5
Team Name:               92.0           The Blues Brothers                             92.0
Years of Experience      91.5           10                                             91.5
E-mail Address:          91.0           thebluesbrothers@theawscookbook.com            91.0
Signature                90.5           Elwood Blues                                   90.5
Date                     89.0           2/9/2021                                       89.0
Number of Team Members   81.0           2                                              81.0
```

Cleanup

Follow the steps in this recipe's folder in the chapter code repository (*https://github.com/AWSCookbook/ArtificialIntelligence*).

Discussion

Automated document processing opens up many new avenues for innovation and efficiency for organizations. Instead of having to manually interpret fields and tables in a document, tools like Textract can be used to digitize and speed up the process. Now that you are able to associate data values and fields with each other, additional processing is able to happen effectively.

Challenge

Print out the blank form provided in the repo. Fill in responses by hand. Take a photo/scan of the document and analyze it with Textract.

8.4 Redacting PII from Text Using Comprehend

Problem

You have a document with potential personally identifiable information (PII) in it. You would like to remove the PII before more processing of the document occurs.

Solution

Create sample data and store it in an S3 bucket. Launch an Amazon Comprehend job to detect and redact PII entities. Finally, view the results (see Figure 8-4).

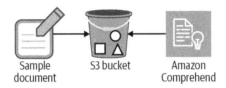

Sample   S3 bucket   Amazon
document   Comprehend

Figure 8-4. Redacting PII data from a document with Amazon Comprehend

Prerequisite

- S3 bucket with file for analysis and path for output

Preparation

Follow the steps in this recipe's folder in the chapter code repository (*https://github.com/AWSCookbook/ArtificialIntelligence*).

Steps

1. Create a file named *assume-role-policy.json* with the following content (file provided in the repository):

   ```
   {
     "Version": "2012-10-17",
     "Statement": [
     {
       "Effect": "Allow",
       "Principal": {
         "Service": "comprehend.amazonaws.com"
       },
       "Action": "sts:AssumeRole"
     }
     ]
   }
   ```

2. Create a role for the Comprehend job to use to read and write data from S3:

   ```
   aws iam create-role --role-name AWSCookbook804Comprehend \
       --assume-role-policy-document file://assume-role-policy.json
   ```

   You should see output similar to the following:

   ```
   {
     "Role": {
     "Path": "/",
     "RoleName": "AWSCookbook804Comprehend",
     "RoleId": "<<RoldID>>",
     "Arn": "arn:aws:iam::111111111111:role/AWSCookbook804Comprehend",
     "CreateDate": "2021-09-22T13:12:22+00:00",
     "AssumeRolePolicyDocument": {
       "Version": "2012-10-17",
       "Statement": [
         {
   ...
   ```

3. Attach the IAM managed policy for `AmazonS3FullAccess` to the IAM role:

```
aws iam attach-role-policy --role-name AWSCookbook804Comprehend \
    --policy-arn arn:aws:iam::aws:policy/AmazonS3FullAccess
```

4. Create some sample PII data using Faker (*https://faker.readthedocs.io*) (or by hand):

```
pip install faker
faker -r=10 profile > sample_data.txt
```

5. Copy your sample data to the bucket (file provided in the repository)

```
aws s3 cp ./sample_data.txt s3://awscookbook804-$RANDOM_STRING
```

You should see output similar to the following:

```
upload: ./sample_data.txt to s3://awscookbook804-<<unique>>/sample_data.txt
```

6. Create a `start-pii-entities-detection-job` with Comprehend:

```
JOB_ID=$(aws comprehend start-pii-entities-detection-job \
    --input-data-config S3Uri="s3://awscookbook804-$RANDOM_STRING/
sample_data.txt" \
    --output-data-config S3Uri="s3://awscookbook804-$RANDOM_STRING/
redacted_output/" \
    --mode "ONLY_REDACTION" \
    --redaction-config
PiiEntityTypes="BANK_ACCOUNT_NUMBER","BANK_ROUTING","CREDIT_DEBIT_NUMBER",
"CREDIT_DEBIT_CVV",
"CREDIT_DEBIT_EXPIRY","PIN","EMAIL","ADDRESS","NAME","PHONE","SSN",MaskMode="REPL
ACE_WITH_PII_ENTITY_TYPE" \
    --data-access-role-arn "arn:aws:iam::${AWS_ACCOUNT_ID}:role/
AWSCookbook804Comprehend" \
    --job-name "aws cookbook 804" \
    --language-code "en" \
    --output text --query JobId)
```

 You can alternatively use the detect-pii-entities (*https://oreil.ly/ pdrQC*) command if you are interested in the location of PII data in a document. This is helpful if you need to process the PII in a certain way.

7. Monitor the job until it is COMPLETED; this will take a few minutes:

```
aws comprehend describe-pii-entities-detection-job \
    --job-id $JOB_ID
```

You should see output similar to the following:

```
{
  "PiiEntitiesDetectionJobProperties": {
  "JobId": "<<hash>>",
  "JobName": "aws cookbook 804",
  "JobStatus": "COMPLETED",
  "SubmitTime": "2021-06-29T18:35:14.701000-04:00",
  "EndTime": "2021-06-29T18:43:21.200000-04:00",
  "InputDataConfig": {
    "S3Uri": "s3://awscookbook804-<<string>>/sample_data.txt",
    "InputFormat": "ONE_DOC_PER_LINE"
```

```
        },
        "OutputDataConfig": {
          "S3Uri": "s3://awscookbook804-<<string>>/redacted_output/<<Account Id>>-PII-
    <<hash>>/output/"
        },
```

Validation checks.   When the job is complete, get the location of the outputted data in S3:

```
S3_LOCATION=$(aws comprehend describe-pii-entities-detection-job \
    --job-id $JOB_ID --output text \
    --query PiiEntitiesDetectionJobProperties.OutputDataConfig.S3Uri)
```

Get the output file from S3:

```
aws s3 cp ${S3_LOCATION}sample_data.txt.out .
```

You should see output similar to the following:

```
download: s3://awscookbook804-<<unique>>/redacted_output/111111111111-PII-
cb5991dd58105db185a4cc1906e38411/output/sample_data.txt.out to ./sample_data.txt.out
```

View the output:

```
cat sample_data.txt.out
```

You should see output similar to the following. Notice the PII has been redacted:

```
{'job': 'Arts development officer', 'company': 'Vance Group', 'ssn': '[SSN]',
'residence':
'[ADDRESS]\[ADDRESS]', 'current_location': (Decimal('77.6093685'),
Decimal('-90.497660')), 'blood_group':
'O-', 'website': ['http://cook.com/', 'http://washington.biz/', 'http://owens.net/',
'http://www.benson.com/'], 'username': 'rrobinson', 'name': '[NAME]', 'sex': 'M',
'address':
'[ADDRESS]\[ADDRESS]', 'mail': '[EMAIL]', 'birthdate': datetime.date(1989, 10, 27)}
```

Cleanup

Follow the steps in this recipe's folder in the chapter code repository (*https://github.com/AWSCookbook/ArtificialIntelligence*).

Discussion

PII is closely associated with many security and compliance standards that you may come across in your career responsibilities. Generally, if you are responsible for handling PII for your customers, you need to implement security mechanisms to ensure the safety of that data. Furthermore, you may need to detect and analyze the kind of PII you store. While Amazon Macie (*https://aws.amazon.com/macie*) can do this at scale within your S3 buckets or data lake, you may want to detect PII within your application to implement your own checks and workflows. For example, you may have a user fill out a form and submit it, and then detect if they have accidentally disclosed specific types of PII that you are not allowed to store, and reject the upload.

You can leverage Amazon Comprehend to detect this type of information for you. When you use Comprehend, the predefined feature detection is backed by detection models that are trained using large datasets to ensure quality results.

Challenge

Use Comprehend to label the type of PII rather than just redacting it. (This article (*https://oreil.ly/u3kJq*) provides a hint.)

8.5 Detecting Text in a Video

Problem

You have a video and would like to extract any text from scenes in it for analysis.

Solution

Upload the video file to S3 and start a text detection job in Amazon Rekognition Video (see Figure 8-5).

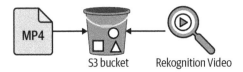

Figure 8-5. Using Rekognition Video to detect text in an MP4

Prerequisite

- S3 bucket

Preparation

Follow the steps in this recipe's folder in the chapter code repository (*https://github.com/AWSCookbook/ArtificialIntelligence*).

Steps

1. Copy the provided *sample_movie.mp4* file to the S3 bucket you created:
   ```
   aws s3 cp ./sample_movie.mp4 s3://awscookbook805-$RANDOM_STRING
   ```

   You should see output similar to the following:
   ```
   upload: ./sample_movie.mp4 to s3://awscookbook805-utonl0/sample_movie.mp4
   ```

Regarding supported video formats, the Amazon Rekognition FAQs (*https://aws.amazon.com/rekognition/faqs*) states, "Amazon Rekognition Video supports H.264 files in MPEG-4 (.mp4) or MOV format. If your video files use a different codec, you can transcode them into H.264 using AWS Elemental MediaConvert (*https://aws.amazon.com/mediaconvert*)."

2. Begin the text detection job:

```
JOB_ID=$(aws rekognition start-text-detection \
    --video '{"S3Object":{"Bucket":"'"awscookbook805-
$RANDOM_STRING"'","Name":"sample_movie.mp4"}}' \
    --output text --query JobId)
```

Wait until `JobStatus` changes from `IN_PROGRESS` to `SUCCEEDED`, and then the results will be displayed:

```
aws rekognition get-text-detection \
    --job-id $JOB_ID
```

You should see text similar to the following:

```
{
  "JobStatus": "SUCCEEDED",
  "VideoMetadata": {
  "Codec": "h264",
  "DurationMillis": 10051,
  "Format": "QuickTime / MOV",
  "FrameRate": 30.046607971191406,
  "FrameHeight": 240,
  "FrameWidth": 320,
  "ColorRange": "LIMITED"
  },
  ...
```

Validation checks. Run the command again with this query to get the `DetectedText` values:

```
aws rekognition get-text-detection \
    --job-id $JOB_ID \
    --query 'TextDetections[*].TextDetection.DetectedText'
```

You should see text similar to the following:

```
[
  "COPYRIGHT, 1901",
  "THOMAB A. EDISON.",
  "PATENTED AuOUST 31ST. 1897",
  "COPYRIGHT,",
  "1901",
  "THOMAB",
  "A.",
  "EDISON.",
  "PATENTED",
  "AuOUST",
```

```
"31ST.",
"1897",
```

Cleanup

Follow the steps in this recipe's folder in the chapter code repository (*https://github.com/AWSCookbook/ArtificialIntelligence*).

Discussion

You used Rekognition to detect text within a video file and saved the output to a report accessible within the Rekognition service. The output of the text detection job contains time markers for the text detected, the detected text itself, and other features. You can also detect text within images, have batch processing jobs run on large sets of files, and detect other features (*https://oreil.ly/Y3pzt*) within videos and images. This fully managed service allows you to use reliable detection models without having to train your own.

 Rekognition supports Custom Labels, a feature of the service that allows you to train specific models to recognize particular features in video and images specific to your needs. You can accomplish this all within the Rekognition service itself for an end-to-end implementation. For more information, see the support document (*https://oreil.ly/TDARq*).

You can integrate Rekognition directly into your application or hardware by using the AWS SDK for a reliable feature and text detection mechanism.

Challenge

Configure a text detection job to automatically start when a file is uploaded to a specific S3 bucket by using EventBridge.

8.6 Physician Dictation Analysis Using Amazon Transcribe Medical and Comprehend Medical

Problem

You need to build a solution that recognizes medical professional dictation audio files. The solution needs to be able to categorize things like protected health information (PHI) for further analysis.

Solution

Use Amazon Transcribe Medical to analyze your audio file. Then, use Amazon Comprehend Medical to generate the analysis of the physician's speech in a medical context (see Figure 8-6).

S3 bucket   Amazon Transcribe   Amazon Comprehend
             Medical   Medical

Figure 8-6. Using Transcribe Medical and Comprehend Medical with physician dictations

Prerequisite

- An audio file with speech (human or computer-generated) in it that contains medical jargon

Preparation

Follow the steps in this recipe's folder in the chapter code repository (*https:// github.com/AWSCookbook/ArtificialIntelligence*).

Steps

1. Create a JSON file named *awscookbook806-template.json* with the parameters specifying your physician's specialty, language, S3 bucket, and dictation audio file (file provided in the repository):

   ```
   {
       "MedicalTranscriptionJobName": "aws-cookbook-806",
       "LanguageCode": "en-US",
       "Specialty": "PRIMARYCARE",
       "Type": "DICTATION",
       "OutputBucketName":"awscookbook806-RANDOM_STRING",
       "Media": {
         "MediaFileUri": "s3://awscookbook806-RANDOM_STRING/dictation.mp3"
       }
   }
   ```

2. Use the **sed** command to replace the values in the *awscookbook806-template.json* file with the *RANDOM_STRING* value for your S3 bucket:

   ```
   sed -e "s/RANDOM_STRING/${RANDOM_STRING}/g" \
       awscookbook806-template.json > awscookbook806.json
   ```

3. Start a medical transcription job using the JSON file that you created:

   ```
   aws transcribe start-medical-transcription-job \
       --cli-input-json file://awscookbook806.json
   ```

You should see output similar to the following:

```
{
  "MedicalTranscriptionJob": {
    "MedicalTranscriptionJobName": "aws-cookbook-806",
    "TranscriptionJobStatus": "IN_PROGRESS",
    "LanguageCode": "en-US",
    "Media": {
      "MediaFileUri": "s3://awscookbook806-<<unique>>/dictation.mp3"
    },
    "StartTime": "2021-07-14T20:24:58.012000-04:00",
    "CreationTime": "2021-07-14T20:24:57.979000-04:00",
    "Specialty": "PRIMARYCARE",
    "Type": "DICTATION"
  }
}
```

Check the status of the Transcribe Medical job. Wait until it is COMPLETED:

```
aws transcribe get-medical-transcription-job \
    --medical-transcription-job-name aws-cookbook-806 \
    --output text \
    --query MedicalTranscriptionJob.TranscriptionJobStatus
```

4. Get the output from your previous job by downloading the file from S3:

```
aws s3 cp s3://awscookbook806-${RANDOM_STRING}/medical/aws-cookbook-806.json \
    ./aws-cookbook-806.json
```

You should see output similar to the following:

```
download: s3://awscookbook806-<<unique>>/medical/aws-cookbook-806.json to ./aws-
cookbook-806.json
```

5. Display the transcribed speech from the downloaded file:

```
cat aws-cookbook-806.json | jq .results.transcripts
```

You should see output similar to the following:

```
[
  {
    "transcript": "patient jane doe experiencing symptoms of headache,
administered 200 mg ibuprofen
twice daily."
  }
]
```

> The resulting JSON file that you downloaded contains time markers for each word that was transcribed. You can use this information within your application to provide additional context and functionality.

Validation checks. Start an entities detection job using the Comprehend Medical detect entities API. This will show the location of things like medical conditions and PHI:

```
aws comprehendmedical detect-entities-v2 \
    --text "$(cat aws-cookbook-806.json | jq .results.transcripts[0].transcript | tr
-d '"')"
```

You should see output similar to the following:

```
{
  "Entities": [
    {
      "Id": 4,
      "BeginOffset": 8,
      "EndOffset": 12,
      "Score": 0.8507962226867676,
      "Text": "jane",
      "Category": "PROTECTED_HEALTH_INFORMATION",
      "Type": "NAME",
      "Traits": []
    },
    ...
```

Cleanup

Follow the steps in this recipe's folder in the chapter code repository (*https://github.com/AWSCookbook/ArtificialIntelligence*).

Discussion

You were able to use Amazon Transcribe Medical and Amazon Comprehend Medical to take a physician's dictation audio file, turn it into text, and then detect the medical-context entities within the audio file. The final result provided patient data, symptoms, and medication and dosage information, which can be extremely useful in building medical applications for patients and medical professionals. Comprehend Medical also provides batch analysis and feature detection for multiple types of PHI and can determine dictation versus patient/physician conversation. With the advent of telemedicine, these powerful features can be used to provide immediate transcriptions to patients using app-based medical services to receive healthcare from medical professionals.

Both of these services you used for the solution are HIPAA compliant. You can confidently build solutions with these services for medical use cases that need to conform with HIPAA compliance. For more information on AWS services that conform to compliance standards, see the Services in Scope web page (*https://oreil.ly/DJi29*).

Challenge

Use EventBridge to automate the processing of new objects uploaded to your S3 bucket.

8.7 Determining Location of Text in an Image

Problem

You need to determine in which quadrant of an image the text "AWS" appears.

Solution

We'll use Textract to analyze the image from an S3 bucket and then parse the output to calculate the location of the text (see Figure 8-7).

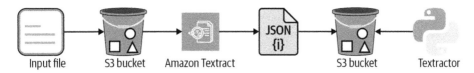

Input file   S3 bucket   Amazon Textract   S3 bucket   Textractor

Figure 8-7. Using Textractor to analyze output from Amazon Textract

Prerequisite

- S3 bucket

Preparation

Follow the steps in this recipe's folder in the chapter code repository (*https:// github.com/AWSCookbook/ArtificialIntelligence*).

Steps

1. Copy the provided *book_cover.png* file to the S3 bucket you created:

   ```
   aws s3 cp ./book_cover.png s3://awscookbook807-$RANDOM_STRING
   ```

   You should see output similar to the following:

   ```
   upload: ./book_cover.png to s3://awscookbook807-<<unique>>/book_cover.png
   ```

2. Analyze the file with Textract and output the results to a file called *output.json*:

   ```
   aws textract analyze-document \
       --document '{"S3Object":{"Bucket":"'"awscookbook807-
   $RANDOM_STRING"'","Name":"book_cover.png"}}' \
       --feature-types '["TABLES","FORMS"]' > output.json
   ```

Validation checks.   Examine the `BoundingBox` values for the Practical text to find the location:

```
jq '.Blocks[] | select(.Text == "Practical") | select(.BlockType == "WORD")
| .Geometry.BoundingBox' output.json
```

If the left and top values are both less than 0.5, the word Practical is located in the top left of the page (see Figure 8-8).

You should see output similar to the following:

```
{
  "Width": 0.15338942408561707,
  "Height": 0.03961481899023056,
  "Left": 0.06334125995635986,
  "Top": 0.39024031162261963
}
```

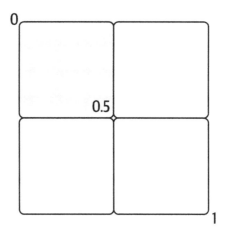

Figure 8-8. Reference BoundingBox coordinate diagram

Per the Textract Developer Guide (*https://oreil.ly/Xh9Bk*), each BoundingBox property has a value between 0 and 1. The value is a ratio of the overall image width (applies to left and width) or height (applies to height and top). For example, if the input image is 700 × 200 pixels, and the top-left coordinate of the bounding box is (350,50) pixels, the API returns a left value of 0.5 (350/700) and a top value of 0.25 (50/200).

Cleanup

Follow the steps in this recipe's folder in the chapter code repository (*https://github.com/AWSCookbook/ArtificialIntelligence*).

Discussion

You may have used traditional optical character recognition (OCR) software in the past when you have scanned physical documents and used the OCR output to get text-based output of the content. Amazon Textract (*https://aws.amazon.com/textract*) takes this a step further using ML models for even more accurate text recognition with additional feature and context information you can use in your applications. You were able to determine the location of a string of text within an image by using this recipe. You could use similar functionality in Textract to forward certain portions of text from images (or scanned forms) to different teams for human review or automating sending certain parts of forms to different microservices in your application for processing or persisting. Application developers do not need to train a model before using Textract; Textract comes pretrained with many datasets to provide highly accurate (*https://oreil.ly/X07aq*) character recognition.

Challenge

Determine the location of two different words in an image and calculate the distance between them.

CHAPTER 9

Account Management

9.0 Introduction

While the previous chapters have focused on deploying and configuring resources *inside* your AWS account, we want to provide some recipes that show examples of what you can do at the whole account level.

As you continue to scale your AWS usage, you will find it useful to have tools and services available to ease the burden of management, especially if you start to add additional AWS accounts to your environment. We are seeing more and more people choose to use AWS accounts as "containers" for their specific applications. Some companies provide individual accounts for production and nonproduction work-loads to business units within a company; some even set up "shared services" accounts to provide internal services to business units within a company to share common resources across the many accounts they may be managing. Your AWS account spans Regions (*https://oreil.ly/INVpe*) to give you global capabilities, as shown in Figure 9-1.

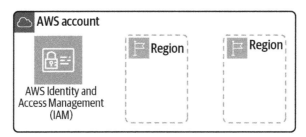

Figure 9-1. AWS account perspective

We like to think of the tools and services that AWS provides as building blocks that you can use to customize your cloud environment to meet your specific needs. Some of these can be used at an account level to give you more management capabilities over your environments as you scale (i.e., adding additional team members or adding additional AWS accounts). You can organize and consolidate billing for many accounts by using AWS Organizations (*https://aws.amazon.com/organizations*) and provide centralized access management through AWS Single Sign-On (*https://aws.amazon.com/single-sign-on*), both of which you will explore in the recipes in this chapter, in addition to some recipes to help you configure and maintain a secure environment at the account level.

 You should always keep an eye on the AWS Prescriptive Guidance (*https://aws.amazon.com/prescriptive-guidance*) website for the most up-to-date guidance on account-level capabilities and recommendations.

Workstation Configuration

You will need a few things installed to be ready for the recipes in this chapter.

General setup

Follow the "General workstation setup steps for CLI recipes" on page xvii to validate your configuration and set up the required environment variables. Then, clone the chapter code repository:

```
git clone https://github.com/AWSCookbook/AccountManagement
```

9.1 Using EC2 Global View for Account Resource Analysis

Problem

You have been presented with an AWS account for a client. You need to export a CSV file containing all provisioned compute instances, disk volumes, and network resources across all Regions within an AWS account.

Solution

Navigate to EC2 Global View in the AWS Console. Export a CSV of resources in your account (see Figure 9-2).

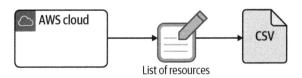

Figure 9-2. Generating a CSV of resources with EC2 Global View

Prerequisite

- AWS account with resources deployed

Steps

1. In the AWS Console, search for and then click EC2 Global View, as shown in Figure 9-3.

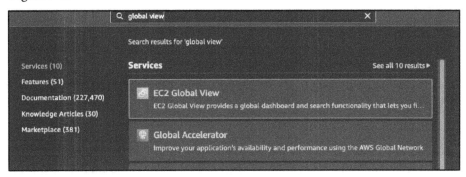

Figure 9-3. Searching for Global View

2. Navigate to the "Global search" menu and click Download CSV (see Figure 9-4).

Figure 9-4. Downloading a CSV from Global View

Validation checks. Open the downloaded CSV file in your favorite editor on your workstation. From there, you should be able to scroll through resources in your AWS account.

Discussion

You may find yourself often working in new AWS accounts as part of your job. If you are in a lab environment or a hackathon, using Global View is a great way for you to get an idea of what an AWS account contains. Before you begin to make changes in an account, it is important to take stock of what is already deployed across all Regions. Having this knowledge will allow you to ensure that you don't mistakenly cause any outages.

While you should use tools like AWS Config (*https://aws.amazon.com/config*) and the AWS Billing console for inspecting the configuration of resources inside your AWS account and keeping an eye on your bill, respectively, it is good to know that you can easily generate a list of EC2 and VPC resources. Routine CSV exports at different times can be used to provide a point-in-time snapshot.

Challenge

Use the Global search functionality to list all default VPC security groups. You can then double-check inbound rules for extraneous permissions.

9.2 Modifying Tags for Many Resources at One Time with Tag Editor

Problem

You need to add a tag to multiple resources in your AWS account where it doesn't already exist.

Solution

Launch the Tag Editor in the AWS Console. Find all resources that have an Environment key with nonexisting value. Add the tag (see Figure 9-5).

Tag   Multiple resources

Figure 9-5. Adding a tag to multiple resources

Prerequisite

- AWS account with resources deployed and tagged

Steps

1. In the AWS Console, search for Tag Editor and then click Resource Groups & Tag Editor, as shown in Figure 9-6.

Figure 9-6. Searching for Tag Editor in the AWS Console

2. From the lefthand menu, click Tag Editor under the Tagging heading (see Figure 9-7).

Figure 9-7. Launching Tag Editor

3. Set "Resource types" to "All supported resource types," enter a Tag key named **Environment**, use the drop-down menu to select "(not tagged)" for the value, and then click "Search resources" (see Figure 9-8).

Figure 9-8. Launching Tag Editor

4. Wait a few moments for the search to complete. Then view the results, select the resources that you wish to tag, and click "Manage tags of selected resources" (see Figure 9-9).

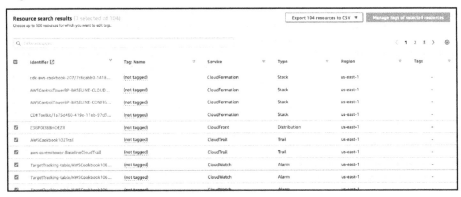

Figure 9-9. Viewing search results in Tag Editor

5. Enter a "Tag key" named **Environment**, enter a "Tag value" **Dev**, and click "Review and apply tag changes" (see Figure 9-10).

Figure 9-10. Tagging multiple resources with Tag Editor

6. In the pop-up window, confirm your selection by clicking "Apply changes to all selected" (see Figure 9-11).

Figure 9-11. Confirming changes to apply to resources in Tag Editor

Validation checks.   Use the CLI to confirm that all EC2 instances have an Environment tag:

```
aws ec2 describe-instances \
  --output text \
  --query 'Reservations[].Instances[?!not_null(Tags[?Key == `Environment`].Value)] |
[].[InstanceId]'
```

You should see no output. You can also repeat step 3 to confirm that all resources now have an Environment tag.

Discussion

A tag consists of a key and a value and can be applied to many resources at the time of creation and almost all resources after creation. You should implement your own tagging strategy as early as possible in your cloud journey. This ensures that you can identify the growing number of resources you deploy over the lifespan of your AWS account. Tags are useful for auditing, billing, scheduling updates, delegating access to resources with specific tags, and so on.

Cost allocation tags (*https://oreil.ly/YvgIT*) can help you make sense of your AWS bill, to see exactly which resources are contributing to certain portions of your bill. In addition to the cost allocation report, you can filter by tags interactively via Cost Explorer in the AWS Billing console to analyze and visualize your costs.

The Tag Editor can help you search and perform batch updates for tags across your AWS resources. Say you might have deployed many resources but forgot to tag them all, or you have historically not used tags and would like to start. You can batch select many resources within the Tag Editor (across all Regions or within a selected set of Regions) and perform these updates to ease the burden of implementing a tagging strategy.

While not an exhaustive list, here are some good tags to include as part of a tagging baseline:

CreatedBy
> The User or Identity that created the resource

Application
> The service or application of which the resource is a component

CostCenter
> Useful for billing identification and to help implement a chargeback model for shared AWS account usage

CreationDate
> The date the resource was created

Contact
> An email address for the team or individual in case of any issues with the resource (also helpful for configuring automated alerts)

MaintenanceWindow
> Useful for defining a window of time that the resource is allowed to not be available in case of patching, updates, or maintenance

DeletionDate
> Useful for development or sandbox environments so that you know when it may be safe to delete a resource

Challenge

Apply a baseline set of tags to your AWS resources and begin to enforce the tags with a tag policy (*https://oreil.ly/7UePx*) by enabling AWS Organizations (*https://oreil.ly/Dg3I6*).

9.3 Enabling CloudTrail Logging for Your AWS Account

Problem

You just set up your AWS account and want to retain an audit log of all activity for all Regions in your account.

Solution

Configure an S3 bucket with a bucket policy allowing CloudTrail to write events. Enable CloudTrail for all Regions in your account and configure CloudTrail to log all audit events to the S3 bucket, as shown in Figure 9-12.

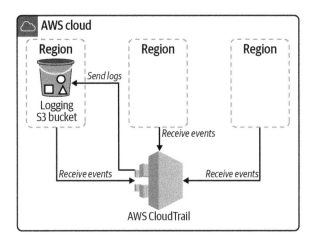

Figure 9-12. Turning on logging for CloudTrail

Prerequisite

- S3 bucket for logging

Preparation

Follow the steps in this recipe's folder in the chapter code repository (*https:// github.com/AWSCookbook/BigData*).

Steps

1. Create a file called *cloudtrail-s3policy-template.json* (file provided in the repository):

```
{
    "Version": "2012-10-17",
    "Statement": [
```

```
      {
        "Sid": "S3CloudTrail",
        "Effect": "Allow",
        "Principal": {"Service": "cloudtrail.amazonaws.com"},
        "Action": "s3:GetBucketAcl",
        "Resource": "arn:aws:s3:::BUCKET_NAME"
      },
      {
        "Sid": "S3CloudTrail",
        "Effect": "Allow",
        "Principal": {"Service": "cloudtrail.amazonaws.com"},
        "Action": "s3:PutObject",
        "Resource": "arn:aws:s3:::BUCKET_NAME/AWSLogs/AWS_ACCOUNT_ID/*",
        "Condition": {"StringEquals": {"s3:x-amz-acl": "bucket-owner-full-
control"}}
      }
    ]
}
```

2. Replace the values in the *cloudtrail-s3policy-template.json* file with values from your deployment. Here is a way to do it quickly with sed:

```
sed -e "s/BUCKET_NAME/awscookbook903-$RANDOM_STRING/g" \
    -e "s|AWS_ACCOUNT_ID|${AWS_ACCOUNT_ID}|g" \
    cloudtrail-s3policy-template.json > cloudtrail-s3policy.json
```

3. Add the S3 bucket policy to your S3 bucket:

```
aws s3api put-bucket-policy \
    --bucket awscookbook903-$RANDOM_STRING \
    --policy file://cloudtrail-s3policy.json
```

4. Enable CloudTrail for all AWS Regions and configure the S3 bucket to send logs to the following:

```
aws cloudtrail create-trail --name AWSCookbook903Trail \
    --s3-bucket-name awscookbook903-$RANDOM_STRING \
    --is-multi-region-trail
```

5. Start the logging of your CloudTrail trail:

```
aws cloudtrail start-logging --name AWSCookbook903Trail
```

 More information can be found on AWS for the required S3 bucket policy (*https://oreil.ly/jhcXQ*) for CloudTrail logging.

Validation checks.   Describe the trail:

```
aws cloudtrail describe-trails --trail-name-list AWSCookbook903Trail
```

You should see output similar to the following:

```
{
  "trailList": [
  {
```

```
    "Name": "AWSCookbook903Trail",
    "S3BucketName": "awscookbook903-<<string>>",
    "IncludeGlobalServiceEvents": true,
    "IsMultiRegionTrail": true,
    "HomeRegion": "us-east-1",
    "TrailARN": "arn:aws:cloudtrail:us-east-1:<<Account Id>>:trail/
AWSCookbook903Trail",
    "LogFileValidationEnabled": false,
    "HasCustomEventSelectors": false,
    "HasInsightSelectors": false,
    "IsOrganizationTrail": false
  }
 ]
}
```

Get the trail status:

```
aws cloudtrail get-trail-status --name AWSCookbook903Trail
```

You should see output similar to the following:

```
{
  "IsLogging": true,
  "StartLoggingTime": "2021-06-28T21:22:56.308000-04:00",
  "LatestDeliveryAttemptTime": "",
  "LatestNotificationAttemptTime": "",
  "LatestNotificationAttemptSucceeded": "",
  "LatestDeliveryAttemptSucceeded": "",
  "TimeLoggingStarted": "2021-06-29T01:22:56Z",
  "TimeLoggingStopped": ""
}
```

Cleanup

Follow the steps in this recipe's folder in the chapter code repository (*https:// github.com/AWSCookbook/Security*).

Discussion

You can use CloudTrail to log and continuously monitor all events in your AWS account. Specifically, events refer to all API activity against the AWS APIs. These include actions that you (and all authenticated entities) take in the console, via the command line, API activity from your applications, and other AWS services performing actions (automatic actions like autoscaling, EventBridge triggers, replication, etc.).

 You can query your logs in place on S3 using Amazon Athena if you are looking for specific events, and you can index your logs with Amazon OpenSearch (*https://oreil.ly/gdkRW*) to perform complex queries against your historical data.

You should use CloudTrail from a security standpoint, but you can also use it from an application debugging standpoint. Say you have an event-driven application that triggers a Lambda function when you upload files to an S3 bucket (see Recipe 5.7). If your IAM policy is incorrect for the Lambda function invocation, you will be able to see the Deny in the CloudTrail logs. This is helpful for application developers and architects who are building and designing event-driven applications powered by Amazon EventBridge.

Challenge

Configure an organizational trail (*https://oreil.ly/4qAbK*) if you have an AWS Organization with multiple accounts. (See Recipe 9.6 to set up an AWS Organization.)

9.4 Setting Up Email Alerts for Root Login

Problem

You want to be notified by email when the root user logs into an AWS account.

Solution

Create an SNS topic and subscribe to it. Then create an Amazon EventBridge rule with a pattern that searches for root logins and triggers the SNS topic, as shown in Figure 9-13.

Root login   AWS CloudTrail   Amazon EventBridge   Email notification

Figure 9-13. Logging and alerting for root logins

Prerequisite

- AWS account with CloudTrail enabled (see Recipe 9.3)

Steps

1. Create an SNS topic:

```
TOPIC_ARN=$(aws sns create-topic \
    --name root-login-notify-topic \
    --output text --query TopicArn)
```

2. Subscribe to the SNS topic. This will send a confirmation email to the address you specify:

```
aws sns subscribe \
    --topic-arn $TOPIC_ARN \
    --protocol email \
    --notification-endpoint your-email@example.com
```

3. Locate the confirmation email in your inbox that AWS sent and click "Confirm subscription."

In the root of this chapter's repository, cd to the *904-Setting-Up-Email-Alerts-for-Root-Login* directory and follow the subsequent steps.

4. Now create an assume-role policy JSON statement called *assume-role-policy.json* to use in the next step (this file is provided in the repository):

```
{
  "Version": "2012-10-17",
  "Statement": [
    {
      "Effect": "Allow",
      "Principal": {
        "Service": "events.amazonaws.com"
      },
      "Action": "sts:AssumeRole"
    }
  ]
}
```

5. Create the role and specify the *assume-role-policy.json* file:

```
aws iam create-role --role-name AWSCookbook904RuleRole \
    --assume-role-policy-document \
    file://assume-role-policy.json
```

6. Now attach the managed `AmazonSNSFullAccess` IAM policy to the IAM role:

```
aws iam attach-role-policy \
    --policy-arn arn:aws:iam::aws:policy/AmazonSNSFullAccess \
    --role-name AWSCookbook904RuleRole
```

7. Create a file called *event-pattern.json* for AWS Console sign-in events (file provided in the repository):

```
{
  "detail-type": [
  "AWS API Call via CloudTrail",
  "AWS Console Sign In via CloudTrail"
  ],
  "detail": {
  "userIdentity": {
    "type": [
      "Root"
    ]
  }
  }
}
```

8. Create an EventBridge rule that monitors the trail for root login activity:

```
aws events put-rule --name "AWSCookbook904Rule" \
    --role-arn "arn:aws:iam::$AWS_ACCOUNT_ID:role/AWSCookbook904RuleRole" --
event-pattern file://event-
pattern.json
```

9. Set the target for your EventBridge rule to your SNS topic:

```
aws events put-targets --rule AWSCookbook904Rule \
    --targets "Id"="1","Arn"="$TOPIC_ARN"
```

Validation checks. Log in to your AWS account using your root account, wait a few minutes, and check your email for a message from SNS.

Cleanup

Follow the steps in this recipe's folder in the chapter code repository (*https://github.com/AWSCookbook/Security*).

Discussion

Setting up an alert to notify you on root user sign-ins is a detective mechanism you can layer into your security strategy to keep aware of unwelcome activity within your account. This method is a cost-effective solution to monitor your AWS account for unintended access via the root user. Since the root user is the most powerful and privileged identity (and should be used only for specific infrequent tasks), it is important to know when it is accessed.

 In some cases, the root user is needed to perform specific privileged actions and tasks within an AWS account. For a list of these actions requiring the root user, refer to the AWS support document (*https://oreil.ly/NvidX*).

Challenge

Add another EventBridge rule that notifies the same SNS topic when the root password is changed (here is a hint (*https://oreil.ly/vzvwz*)).

9.5 Setting Up Multi-Factor Authentication for a Root User

Problem

You need to enable multi-factor authentication for the root user of your AWS account.

Solution

Log in to your AWS account with your root user credentials. Navigate to the IAM console and enable multi-factor authentication using a U2F-compatible hardware device or a Time-Based One-Time Password (TOTP) (*https://oreil.ly/TtQtd*)–compliant virtual device (see Figure 9-14).

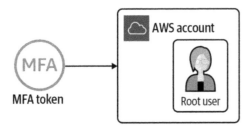

Figure 9-14. Enabling MFA for the root user in your AWS account

Steps

1. Log in to the AWS Console (*https://console.aws.amazon.com*) by using the email address associated with your root user. You can reset the password for the root user by using the "Forgot password" link displayed after you enter the root user email address; click Next. The login dialog you should see is shown in Figure 9-15.

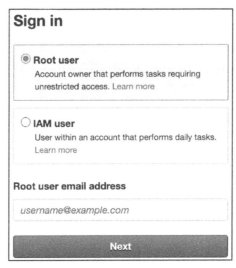

Figure 9-15. Selecting the root user login option

Since you will log in with the root user infrequently, you do not need to store the password for the user once you enable MFA. You can reset the password (*https://oreil.ly/ar0H9*) each time you need to access the account; take care to secure access to the mailbox associated with your root user.

2. Once you are logged in to the AWS Console, select My Security Credentials (*https://oreil.ly/z5xsh*) from the top right of the user interface, as shown in Figure 9-16.

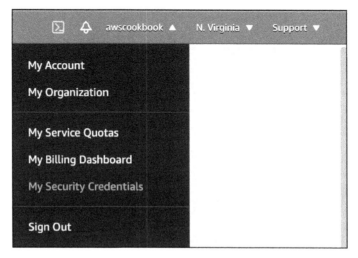

Figure 9-16. Navigating to the My Security Credentials menu

3. Expand the "Multi-factor authentication" pane on the Your Security Credentials page within the IAM console and click the Activate MFA button. Choose the type of device (*https://oreil.ly/VVL9g*) you will use and click Continue (see Figure 9-17).

 If you use a software-based password manager utility to store your virtual MFA device information, do not store your root user password in that same password manager. If your password manager utility or vault is compromised, your second factor and password together give the ability to access your AWS account. Similarly, the password information for your email account should not be stored in the same place as your virtual MFA device, since the root user password-reset procedure can be performed successfully with access to the mailbox associated with your root user.

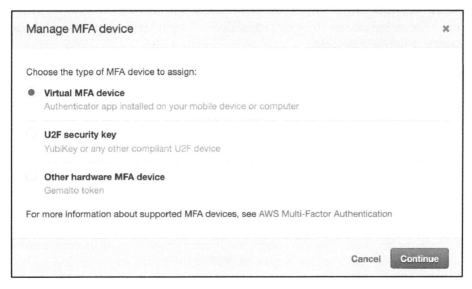

Figure 9-17. Selecting a virtual MFA device

4. Follow the prompts to either display a QR code that you can scan with your virtual device or plug in your hardware token and follow the prompts. Once you enter the code, you will see a window indicating that you have completed the MFA setup (see Figure 9-18).

Figure 9-18. Confirmation of MFA device setup

 You can print out a copy of the QR code displayed and keep this in a physically secure location as a backup in case you lose access to your virtual MFA device.

Validation checks. Sign out of your AWS account and sign back in with the root user. Enter the code generated by your virtual device (or plug in your hardware token) and complete the login process.

Cleanup

You should always keep MFA enabled for your root user. If you would like to disable the MFA device associated with your root user, follow the steps for deactivating the device (*https://oreil.ly/pvpVw*).

Discussion

The root user (*https://oreil.ly/qNtiE*) is the most powerful and privileged identity of an AWS account. The username is an email address that you configure when you first establish your AWS account, and password-reset requests can be made from the AWS Console or by contacting AWS support. If your email account is compromised, a malicious actor could request a reset of your root account password and gain access to your account. The root user should always be protected with a second factor of authentication to prevent unauthorized access to your account. Since the root user is needed on only rare occasions (*https://oreil.ly/Em4TW*), you should never use it for routine tasks.

 You need to enable IAM user and role access to the Billing console. You can follow the AWS steps (*https://oreil.ly/DVPbZ*) to perform that action and further reduce your dependency on using the root user for tasks.

It is extremely important to configure an IAM user (or set up federated access using ADFS with IAM, SAML with IAM, or AWS Single Sign-On) rather than use the root user to log in to your AWS account for your routine usage. AWS recommends immediately creating an administrative IAM user (*https://oreil.ly/MuSdE*) as one of the first things you do when you open an AWS account, shortly after you enable MFA for the root user. For a scalable approach, you can follow Recipe 9.6 to enable and use AWS Single Sign-On for your own (and delegated) access requirements.

Challenge

Configure MFA protection for other IAM roles (using trust policies) in your account (here is a hint (*https://oreil.ly/e8YMQ*)).

9.6 Setting Up AWS Organizations and AWS Single Sign-On

Problem

You need a scalable way to centrally manage usernames and passwords to access your AWS accounts.

Solution

Enable AWS Organizations, configure AWS Single Sign-On, create a group, create a permission set, and create a user in the AWS SSO directory for you to use, as shown in Figure 9-19.

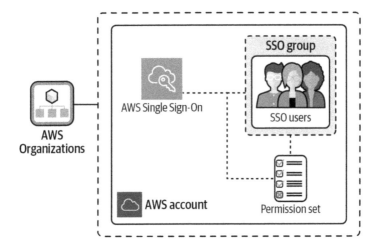

Figure 9-19. AWS SSO view of permissions and users

Steps

1. Navigate to AWS Organizations (*https://console.aws.amazon.com/organizations*) in the AWS Console and click "Create an organization."

    AWS Organizations provides many features that enable you to work with multiple AWS accounts at scale. For more information, see the AWS Organizations documentation (*https:// oreil.ly/Wdaa4*).

2. The organization creation will trigger an email to be sent to the email address associated with the root user of your account. Confirm the creation of the organization by clicking the "Verify your email address" button.

3. Navigate to the AWS SSO console (*https://console.aws.amazon.com/singlesignon*) in your Region and click the Enable SSO button.

 The initial configuration of AWS SSO uses a local directory for your users. You can federate to an existing user directory you may have, like Active Directory or a SAML provider. For information on configuring federation, the user guide for AWS SSO (*https://oreil.ly/PeusI*) provides details.

4. Go to the Groups portion of the SSO console and click "Create group." Enter the required Group name and click Create, as shown in Figure 9-20.

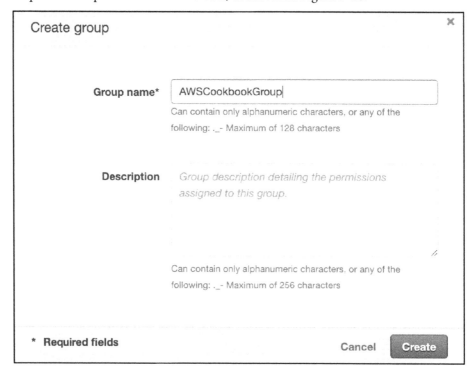

Figure 9-20. Creating a group in AWS SSO

5. Go to the Users portion of the SSO console and select "Add user." Enter the information required in the fields, add the user to the group you created, and select Create. You can have the AWS SSO console generate the initial password for you or send an email to the address provided in the required "Email address" field.

Assign the user to the group that you created in step 4 on the second page of the "Add user" wizard (see Figure 9-21).

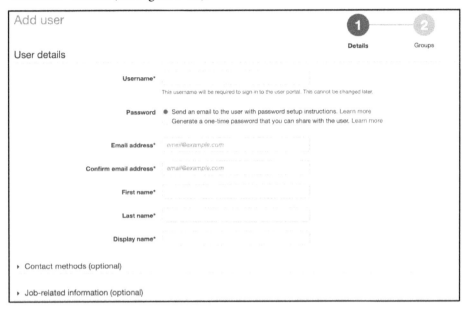

Figure 9-21. Creating a user in AWS SSO

6. Go to the AWS Accounts portion of the SSO console (in the left navigation menu of the console), choose the "Permission sets" tab, and select "Create permission set." Choose the "Use an existing job function policy" option and select PowerU serAccess (see Figure 9-22).

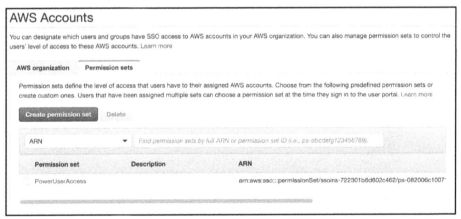

Figure 9-22. Creating a permission set in AWS SSO

7. To assign the permission set to the group you created for your AWS account, click the AWS accounts link in the left navigation menu, choose the "AWS organization" tab, select your AWS account from the list of accounts, and click "Assign users." Click the Groups tab and choose the group that you added your user to in step 4, as shown in Figure 9-23. Click "Next: Permission sets."

Figure 9-23. Adding a group to an assignment

8. Select the permission set you created in step 6 and click Finish (see Figure 9-24).

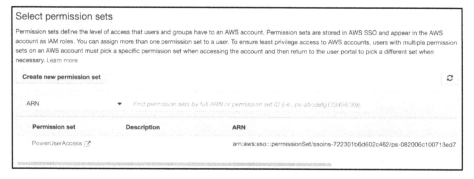

Figure 9-24. Assigning a permission set in AWS SSO

When you click Finish, members of this group can access the AWS account you specified using with permissions of the Pow erUserAccess IAM policy. AWS SSO provisions a role that can be assumed in your AWS account for this purpose. Do not modify this role via IAM in your AWS account, or the permission set will not be able to be used through AWS SSO.

Validation checks. Go to the URL provided on the AWS SSO console dashboard page and log in with the username and password of the user that you created in step 5. Choose either "Management console" or "Command line or programmatic access" to gain PowerUserAccess to your AWS account.

 The default URL is generated when you first enable AWS SSO. You can create a customized URL for your own purposes by clicking the Customize link next to the default URL in the SSO console.

Cleanup

Go to the AWS SSO console and select Settings from the left navigation menu. Scroll down to the bottom of the settings page and select "Delete AWS SSO Configuration." Confirm the deletion by selecting the checkboxes and clicking "Delete AWS SSO."

Go to AWS Organizations, select your organization, open the settings for your organization, and select "Delete organization." You will need to verify the organization ID and confirm the deletion of the organization from the email address associated with the root user of your AWS account.

Discussion

When you enable AWS Organizations, the account where you initially create your organization is known as the management account (*https://oreil.ly/UTrvA*). While you enabled AWS Organizations so that you could use AWS Single Sign-On in this recipe, it primarily exists for governing, organizing, and managing AWS accounts at scale. Some account management capabilities that you might be interested in include, but are not limited to, these:

- Consolidating billing for multiple AWS accounts
- Managing group accounts using organizational units (*https://oreil.ly/ZLn6v*) (OUs)
- Applying service control policies (*https://oreil.ly/DeR3h*) (SCPs) to individual accounts or OUs
- Centralizing policies (*https://oreil.ly/4s2Nx*) for tagging and backups for all accounts within your organization
- Sharing resources across accounts using Resource Access Manager (*https://oreil.ly/eiNlp*) (RAM)

AWS Organizations and AWS SSO are free to enable and provide a scalable way for you to begin to manage AWS accounts and user access to your entire AWS environment. As a best practice (*https://oreil.ly/rZ02g*), using the management account for management functions only (and not running workloads) is a pattern you should adopt. Creating specific AWS accounts for your production and nonproduction workloads that are members of your AWS Organization helps you isolate your workloads and reduce blast radius, delegate access, manage your billing, and so on.

 These concepts begin to define the concept of a *landing zone* (*https://oreil.ly/X9vg1*). Rather than build your own, you can use AWS Control Tower (*https://oreil.ly/DzWXI*) to configure a fully managed landing zone. There are advantages of using Control Tower when you plan to scale your AWS usage beyond just a few accounts.

AWS Single Sign-On provides a secure and scalable way to manage user access to your AWS accounts. You can integrate with an external identity provider (IdP) or use the built-in directory within AWS SSO, depending on how many users you need to manage and if you already have an external user directory.

When you successfully authenticate with AWS SSO, you are presented with a choice of access levels defined by permission sets (*https://oreil.ly/t3wOC*). Permission sets use an IAM policy definition that SSO uses to manage a role, which you can assume upon successful login. AWS provides permission sets within SSO that align with common job functions, but you can also create your own custom permission sets by writing IAM policy statements and saving them as a permission set. A temporary session is created once you choose your access level into an account. You can use the session within the AWS Console, or via the command line with the temporary access key ID, secret access key, and session token variables (*https://oreil.ly/Uz8BT*), or by using the AWS CLI v2 to authenticate with SSO from the command line (*https://oreil.ly/qLcUl*). You can adjust the length of the session duration (*https://oreil.ly/nXfAi*) within the AWS SSO console.

Security around the access to your AWS environments should be your top priority, and as you scale the number of users and accounts, and level of access delegated, this becomes a challenge. AWS SSO gives you a mechanism to implement security at scale for your AWS environments. Since the session you initiate with your account via AWS SSO is temporary, you do not need to create long-lived IAM access keys (*https:// oreil.ly/bk0L7*) to use in your command-line environment, which is one less secret to have to rotate and manage. You can also use multi-factor authentication with AWS SSO and require MFA for login.

Challenge 1

Connect AWS SSO to an external identity provider (*https://oreil.ly/Ra2r6*) for an existing IdP-like Active Directory or Okta.

Challenge 2

Apply a service control policy (*https://oreil.ly/6KWR4*) (SCP) to limit the Regions you can use within your AWS account.

Fast Fixes

These useful small bits of code will help you save time and get the most out of AWS.

Set your `AWS_ACCOUNT_ID` to a bash variable:

```
export AWS_ACCOUNT_ID=$(aws sts get-caller-identity \
--query Account --output text)
```

Get the most recently created CloudWatch log group name:

```
aws logs describe-log-groups --output=yaml \
--query 'reverse(sort_by(logGroups,&creationTime))[:1].{Name:logGroupName}'
```

Tail the logs for the CloudWatch group:

```
aws logs tail <<LOGGROUPNAME>> --follow --since 10s
```

Delete all log groups that match a text pattern and prompt yes/no for confirmation:

```
aws logs describe-log-groups | \
jq ".logGroups[].logGroupName" | grep -i <<pattern>> | \
xargs -p -I % aws logs delete-log-group --log-group-name %
```

Stop all running instances for your current working Region (H/T: Curtis Rissi):

```
aws ec2 stop-instances \
--instance-ids $(aws ec2 describe-instances \
--filters "Name=instance-state-name,Values=running" --query
"Reservations[].Instances[].[InstanceId]"
--output text | tr '\n' ' ')
```

Determine the user making CLI calls:

```
aws sts get-caller-identity --query UserId --output text
```

Generate YAML input for your CLI command and use it:

```
aws ec2 create-vpc --generate-cli-skeleton yaml-input > input.yaml
#Edit input.yaml - at a minimum modify CidrBlock, DryRun, ResourceType, and Tags
aws ec2 create-vpc --cli-input-yaml file://input.yaml
```

List the AWS Region names and endpoints in a table format:

```
aws ec2 describe-regions --output table
```

Find interface VPC endpoints for the Region you are currently using:

```
aws ec2 describe-vpc-endpoint-services \
--query ServiceDetails[*].ServiceName
```

Populate data into a DynamoDB table:

```
aws ddb put table_name '[{key1: value1}, {key2: value2}]'
```

Determine the current supported versions for a particular database engine (e.g., aurora-postgresql):

```
aws rds describe-db-engine-versions --engine aurora-postgresql \
--query "DBEngineVersions[].EngineVersion"
```

Delete network interfaces associated with a security group and prompt for each delete (answer yes/no to delete or skip):

```
aws ec2 describe-network-interfaces \
--filters Name=group-id,Values=$SecurityGroup \
--query NetworkInterfaces[*].NetworkInterfaceId \
--output text | tr '\t' '\n' | xargs -p -I % \
aws ec2 delete-network-interface --network-interface-id %
```

Find your default VPC (if you have one) for a Region:

```
aws ec2 describe-vpcs --vpc-ids \
--query 'Vpcs[?IsDefault==`true`]'
```

Enable encryption by default for new EBS volumes in a Region:

```
aws ec2 enable-ebs-encryption-by-default
```

List all AWS Regions:

```
aws ssm get-parameters-by-path \
--path /aws/service/global-infrastructure/regions \
--output text --query Parameters[*].Name | tr "\t" "\n"
```

List all AWS services:

```
aws ssm get-parameters-by-path \
--path /aws/service/global-infrastructure/services \
--output text --query Parameters[*].Name \
| tr "\t" "\n" | awk -F "/" '{ print $6 }'
```

List all services available in a region (e.g., us-east-1):

```
aws ssm get-parameters-by-path \
--path /aws/service/global-infrastructure/regions/us-east-1/services \
--output text --query Parameters[*].Name | tr "\t" "\n" \
| awk -F "/" '{ print $8 }'
```

List all Regions that have a particular service available (e.g., SNS):

```
aws ssm get-parameters-by-path \
--path /aws/service/global-infrastructure/services/sns/regions \
--output text --query Parameters[*].Value | tr "\t" "\n"
```

Create a presigned URL for an object in S3 that expires in a week:

```
aws s3 presign s3://<<BucketName>>/<<FileName>> \
--expires-in 604800
```

Find Availability Zone IDs for a Region that are consistent across accounts:

```
aws ec2 describe-availability-zones --region $AWS_REGION
```

Set the Region by grabbing the value from an EC2 instance's metadata:

```
export AWS_DEFAULT_REGION=$(curl --silent http://169.254.169.254/latest/dynamic/
instance-
identity/document \
| awk -F'"' ' /region/ {print $4}')
```

Index

A

Access Analyzer
  list of services supported, 9
  using to generate IAM policy based on
    CloudTrail activity, 6
access points (S3), configuring application-
  specific access to buckets with, 110-114
access policies for common job functions, 4
  creating policy for secret access, 34
account management, 289-313
  enabling CloudTrail logging for AWS
    account, 297-300
  modifying tags for many resources at one
    time with Tag Editor, 292-296
  setting AWS ACCOUNT ID to bash vari-
    able, 315
  setting up AWS Organization and AWS Sin-
    gle Sign-On, 307-313
  setting up email alerts for root login,
    300-302
  setting up multi-factor authentication for
    root user in, 302-306
  using EC2 Global View for account resource
    analysis, 290-292
administrative access for routine development
  tasks, not recommended, 5
administrative capabilities, delegating for IAM
  using permissions boundaries, 17-25
administrative IAM user, 306
AI/ML, 267-287
  computer vision analysis of form data,
    272-275
  converting text to speech, 270-272
  detecting text in a video, 279-281

determining location of text in an image,
  285-287
physician dictation analysis, 281-284
redacting PII from text using Comprehend,
  275-279
transcribing a podcast, 268-270
ALBs (see Application Load Balancers)
alerts (email) for root login, setting up, 300-302
Amazon Certificate Manager (ACM), 42
Amazon Cloud Watch (see Cloud Watch)
Amazon Comprehend, using to redact PII from
  text, 275
Amazon ECS (see ECS)
Amazon Elastic Cloud Compute (see EC2)
Amazon Elastic Kubernetes Service (Amazon
  EKS), 207
  (see also EKS)
Amazon Lightsail (see Lightsail, deploying con-
  tainers with)
Amazon Machine Image (AMI), AWS Backup
  handling process of building, 124
Amazon Managed Service for Prometheus, 208
Amazon OpenSearch, 299
Amazon Polly, converting text to speech,
  270-272
Amazon Rekognition Video, using to detect
  text in a video, 279-281
Amazon Textract and textractor tool
  determining location of text in an image,
    285-287
  using for computer vision analysis of form
    data, 272-275

Amazon Transcribe Medical and Amazon Comprehend Medical, using to analyze physician dictation, 281-284
Amazon Transcribe, using with MP3 file, 268-270
AmazonDynamoDBFullAccess policy, 23, 199
AmazonEC2ReadOnlyAccess policy, 14
AmazonS3ReadOnlyAccess policy, 199
AmazonSSMManagedInstanceCore policy, 26, 27
Application Load Balancers (ALBs)
    configuring ALB to invoke Lambda function, 179-181
    creating new ALB target group to use as Green target with CodeDeploy, 225
    redirecting HTTP traffic to HTTPS with, 67-74
Archive Access storage tier, 99
ARN (Amazon Resource Names)
    finding for ECS task, 237
    retrieving ARN for user, 3
artificial intelligence (see AI/ML)
AssumeRole API, 4
AssumeRole policy, 4
assuming a role, 4
Athena service
    querying files on S3 with, 256-260
    querying logs in place on S3 with, 299
audio, transcribing to text, 268-270
auditing session activity, 30
Aurora Serverless
    creating PostgreSQL database, 134-140
    enabling REST access to, using RDS Data API, 171-176
authentication
    IAM, using with RDS database, 140-146
    multi-factor, 13
        requiring in AssumeRole policies, 5
        setting up for root user, 302-306
authorization tokens, 212
AutoPause, 137
Availability Zones (AZs), 46
    ENI in, 50
    finding AZ IDs for Region that is consistent across accounts, 317
    NAT gateways in, 58
    subnets in a VPC, spreading across AZs, 50
available state for VPC, verifying, 45

AWS ACCOUNT ID, setting to bash variable, 315
AWS account management (see account management)
AWS Backup, 127
    creating and restoring EC2 backups to another Region using, 118-125
AWS Backup Managed Policy, 119
AWS CLI
    automating process of token retrieval, 36
    configuring credentials for, 4
    determining user making calls, 315
    generating Yaml input for command, 315
    installing Lightsail Control plugin for, 217
    starting Transcribe transcription job, 269
AWS Cloud Map, 208
AWS CodeDeploy, using to orchestrate application deployments to ECS, 223-227
AWS Config, 292
AWS Control Tower, 312
AWS Copilot, deploying containers with, 220-223
AWS Database Migration Service (AWS DMS), 139
AWS Glue crawlers, automatically discovering metadata with, 249-256
AWS KMS CMK, configuring S3 buckets to use keys referencing, 115
AWS Lake Formation, 260
AWS Organizations, 290
AWS Organizations and Single Sign-On, setting up, 307-313
AWS Policy Generator, 16
AWS Schema Conversion Tool, 171
AWS SDK, 36
    using specific access points with, 112
AWS Security Token Service (see Security Token Service)
AWS security topics, resources for, 1
AWS services, listing all, 316
AWS Signer, using to run trusted code in Lambda function, 191-194
AWS Single Sign-On, 10, 290, 306
    setting up AWS Organizations and, 307-313
AWS SSM Session Manager
    connecting to EC2 instance in subnet of VPC via, 53
    connecting to EC2 instances with, 25-30
AWS Systems Manager (SSM) API, 29

AWS-managed (aws/ebs) KMS keys, 32
AWSLambdaBasicExecutionRole policy, 178, 199
AWSLambdaVPCAccess IAM policy, 160

B

backups
    automated in Aurora Serverless, 140
    creating and restoring EC2 backups to another Region using AWS Backup, 118-125
big data, 241-265
    automatically discovering metadata with AWS Glue crawlers, 249-256
    querying files on S3 using Amazon Athena, 256-260
    streaming data to S3 using Kinesis Data Firehose, 245-249
    transforming data with AWS Glue Data-Brew, 261-265
    using Kinesis Stream for ingestion of streaming data, 242-244
    workstation configuration, 242
Block Public Access feature (S3), 36
blue/green deployments, updating containers with, 223-227
Border Gateway Protocol (BGP), 88
bucket policy template to enforce encryption on all objects, 116

C

capacity for databases, 137
    Aurora Serverless scaling measured in capacity units, 139
    automatically scaling capacity targets, 137
    autoscaling DynamoDB table provisioned capacity, 163-167
    checking for RDS cluster, 138
    DynamoDB provisioned capacity , use of capacity units, 165
    scaled down to 0, 137
    setting at upper limit, 139
    when database activity resumes, 137
CDNs (content delivery networks), 39
certificate authority (CA), RDS Root CA, 144
certificates
    CloudFront HTTPS certificate on default hostname , 42
    creating for HTTPS, 69

SSL, 146
CI/CD pipelines
    AWS Copilot commands embedded in, 223
    blue/green deployments pattern, 227
CIDR (classless inter-domain routing) blocks, 44
    choosing carefully for your VPC, 46
    creating VPC with IPv6 CIDR block, 46
    nonoverlapping ranges when connecting VPCs, 91
    quotas for IPv4 and IPv6, 46
    simplifying management of CIDRs in security groups with prefix lists, 74-78
    specifying CIDR notation for authorizations, 63
CLI (see AWS CLI)
Cloud Map, 208
CloudFront, 39
    serving web content securely from S3 with, 39-42
CloudTrail logging, 6
    configuring to log events on S3 bucket, 232
    enabling, 7
    enabling for your AWS account, 297-300
CloudWatch, 22
    configuring alarm and scaling policy for ECS service, 228
    getting most recently created log group name, 315
    Glue crawlers logging information to, 254
    metrics service, 231
    streaming container logs to, 235-239
    tailing log group to observe Lambda function invoked, 186
    tailing logs for CloudWatch group, 315
CloudWatch Events (see EventBridge)
CloudWatchFullAccess policy, 23
clusters
    creating database cluster with engine mode of serverless, 136
    database, checking capacity of, 138
    deleting RDS cluster, 139
CMK (see customer-managed KMS key)
code signing configuration, 192
CodeDeploy, using to orchestrate application deployments to ECS, 223-227
CodeDeployRoleForECS policy, 224
CodeSigningPolicies, changing, 194

Common Vulnerabilities Scoring System (CVSS), 216
Comprehend, using to redact PII from text, 275-279
computer vision analysis of form data, 272-275
concurrency (provisioned), reducing Lambda startup times with, 201-204
connection pooling, leveraging RDS Proxy for database connections from Lambda, 146-152
consumers and producers (streaming data), 244
containers, 207-239
    autoscaling container workloads on ECS, 228-231
    building, tagging and pushing container image to Amazon ECR, 209-214
    capturing logs from containers running on ECS, 235-239
    deploying using Amazon Lightsail, 217-220
    deploying using AWS Copilot, 220-223
    launching Fargate container task in response to an event, 231-235
    networked together, 43
    orchestrators, 207
    packaging Lambda code in container image, 194
    prerequisite, installing Docker, 208
    scanning images for security vulnerabilities on push to ECR, 214-217
    updating with blue/green deployments, 223-227
Control Tower, 312
Copilot, deploying containers with, 220-223
cost allocation tags, 296
CreateInternetGateway action (EC2), testing, 14
credentials
    temporary, for a role, returned by AssumeRole API, 4
    temporary, from AWS STS instead of IAM user, 5
cross-account access to AWS resources, 5
Cross-Region Replication (CRR), 104
CSV files
    generating and exporting CSV of resources with EC2 Global View, 290-292
    transforming data in, using Glue DataBrew, 261-265
customer-managed KMS key, 30, 114, 117

CVSS (Common Vulnerability Scoring System), 216

D
dashboard, creating for S3 Storage Lens, 106-109
data, 241
    (see also big data)
Data Catalog
    creating in Athena, 258
    using Glue Data Catalog in Athena service, 260
data lakes, 260
Data Lifecycle Manager, 124
    automating EBS snapshots with, 127
database engines, determining current supported versions for, 316
Database Migration Service (see DMS)
databases, 133-176, 260
    automating password rotation for RDS databases, 157-163
    autoscaling DynamoDB table provisioned capacity, 163-167
    AWS managed database services, 133
    creating Amazon Aurora serverless PostgreSQL database, 134-140
    enabling REST access to Aurora Serverless using RDS Data API, 171-176
    encrypting storage of existing RDS for MySQL database, 153-156
    leveraging RDS Proxy for database connections from Lambda, 146-152
    migrating to Amazon RDS using DMS, 167-171
    using IAM authentication with RDS database, 140-146
DataSync, replicating data between EFS and S3 with, 128-131
Days in Transition action, 96
db-connect action, 145
DBAppFunction Lambda function's role, 149
DBInstanceStatus, 154
DBProxyTargets, 150
Deep Archive Access storage tier, 99
deploying containers
    updating containers with blue/green deployments, 223-227
    using Amazon Lightsail, 217-220
    using AWS Copilot, 220-223

DescribeInstances action (EC2), testing, 15
Destination S3 bucket, 101
DHCP server (AWS-managed), options set, 50
DMS (Database Migration Service), 139
    migrating databases to Amazon RDS using
        DMS, 167-171
dms.t2.medium replication instance size, 169
Docker
    creating a Dockerfile, 211
    installation and validation, 208
Docker container image, pushing to ECR
    repository, 194-197
Docker Desktop, 208
Docker Linux Engine, 208
Docker Swarm, 207
DynamoDB
    automating CSV import from S3 with
        Lambda, 198-201
    autoscaling DynamoDB table provisioned
        capacity, 163-167
    populating data into a table, 316
    using Glue crawlers to scan tables, 256

E
EBS snapshots, 124
    restoring a file from, 125-128
EBS volumes
    enabling encryption by default for new vol-
        umes in Region, 316
    encrypting using KMS keys, 30-32
ebs-encryption-by-default option, 32
EC2, 207
    connecting to instances using AWS SSM
        Session Manager, 25-30
    creating and restoring EC2 backups to
        another Region using AWS Backup,
        118-125
    granting instance the ability to access a
        secret, 35
    instance in subnet of a VPC, connecting to
        the internet, 51
    retrieving secret from Secrets Manager, 35
    storing, encrypting, and accessing pass-
        words with Secrets Manager, 33-36
    using EC2 Global View for account resource
        analysis, 290-292
ECR (Elastic Container Registry), 208
    container images supported, 214
    deleting repositories containing images, 216

Docker Credential Helper, 212
    pushing container image to, 194-197,
        209-214
    scanning container images for vulnerabili-
        ties on push to ECR, 214-217
    storage of container images on, 197
ECS (Elastic Container Service), 207
    autoscaling container workloads on,
        228-231
    capturing logs from containers running on,
        235-239
    Copilot requirement for ECS service-linked
        role, 221
    using EventBridge to trigger launch of con-
        tainer tasks on Fargate, 232-235
ECSRunTaskPermissionsForEvents policy, 233
EFS
    configuring Lambda function to access,
        188-191
    replicating data between EFS and S3 with
        DataSync, 128-131
EIP (Elastic IP address), 53
    associated with NAT gatway, 58
    creating and associating to EC2 instance, 51
    creating for use with NAT gateway, 56
Elastic Cloud Compute (see EC2)
Elastic Container Registry (see ECR)
Elastic Container Service (Amazon ECS) (see
    ECS)
Elastic Load Balancing (ELB) service, 208
    giving permission to invoke Lambda func-
        tions, 179
elastic network interfaces (see ENIs)
ElastiCache, accessing cluster having endpoint
    on a VPC, 204-206
email alerts for root login, setting up, 300-302
encryption
    enabling by default for new EBS volumes in
        a Region, 316
    encrypting EBS volumes using KMS keys,
        30-32
    encrypting storage of existing RDS for
        MySQL database, 153-156
    SSL encryption in transit, support by RDS
        Proxy, 152
    traffic in transit and at rest using TLS with
        DataSync, 131
    using S3 bucket keys with KMS to encrypt
        objects, 114-117

endpoint policies (S3 VPC), 80
engine-mode of serverless, 136
ENIs (elastic network interfaces)
    database subnet groups simplifying palce-
        ment of RDS ENIs, 135
    of two EC2 instances, security group associ-
        ated with, 59
    security group acting as stateful virtual fire-
        wall for, 63
    subnets used for placement of, 50
EvalDecision, 14
event-driven applications, 201, 234
EventBridge
    invoking a Lambda function on a schedule,
        185-188
    rule searching for root logins and triggering
        SNS topic, 300-302
    using to trigger launch of ECS container
        tasks on Fargate, 232-235
events in your AWS account, monitoring with
    CloudTrail, 299

F

Fargate, 68, 208
    launching Fargate container task in
        response to an event, 231-235
fast fixes, 315-317
federation
    AWS accounts leveraging, 5
    identity, 10
form data, computer vision analysis of, 272-275
Frequent Access storage tier, 99
full-load-and-cdc, 170

G

gateway endpoint in your VPC, creating and
    associating with route tables, 80
Gateway Load Balancers, 73
Gateway VPC endpoints, 82
get-secret-value API call, 36
Glacier archive (S3), automating archival of S3
    objects to, 97
global condition context keys (IAM), 14
Glue service
    automatically discovering metadata with
        Glue crawlers, 249-256
        crawler configuration summary, 252
        creating Glue Data Catalog database, 250

transforming data with Glue DataBrew,
        261-265
groups (IAM), 10

H

HIPAA compliance for PHI, 284
HTTP
    HTTP 301 response, 72
    security group rules allowing HTTP traffic,
        70
HTTPS
    redirecting HTTP traffic to with application
        load balancer, 67-74
    Session Manager, communicating with AWS
        Systems Manager (SSM) via, 29

I

IAM (Identity and Access Management)
    access keys, AWS SSO and, 312
    access point policies, 111, 114
    creating and assuming role for developer
        access, 2-6
    creating policy for secret access, 34, 34
    creating role for Kinesis Data Firehose, 247
    creating role for RDS Proxy, 147
    delegating administrative capabilities using
        permissions boundaries, 17-25
    enabling IAM user and role access to Billing
        console, 306
    generating least privilege IAM policy based
        on access patterns, 6-9
    role allowing S3 to copy objects from source
        to destination bucket, 101
    role for Lambda function execution, 178
    service-linked roles, 222
    setting up multi-factor authentication for
        root user in AWS account, 304
    testing policies with IAM Policy Simulator,
        13-16
    user password policies, enforcing in AWS
        account, 9-13
    using IAM authentication with RDS data-
        base, 140-146
IAM Access Analyzer (see Access Analyzer)
identity federation, using to access AWS
    accounts, 10
IGW (see internet gateway)
Infrequent Access storage class, 94, 96, 99
instance metadata (EC2), 28

---

instance profiles (EC2), 27
    creating and associating profile allowing
        access to secret, 33
Intelligent-Tiering archive policies, using to
    automatically archive S3 objects, 97-100
internet gateway
    egress-only, for private subnets on VPC
        with IPv6 capability, 58
    using to connect VPC to the internet, 51-55
internet, using NAT gateway for outbound
    access from private subnets, 55-58
IP addresses
    AWS-provided ranges list, 74
    Elastic IP address in IPv4, 53
    for ENIs, 50
    option to auto-assign on newly launched
        EC2 instances in a subnet, 54
    retrieving public IP from EC2 instance's
        metadata, 54
IPv4 CIDR blocks, 45
    additional, associating with your VPC, 46
    quota for, 46
IPv6 CIDR blocks
    configuring for Amazon VPC , 46
    quota, 46

J

Java Database Connectivity (JDBC) data stores,
    using Glue crawlers to scan, 256
jq utility, 75, 268

K

Key Management Service (KMS), 208
    creating KMS key to encrypt database snap-
        shot, 153
    encrypting EBS volumes using KMS keys,
        30-32
    specifying key for encyrpting RDS data-
        base snapshot, 155
    using with S3 bucket keys to encrypt
        objects, 114-117
key rotation, automatic, on KMS service, 32
Kinesis Client Library (KCL), 244
Kinesis Data Analytics, 244
Kinesis Data Firehose, streaming data to S3
    with, 245-249
Kinesis Producer Library (KPL), 244
Kinesis Stream, using for ingestion of stream-
    ing data, 242-244

KMS (see Key Management Service)
KMS.NotFoundException error, 116
Kubernetes, 207

L

Lambda functions
    accessing VPC resources with, 204-206
    configuring application load balancer to
        invoke, 179-181
    configuring to access EFS file system,
        188-191
    connection to RDS database, leveraging
        RDS Proxy for, 146-152
    IAM role for execution, 178
    integrating function with Secrets Manager
        to rotate RDS database passwords,
        157-163
    invoking on a schedule, 185-188
    packaging Lambda code in container image,
        194-197
    packaging libraries with Lambda Layers,
        181-185
    reducing startup times with provisioned
        concurrency, 201
    running trusted code in, using AWS Signer,
        191-194
    time out after 900 seconds, 201
    transforming data with, 249
    using EventBridge instead of for long-
        running jobs, 235
landing zone, 312
least privilege access
    implementing based on access patterns, 6-9
    principle of least privilege, 5
libraries, packaging with Lambda Layers,
    181-185
lifecycle policies (S3), using to reduce storage
    costs, 94-97
Lightsail, deploying containers with, 217-220
Linux, installing Docker on, 209
load balancers
    redirecting HTTP traffic to HTTPS with
        application load balancer, 67-74
    types other than ALB offered by AWS, 73
logging
    capturing logs from containers running on
        ECS, 235-239
    CloudTrail, enabling for your account, 6

deleting all log groups matching text pattern, 315
enabling CloudTrail logging for AWS account, 297-300
Glue crawlers automatically logging information to CloudWatch Logs, 254
login profile, creating for a user, 11
low-code development platforms (LCDPs), 265

M

machine learning (ML) (see AI/ML)
MacOS, installing Docke Desktop on, 209
management account, 311
metadata, 260
  automatically discovering with AWS Glue crawlers, 249-256
  EC2 instance, retrieving public IP from, 54
  EC2 instances, 28
metrics
  autoscaling metrics on CloudWatch, 231
  ECS service, on AWS Console, 230
  observing for S3 storage using Storage Lens, 109
migration of databases
  migrating databases to Amazon RDS using DMS, 167-171
  provisioned capacity type on RDS to Aurora Serverless, 139
mounting and unmounting EBS volumes, 127
MP3-based audio, transcribing to text, 268-270
multi-factor authentication (MFA), 5, 13
  setting up for root user in your AWS account, 302-306
MySQL
  RDS instance, encrypting storage of, 153-156
  RDS instance, leveraging RDS Proxy for database connections from Lambda, 146
  RDS instance, using IAM authentication with, 140-146

N

NAT gateway
  sharing of, enabled by Transit Gateway, 85
  using for outbound internet access from private subnets, 55-58
Ncat utility, 66
network insights path, creating for EC2 instances, 64

Network Load Balancers, 73
networking, 43-92
  AWS services providing, 208
  connecting VPC to the internet using internet gateway, 51-55
  controlling network access to S3 from VPC using VPC endpoints, 78-82
  creating network tier with subnets and route table in a VPC, 47-51
  defining private virtual network in the cloud with Amazon VPC, 44-47
  deleting network interfaces associated with a security group, 316
  enabling transitive cross-VPC connections using Transit Gateway, 82-88
  granting dynamic access by referencing security groups, 59-63
  innovations at AWS, resources on, 43
  peering VPCs together for inter-VPC network communication, 88-92
  redirecting HTTP traffic to HTTPS with application load balancer, 67-74
  simplifying management of CIDRs in security groups with prefix lists, 74-78
  using NAT gateway for outbound internet access from private subnets, 55-58
  using VPC Reachability Analyzer to verify and troubleshoot network paths, 63-67
NGINX containers
  deploying using Amazon Lightsail, 217-220
  nginx:latest image, 212
notifications (S3), 199

O

OpenSearch, 299
OpenSSL CLI, generating self-signed certificate with, 69
orchestrators (container), 207
Organizations (AWS), setting up, 290, 307-313
origin access identity (OAI)
  configuring to require S3bucket to be accessible only from CloudFront, 40
  creating for CloudFront to reference S3 bucket polity, 40
OS X CLI, listening to MP3 file on, 271

P

passwords

automating rotation for RDS databases, 157-163

complex, generating with Secrets Manager, 135

enforcing IAM user password policies in AWS account, 9-13

storing, encrypting, and accessing with Secrets Manager, 33-36

peering VPCs for inter-VPC network communication, 88-92

permissions

locking down for SSM users, 30

permission sets, 312

permissions boundaries, using to delegate IAM administrative capabilities, 17-25

PHI (protected health information), categorizing for further analysis, 281-284

physician dictation analysis using Transcribe Medical and Comprehend Medical, 281-284

PII (personally identifiable information), redacting from text using Comprehend, 275-279

Policy Simulator (IAM), testing IAM policies with, 13-16

Polly service, converting text to speech, 270-272

PostgreSQL

Aurora Serverless database, allowing REST access using RDS Data API, 171-176

creating Amazon Aurora serverless PostgreSQL database, 134-140

PostgreSQL package, installing, 138

PowerUserAccess IAM policy, 2, 5

attaching to role, 4

prefix lists in security groups, managing CIDRs with, 74-78

principle of least privilege, 5, 9

(see also least privilege access)

privilege escalation, IAM service mitigating risk of, 3

producers and consumers (streaming data), 244

Prometheus, Amazon Managed Service for, 208

protected health information (PHI), categorizing for further analysis, 281-284

provisioned capacity for DynamoDB table, autoscaling, 163-167

provisioned concurrency, reducing Lambda startup times with, 201-204

Proxy ID, 148

public access, blocking for S3 bucket, 36-39

Q

Query Editor in RDS Console, 173, 176

quotas and limits (Kinesis service), 244

R

RDS Data API

short-lived database connections, 152

using to enable REST access to Aurora Serverless, 171-176

rds-data:CommitTransaction permission, 176

rds-data:RollbackTransaction permission, 176

Reachability Analyzer (VPC), using to verify and troubleshoot network paths, 63-67

ReadCapacityUnits scaling target, 164

recovery point (backup), 120

recovery point objectives, replicating S3 buckets to meet, 100-105

recovery time objective (RTO), decreasing for EC2 instance using AWS Backups, 125

redirect response for all HTTP traffic to HTTPS, 72

Redis Python package, installing, 205

Redis, Lambda function with Redis client, accessing VPC resources, 204-206

Regions

creating and restoring EC2 backups to another Region using AWS Backup, 118-125

creating VPC in, spreading subnets across Availability Zones, 50

listing all, 316

listing all that have a particular service, 317

listing Region names and endpoints in table, 316

setting by grabbing value from EC2 instance metadata, 317

stopping all running instances for current working Region, 315

for VPCs, 46

Rekognition Video, using to detect text in a video, 279

Relational Database Service (RDS), 133

automating password rotation for RDS databases, 157-163

deleting RDS cluster, 139

leveraging RDS Proxy for database connections from Lambda, 146-152

migrating databases to, using DMS, 167-171

naming constraints, 135

using IAM authentication with RDS database, 140-146
replication
    Aurora Serverless databases, 140
    DMS replication tasks, 167-171
    replicating data between EFS and S3 with DataSync, 128-131
    replicating S3 buckets to meet recovery point objectives, 100-105
ReplicationStatus, 104
Resource Access Manager, 311
REST
    enabling REST access to Aurora Serverless using RDS Data API, 171-176
    REST API exposed by RDS, 152
restores
    restoring a file from an EBS snapshot, 125
    restoring EC2 backups to another Region using AWS Backup, 123
roles
    creating, 4
    retrieving for a user, 3
root user
    email alerts for root login, setting up, 300-302
    setting up multi-factor authentication for, 302-306
rotate-secret command (Secrets Manager), 162
Route 53 DNS records, 156
route tables
    associated with each subnet, route to direct traffic for peered VPCs to peering connection, 90
    associating gateway endpoint in VPC with, 80
    creating network tier with subnets and route table in a VPC, 47-51
    prefix lists associated wtih, 78
    priority given to most specific route, 54
routing, 44
    (see also CIDR blocks)
    for Transit Gateway, 85
runtime interface client, 197

S

S3
    automatically archiving S3 objects using Intelligent-Tiering, 97-99
    AWS support for S3 interface endpoints, 81
    blocking public access for a bucket, 36-39
    configuring application-specific access to buckets with S3 access points, 110-114
    controlling network access to S3 from VPC using VPC endpoints, 78-82
    creating presigned URL for object that expires in a week, 317
    CSV import into DynamoDB from S3 with Lambda, 198-201
    lifecycle policies, using to reduce storage costs, 94-97
    observing storage and access metrics using Storage Lens, 105-110
    querying files using Amazon Athena, 256-260
    replicating buckets to meet recovery point objectives, 100-105
    replicating files from S3 to EFS using DataSync, 128-131
    serving web content securely from using CloudFront, 39-42
    streaming data to, using Kinesis Data Firehose, 245-249
    using bucket keys with KMS to encrypt objects, 114-117
S3:GetObject action, 110
S3:PutObject action, 110
Same-Region Replication (SRR), 104
scaling
    autoscaling by Kinesis Data Firehose, 249
    autoscaling capacity for database, 137
    autoscaling container workloads on ECS, 228-231
    autoscaling DynamoDB table provisioned capacity, 163-167
Schema Conversion Tool (SCT), 171
schemas, 260
secrets
    creating using AWS CLI, 33
    SECRET_ARN role, replacing, 34
    storing, encrypting, and accessing passwords with Secrets Manager, 33-36
Secrets Manager
    creating and storing passwork in, 33
    generating passwords with, 11
    using to generate complex password, 135
    using with Lambda function to automatically rotate RDS database passwords, 157-163

SecretsManagerReadWrite policy, 149, 160
security, 1-42
  administrative access, 5
  blocking public access for S3 bucket, 36-39
  encryption at rest, 156
  endpoint policy to restrict access to S3 buckets, 81
  fine-grained security capabilities on AWS, 208
  IAM role, creating and assuming for developer access, 2-6
  scanning container images for vulnerabilities on push to ECR, 214-217
  security topics on AWS, 1
  serving web content securely from S3 with CloudFront, 39-42
  trusted code, running in Lambda, 194
  workstation configuration, 2
security groups
  CIDR management using prefix lists, 74-78
  creating VPC security group for database, 136
  deleting network interfaces associated with, 316
  EC2 instances's security group allowing ingress traffic from ALB, 70
  granting dynamic access to EC2 instances by referencing, 59-63
  for RDS Proxy, 147
    rule allowing access on TCP port 3306 for Lambda APP function security group, 151
  RDS MySQL database instance, ingress rule allowing access on TCP port 3306, 149
  referencing in peered VPCs, 91
  referencing other security groups, 150
  rules to allow HTTP and HTTPS traffic, 70
  updating rule to allow access SSH access between instances, 65
Security Token Service (STS), 4, 5
self-referencing rule (security group), 62
serverless, 177-206
  accessing VPC resources with Lambda, 204-206
  automating CSV import into DynamoDB from S3 with Lambda, 198-201
  benefits of, on AWS, 177
  configuring ALB to invoke Lambda function, 179-181

configuring Lambda function to access EFS, 188-191
  packaging Lambda code in container image, 194-197
  packaging libraries with Lambda Layers, 181-185
  prerequisite, IAM role for Lambda function execution, 178
  reducing Lambda startup times with provisioned concurrency, 201-204
  running trusted code in Lambda using AWS Signer, 191-194
  services available on AWS, 177
Session Manager (see SSM Session Manager)
shards, 242
signing process for Lambda function code, 191
Single Sign-On (SSO), 10, 290, 306
  setting up AWS Organizations and SSO, 307-313
snapshots
  encrypting storage of RDS database using, 153-156
  skipping final snapshot when deleting RDS cluster, 139
SNS topic, creating and subscribing to it, 300-302
Source S3 bucket, configuring replication policy for, 103
SQL query, running on files stored in S3, 256-260
SSH, allowing between EC2 instances, 59-63
SSL
  certificate, creating, 69
  OpenSSL, 68
SSM Session Manager
  connecting to EC2 instance in subnet of VPC via, 53
  connecting to EC2 instances with, 25-30
SSML (Speech Synthesis Markup Language) tags, 271
SSO (see Single Sign-On)
Standard storage class, 96
storage, 93-131
  creating and restoring EC2 backups to another Region using AWS Backup, 118-125
  ElastiCache service implementing redis or memcached for, 206

encrypting storage of existing RDS for MySQL database, 153-156

restoring a file from an EBS snapshot, 125-128

using Intelligent-Tiering archive policies to automatically archive S3 objects, 97-100

using S3 lifecycle policies to reduce storage costs, 94-97

Storage Lens, observing S3 storage and access metrics with, 105-110

streaming data
  to S3 using Kinesis Data Firehose, 245-249
  using Kinesis Stream for ingestion of, 242-244

subnets
  creating database subnet group, 135
  creating network tier with subnets and route table in a VPC, 47-51
  outbound-only internet access for an EC2 instance in private subnets, 55-58

Switch Role feature, 4

T

tables, 260

Tag Editor, using to modify tags for many resources at one time, 292-296

tagging containers, 212, 214

tags for AWS resources, 295

target groups for Load Balancer, 70

text in an image, determining location of, 285-287

text to speech conversion, 270-272

text, detecting in a video, 279

Textractor tool
  analyzing output from Amazon Textract to determine location of text in an image, 285-287
  using for computer vision analysis of form data, 272-275

tokens (authentication), 145
  IAM policy allowing Lambda function to generate, 148

tokens (authorization), 212

Transcribe Medical and Comprehend Medical, using for physician dictation analysis, 281-284

transcribing a podcast, 268-270

transformations
  Lambda functions for, 249
  transforming data with AWS Glue Data-Brew, 261-265

Transit Gateway, enabling transitive cross-VPC connections, 82-88

U

universally unique identifiers (UUIDs), 127

user password policies, enforcing in AWS account, 9-13

V

video, detecting text in, 279-281

VPC (Virtual Private Cloud), 208
  accessing VPC resources with Lambda, 204-206
  connecting to internet using internet gateway, 51-55
  controlling network access to S3 from VPC using VPC endpoints, 78-82
  creating, 44-47
  creating network tier with subnets and route table in a VPC, 47
  default, finding for a Region, 316
  enabling transitive cross-VPC connections using Transit Gateway, 82-88
  finding interface VPC endpoints for current Region, 316
  peering two VPCs together for inter-VPC network communication, 88-92
  Reachability Analyzer, using to verify and troubleshoot network paths, 63-67
  using NAT gateway for outbound internet access from private subnets, 55-58

VPN Endpoints for Session Manager, 29

W

Windows, installing Docker Desktop on, 209

WorkSpaces gateways, list of CIDR ranges for, 74

Y

Yaml input for CLI command, 315

About the Authors

John Culkin is a senior solutions architect at AWS. He holds all current AWS certifications. Previously, he was a principal cloud architect lead at Cloudreach, where he led the delivery of cloud solutions aligned with organizational needs. A lifelong student of technology, he now focuses on creating transformative business solutions that utilize cloud services.

Mike Zazon is a senior cloud architect at AWS, focused on helping enterprise customers modernize their businesses. He previously held roles as a cloud software developer, software engineer, software architect, IT manager, and data center architect. His passion for technology education blossomed while serving in some of these roles within an engineering research university setting.

Colophon

The animal on the cover of *AWS Cookbook* is the northern goshawk (*Accipiter gentilis*). A powerful predator, the northern goshawk belongs to the Accipitridae family (part of the "true hawk" subfamily) and can be found in the temperate parts of the Northern Hemisphere. The northern goshawk is the only species in the genus *Accipiter* living in coniferous and mixed forests in both Eurasia and North America, generally restricting itself to relatively open wooded areas or along the edges of a forest. It's a migratory bird that ventures south during the winter.

The northern goshawk has relatively short, broad wings and a long tail to enable maneuverability within its forest habitat. For its species, it has a comparatively sizable beak, robust and fairly short legs, and thick talons. It has a blue-gray back and a brownish-gray or white underside with dark barring. These birds tend to show clinal variation in color, which means that goshawks further north are paler than those in warmer areas.

The northern goshawk is amazingly fast, and catches its prey by putting on short bursts of flight, often twisting among branches and crashing through thickets in its intensity. It's a quiet predator that hunts by perching at mid-level heights and attacking quickly when it spots prey. The diet often consists of medium-sized birds, small mammals including squirrels and rabbits, small rodents, snakes, and insects.

This hawk lays around 2–4 bluish white eggs and is very territorial and protective of its nest, diving at intruders (including humans) and sometimes drawing blood. Young goshawks are usually looked after by the female, who remains with them most of the time while the male's primary responsibility is to bring food to the nest. Goshawks typically mate for life and hence they function as a partnership with most things.

Goshawks have a long and noble history. In the Middle Ages, only the nobility were permitted to fly goshawks for falconry. Ancient European falconry literature refers to goshawks as a yeoman's bird or the cook's bird because of their utility as a hunting partner catching edible prey. Currently, the northern goshawk's conservation status is that of least concern as the population remains stable. However, it may falter with increased deforestation, which is a loss of habitat for these mighty birds. Many of the animals on O'Reilly covers are endangered; all of them are important to the world.

The cover illustration is by Karen Montgomery, based on a black and white engraving from *British Birds*. The cover fonts are Gilroy Semibold and Guardian Sans. The text font is Adobe Minion Pro; the heading font is Adobe Myriad Condensed; and the code font is Dalton Maag's Ubuntu Mono.

O'REILLY®

There's much more where this came from.

Experience books, videos, live online training courses, and more from O'Reilly and our 200+ partners—all in one place.

Learn more at oreilly.com/online-learning

©2019 O'Reilly Media, Inc. O'Reilly is a registered trademark of O'Reilly Media, Inc. 1175

Milton Keynes UK
Ingram Content Group UK Ltd.
UKHW032207221123
433106UK00002B/5